MANAGER 3.0

More Advance Praise for *Manager 3.0*

"*Manager 3.0* brings keen insight and practical best practices both to millennials aspiring to be great managers and to managers from other generations who care to effectively groom and train this key contributing generation. As inherent to their nature, Karsh and Templin bring awesome amounts of color, humor, sage advice, and high energy to the book's teachings. A great read."
—**Kevin Sheridan,** *New York Times* **bestselling author of** *Building a Magnetic Culture*

"*Manager 3.0* is an essential book for Generation Y, specifically those high-achieving millennials who want to make a difference on day one as a manager. This book is perfect for its audience—it's all about balance, connection, and fun!"
—**Lindsey Pollak, author,** *Getting from College to Career*

"Brad Karsh has managed to separate the many clichés that now exist around the topic of millennials and produce a breakthrough book that gives insightful and entertaining guidance to lead people to future success."
—**Carter Murray, Global CEO, Draftfcb**

WITHDRAWN

"*Manager 3.0* is a must-read for any millennial looking to get ahead in business as well as those who manage and work alongside this innovative and promising generation. Courtney and Brad break down the stereotypes, both true and untrue, and rather than complaining about what millennials are or are not, give hard-hitting tools to get along and get ahead. It's a thought-provoking read for anyone who has ever complained about a millennial. And it's an incredible pat on the back to millennials who truly want to lead."
—**Marcy Twete, Founder and CEO of Career Girl Network**

"Finally, a book that documents everything I've experienced through the formative stages of my career. The authors combine real-life lessons learned into a practical guide for the aspiring millennial and those who direct them."
—**AJ Brown, Millennial Manager, West Monroe Partners, LLC**

"I thought I knew it all about millennials but was blown away by the powerful insights and sound advice packed in this book. Fun to read, too!"
—**Shelley Wyka, VP of Human Resources, Merge Healthcare**

"*Manager 3.0* will be THE book for managers looking to lead and engage the millennials. This toolkit of practical ideas is a must-read for managers."
—**Bob Kelleher, President and Founder of The Employee Engagement Group**

"There is one undeniable truth in the corporate world today—tomorrow's success is hugely dependent upon today's multigenerational management structures devising solutions that equally meet the needs of its employees and customers."
—**Daryl Sneed, Chief Talent Officer, Sg2**

"For all my students with managerial aspirations, I'll refer them to *Manager 3.0*. Finally, a management book that combines the perspectives of a seasoned manager and a new manager. Filled with practical material that is immediately usable, this is the ultimate guide to understanding how to meet in the middle."
—**Nell Madigan, Associate Dean, University of Illinois School of Labor and Employment Relations**

"A must-read for business school grads preparing to enter the confusing world of management. Karsh and Templin share a much-needed dose of reality with new managers."
—**Leah Stallone, Human Resources, William Blair & Company**

"Moving from an individual contributor to a manager is tough, but *Manager 3.0* gives you countless ideas for making this a smooth and successful transition. You will love all of the specific, tactical management ideas for empowering your team, showing recognition, delegating responsibilities, and navigating sticky situations."
—**Keith Dayton, MBA Core Coordinator, Indiana University Kelley School of Business**

"Millennial leaders are shaking things up—they are kicking the corporate ladder to the curb! *Manager 3.0* gives you all the tips, tools, and techniques to succeed in the new school of management."
—**Claire Leuck, Millennial Manager, ConAgra**

"Brad always seems to have his finger on the pulse of our work lives…what's the latest team dynamic we are faced with and how to recognize and accept changes in our workplace. In this book, Brad has again captured what a lot of us are thinking. With the new wave of millennial managers, is there a new set of rules? Do we adapt to and applaud the strengths they bring to the organization? This book will help everyone who manages the new generation of leaders."
—**Patti Grace, U.S. Director of Learning and Development, OmnicomMediaGroup**

"*Manager 3.0* is a tool I recommend with confidence. It is a relevant and transformative guide for any manager who is willing to manage outside the box."
—**Dom Merritt, Talent Consultant, Health Care Service Corporation**

"This book has it all! Stories, quotes, exercises, and telltale tweets. *Manager 3.0* is teeming with memorable and actionable ideas!"
—**Jeff Ellman, Cofounder, Hireology & UrbanBound**

"*Manager 3.0* signifies the great demise of the corner office and climbing the corporate ladder. Millennial managers are about passion, people, and productivity. If you want to connect, collaborate, and challenge the status quo as a leader, then you must read this book."
—**Bethany Weis, Millennial Manager, MSL**

"Whether you're a millennial manager or someone working with one, you'll find this book a powerful lens for understanding our newest generation of leaders. Brad's insights about the millennial mindset are revealing and spot-on. This book promises to bridge the generation gap and unleash collaboration on the road to high performance."
—**Juan Antonio Ruiz-Hau, VP Director, Learning and Development, DIGITAS**

"Whether you yourself are a millennial or are just baffled by them, this book delivers insight into the new world of management. There is a better way to take care of business in a multigenerational environment, and Courtney and Brad have found it. Read on and Rock on millennials!"
—**Kelly Dowd, Manager of Training and Development, Providential.com**

"Brad Karsh is an expert on the millennial generation and one of the most engaging speakers I've ever heard. His energy, humor, and incredible insight into millennials make his training sessions both informative and fun. I'd highly recommend Brad to anyone looking to better understand the millennial generation."
—**Jon Russell, Learning and Development Manager, Jump Trading**

"*Manager 3.0* is a great resource for both millennial managers and the human resource staff who help coach them on management responsibilities."
—**Ramona Eick, HR Analyst, Huron Consulting Group**

MANAGER 3.0

A Millennial's Guide to
Rewriting the Rules of Management

Brad Karsh • Courtney Templin

AMACOM

New York • Atlanta • Brussels • Chicago • Mexico City
San Francisco • Shanghai • Tokyo •Washington, D.C.

Bulk discounts available. For details visit:
www.amacombooks.org/go/specialsales
Or contact special sales:
Phone: 800-250-5308
Email: specialsls@amanet.org
View all the AMACOM titles at: www.amacombooks.org

This publication is designed to provide accurate and authoritative information in regard to the subject matter covered. It is sold with the understanding that the publisher is not engaged in rendering legal, accounting, or other professional service. If legal advice or other expert assistance is required, the services of a competent professional person should be sought.

Library of Congress Cataloging-in-Publication Data

Karsh, Brad.
    Manager 3.0 : a millennial's guide to rewriting the rules of management /
Brad Karsh and Courtney Templin.
        pages   cm
    Includes index.
    ISBN 978-0-8144-3289-1 — ISBN 0-8144-3289-1
    1. Management.   2. Personnel management.   3. Generation Y—Employment.
4. Generation Y—Attitudes.   5. Intergenerational relations.   I. Templin, Courtney.
II. Title.
HD31.K317   2013
658—dc23   2012051363

About AMA

American Management Association (www.amanet.org) is a world leader in talent development, advancing the skills of individuals to drive business success. Our mission is to support the goals of individuals and organizations through a complete range of products and services, including classroom and virtual seminars, webcasts, webinars, podcasts, conferences, corporate and government solutions, business books, and research. AMA's approach to improving performance combines experiential learning—learning through doing—with opportunities for ongoing professional growth at every step of one's career journey.

Printing number

10 9 8 7 6 5 4 3 2 1

Brad

To Gus and Digby, my medium and youngest guys

Courtney

*To my husband, Joe, who provides me with unconditional
support and those needed laugh breaks*

*And to my mom and dad—of course.
To my mom who has always been my greatest writing champion.
To my dad who taught me that hard work pays off.*

CONTENTS

ACKNOWLEDGMENTS

We would like to thank the many people who made this book possible. We couldn't have done it without all of our clients, colleagues, friends, and the countless millennials who shared their unique stories and anecdotes that truly enriched our book. Additionally, we would like to thank:

Allison Lackey, who helped with interviews, millennial insights, PR, and an amazing communications plan for the book. She was instrumental in making this book a success, and she is a great example of a go-getting millennial.

Nicole Scime, who tracked down our sources and references and helped with all of our logistics. Yet another millennial who makes our team great.

Jeff Hiller, who offered great perspective and ideas for bringing our chapters and advice to life.

Brian Keyes, who shared our love for millennial and generational research and kept us entertained and connected with the latest studies and insights on this riveting topic.

Warren Smith, who said, "When are you going to write a book about millennials?"

Matthew Carnicelli of CLM, who championed our idea and helped our book get published.

Christina Parisi, our editor, who believed in us from the start, and our supportive team at AMACOM. **Barbara Chernow,** our production editor, who had a Mrs. Stanley in her life too.

Joe for putting up with late nights, early mornings, and weekends of writing.

Muriel for being a sounding board and cheerleader through it all.

Milo, Gus, and Digby for sitting through way too many management lessons at very tender ages.

Lisa for being the most supportive, understanding, and compassionate wife I could have ever wished for.

INTRODUCTION: NOT BETTER, NOT WORSE— JUST DIFFERENT

"Each generation imagines itself to be more intelligent than the one that went before it, and wiser than the one that comes after it."
—George Orwell

I will never forget the day I came across my first leaderless team.

In my days as a Vice President/Director of Talent Acquisition at Leo Burnett, I was in charge of recruiting at all levels, but my main focus was entry-level candidates. I had the pleasure of reading more than 10,000 student resumes and interviewing more than 1,000 collegians. One of the standard interview questions I asked was, "Tell me about a group project you worked on in college." I used this question when hiring for the account management department because a huge part of the job was working with diverse groups within the company. We wanted to hire people who had the ability to manage projects and lead teams.

I was seeking candidates who said that they took the role of leader within the group. I would then probe them about their ability to work on diverse teams, handle conflict effectively, and drive results for the group. I must have posed this question hundreds of times in my quest to find the best candidates.

I still remember the day it all changed. It was in the spring of 2001, and I was interviewing a student from Princeton. I asked my standard "group project" question and was immediately stunned by the response. Here's how it went:

BRAD: Tell me about a group project you worked on recently in college.

CANDIDATE: Well, last semester we did some work on creating an economic model for a fictitious company.

BRAD: What role did you play in the group?

CANDIDATE: What do you mean?

BRAD: How was the group structured, and what was your role?

CANDIDATE: I'm sorry, but I'm confused. Do you mean what part of the project was I responsible for?

BRAD (*annoyed*): No, I mean were you the leader of the group or a team member?

CANDIDATE: We didn't have a leader.

BRAD (*dumbfounded*): What do you mean you didn't have a leader? Every group needs to have a leader. How did you get everything done and stay on track?

CANDIDATE: I don't know, we just sort of all did our part. It wasn't really a big deal.

BRAD (*thinking this person will never work at our company and moving on to a new line of questioning*): Okay, now, tell me about your weaknesses.

I shared the story with a few other recruiters, and we all had a good laugh about this fascinating candidate who worked on a leaderless team. Now here's the funny thing. Over the next couple of weeks, it happened again—and again. I heard similar answers regarding leaderless groups from sharp candidates again, and again, and again.

At that point, I knew I was experiencing a fundamental shift, and I recognized that this new generation was not going to play by the same rules. This generation was planning to chart a brave, new course. I was witnessing the formation of the next generation of leaders—*Manager 3.0.*

That is our strong belief at JB Training Solutions. In fact, we consider ourselves the great defender of millennials. One of the best decisions I made for the company was to hire a *real, live* millennial—Courtney —my coauthor. Between working with the millennials on my team and working with thousands of millennials across the country, I know that you're up against some tough preconceptions about your generation. The key problem is that many of your elders *do* assume you're worse—a lot worse. I have conducted over 500 workshops for more than 15,000 senior leaders on the topic of working with millennials. This workshop, *"Dude, What's My Job?" Managing Millennials in Today's Workforce,* is primarily comprised of Xers and boomers who are struggling with "the kids these days". Let me tell you, they are not a happy bunch. Although they leave the course with a sound understanding of your generation, they come into our workshop practically spewing venom about your group:

> *"Why do I always have to hold their hand?"*
> *"Why are they so entitled?"*
> *"Don't they understand that they have to pay their dues?"*

Those are some of the tamer responses. I've also heard:

> *"The worst generation ever!"*
> *"I. Cannot. Stand. Them."*
> *"Can't we just get rid of them?"*

I begin by asking the participants what they think of millennials, and I receive the standard responses like, "You mean those skateboard-riding, Mountain-Dew-drinking, Facebook-posting, Google-searching, YouTube-watching slackers?" I knowingly chuckle, and then I read direct quotes from *Time* magazine to bring a little light to the situation.

The article in *Time* states that this generation truly struggles to make decisions and that they "would rather hike in the Himalayas than climb a corporate ladder."[1] The article goes on to say that when they should be starting a career and a family of their own, "the twenty-something crowd is balking at those rights of passage."[2]

At this point, one of the Xers in the workshop jumps in and says, "You got it, Brad, you understand our pain."

I read on and share how companies feel like they "must cater to a young workforce that is considered overly sensitive at best, and lazy at worse."[3]

"That totally describes Caitlyn!" screams a delighted boomer.

There is more. The article continues to describe a generation of whiners that doesn't want to pay its dues. It really drives it home when I read that this generation has "a reluctance to embrace the dying work ethic of the former generation."[4]

A warm chuckle circulates through the room as boomers and Xers rejoice in my recounting of their daily struggles.

I ask if anyone remembers reading that issue of *Time* magazine. A few hands usually go up. I mention that it's from July, and then I show the cover. The young people on the cover have big bangs, large hoop earrings, and black leather jackets.

It's July alright. July of 1990! My audience is dumbfounded. Jaws drop to the floor. "But how could it be?" they ask. "That totally describes millennials," they protest.

Then I break the obvious news that the article was describing many of them—generation X. I tell them that as they get older, they tend to forget what it's like to be twenty-two or twenty-four and starting a first job or launching a career. This *Time* magazine sting operation really drives the insight home.

I firmly believe that half of the issues that other generations have with millennials is rooted in the fact that they are just *getting old*. Professionals gain experience—and hopefully wisdom—and they forget about how difficult the transition from school to work can be. They also tend to forget that millennials were raised very differently and were brought up in a changed world. Before they learn these insights, older generations just don't get it. As they discover more about millennials, they have several "aha" and "oohhh" moments.

George Orwell hit the nail on the head when he said, "Each generation imagines itself to be more intelligent than the one that went before it, and wiser than the one that comes after it." Every generation likes to complain about those who have followed. Traditionalists railed on about hippie boomers. Boomers decried the horrifying generation Xers, and now all have joined forces to lament the sorry state of the millennials. Likewise, my younger brother isn't as cool as I am. It's a time-honored tradition. I'm sure, like me, you have heard the stories about how your parents trekked five miles to school, uphill *both* ways, in a driving snowstorm—barefoot, no less!

The fact is that every generation loves to complain about those after them and all the advantages they were afforded. There's bound to be a little tension. The real triumph comes when each individual embraces the idea that no generation is better or worse—just different.

Think back to the candidate at Princeton that I interviewed in the spring of 2001. That millennial is now a 32-year-old. Chances are—like you—she's entered the ranks of management and is now leading teams. What is she going to be like? How is she going to manage? How will she show her leadership skills and take her company to the next level? What might she be lacking and where will she be strong? Based on the fact that she is a millennial, how will she (and you) rewrite the rules of management?

You will learn just that.

This book is your essential toolkit for being an effective and inspiring manager. There will be big ideas, small ideas, and everything in between. Groupon, Southwest Airlines, Winston Churchill, your parents, and the Backstreet Boys will all make an appearance at some point, and Sacagawea and another great captain will help show you the way. You will hear extraordinary examples grounded by tangible management strategies that you can put into practice today. There will be reflective exercises, telltale tweets, and some downright hairy ideas. By learning more about each of the generations, you can reach out, bridge the gap, and shatter all of those negative, preconceived notions about millennials. You will gain the insights and skills to bring out the best in each generation, rewrite the rules that aren't working, and forge a path toward a newer and more compelling version of leadership—Manager 3.0.

Let's get into it.

1

TALKIN' 'BOUT
YOUR GENERATION

"We are not on a journey to become the same or to be the same. But we are on a journey to see that in all of our differences, that is what makes us beautiful as a human race, and if we are ever to grow, we ought to learn and always learn some more."

—C. JoyBell C.

As soon as you bring up the topic of the generations at work, over dinner, or with friends, you can see people's eyes light up. Everyone has a fervent perspective of how crazy all the people are who were unlucky enough to be born *outside* of their generation's coveted years. When referring to another generation, the phrase "they just don't get it" comes up at some point—that's boomers talking about Xers, millennials talking about boomers, and Xers complaining about being scrunched in between.

According to a 2011 Society for Human Resource Management (SHRM) poll,[1] 75 percent of respondents reported some level of conflict among the generations. If you think about the different societal trends, the cultures, and world in which each generation grew up, it is apparent why everyone doesn't see eye to eye. Simply think about the most basic components of work in the 1950s and the stark contrast in workplaces today. The manufacturing line that abounded is now replaced by work stations, professional services, and computers. In the amount of time it would have taken to type a paragraph on a typewriter, we have zipped off 23 e-mails, many of them that simply say "Thanks!" or "Sounds good."

Try to envision your world of work without e-mail. For those of you who have desk jobs, e-mail may comprise 70 percent of your work day. Imagine if you actually had to talk to someone face-to-face! Now, I am being a little sarcastic here, but there is a huge, fundamental shift in the way we're doing business. As we move to a "knowledge" economy and as technology changes at breath-taking speeds, we have to take into account the changes traditionalists, boomers, and even Xers have gone through in the workplace.

Over the past 100 years, the world has been through startling changes. In the words of Condoleezza Rice, we live in a country where the "Impossible becomes inevitable"[2]—people flying airplanes across oceans, heroes walking on the moon, and children playing on iPhones at the age of two. Can you imagine there was a time when hearing someone thousands of miles away without the use of a wire seemed impossible? Now, it only seems inevitable that someone invented the radio. Of course. *The impossible becomes inevitable.*[3]

Each of these seemingly impossible inventions and experiences shaped our world. If you think through the last century, a few defining moments and events stand out. There was the Great Depression, World War II, the Civil Rights Movement, the Women's Movement, Vietnam, and September 11th, to name a few. Each of these world events shaped families and children and the lens through which they see the world.

The generations are comprised of unique individuals and, undoubtedly, there are exceptions to the stereotype. We always joke that Courtney is a Traditionalist stuck in the millennial time trap. However, each of the generations is shaped by the society and culture in which its members were raised. Even if Courtney's company loyalty echoes that of a Traditionalist, she grew up trying to memorize the words and remember the trite dance moves of New Kids on the Block and Wilson Phillips, while I nearly cracked my neck rocking out to Nirvana and Boston.

The generations are fascinating, and you will be a better manager for having a firm grasp on this important topic. As a millennial manager, you likely will be working across *all* generations. Maybe you manage employees who are older than you, and you likely will have fellow millennials who report to you. You can't fall into the trap of managing people how *you* would like to be managed. Each of the generations' approaches work differently and, to succeed as manager, you need to understand the driving forces and styles of each group. The more awareness and understanding you have of your bosses, colleagues, and direct reports, the better you can manage, lead, and succeed in the workplace.

As millennials, you probably have some preconceived notions about the *old* people in the workforce. You may even think most of them should retire, but don't worry, some of them wouldn't mind if you decided to return to graduate school. Putting all of these biases aside, let's look at how each generation is simply a product of its times.

At any given time, you are probably working with and even managing people in four different generations, and you likely are part of the 75 percent experiencing intergenerational conflict.[4] Most of this conflict stems from the differences in communication style, expectations, and perspectives of the different generations. If you know what makes individuals in each generation tick, what gets them going, what frustrates them, and what makes them who they are, then you can better work with them. Although there are bound to be some exceptions, on a whole, each generation has some predispositions that I will discuss.

Traditionalists (born 1928–1945)
Baby Boomers (born 1946–1964)
Generation X (born 1965–1980)
Millennials (born 1981–2000)

TRADITIONALISTS (BORN 1928–1945)

First up are the traditionalists. The traditionalists are the oldest generation in the workforce. Since the majority of traditionalists are no longer in the workforce, we won't spend too much time on them here. The traditionalists are the World War II generation, and they are a very loyal group.

Do you have a father or grandfather who worked at the same company for thirty years or more? He is probably a traditionalist. Can you imagine working at only *one* company all your adult life? If you're on par with the statistics of the millennial generation, by the age of 26, you will have had an average of seven jobs. On the contrary, traditionalists mostly stayed with one company, and they may view your job hopping as fickle, unfocused, and irresponsible. It's important to note that companies were also loyal to traditionalists, a two-sided partnership of loyalty that began to deteriorate in the baby boomer generation. For traditionalists, you go to work, you earn a living, and you don't complain or ask for too much. Work is work. Traditionalists go to work at the same company for their entire life, and they retire with a gold watch.*

When you think about traditionalists' work style, it's very hierarchal and respectful. Remember, they grew up either living through or hearing stories of World War I, World War II, and even the Korean War. Chances are they were soldiers or their dad was a soldier. They never went to the commanding officer's commanding officer to talk about a problem. First, they would never really talk about a problem. Second, they would never go around or above their direct authority. There is a very clear line of command and distinction in this generation.

The Great Depression preceded World War II, so traditionalists were happy to have a job and a paycheck. No complaining or pushing for employee rights; a job is a job, and that's good enough. That's the traditionalist generation—conservative and rule followers. As managers, traditionalists are more likely to give orders and resist change. If you're managing traditionalists, learn as much as you can from them. Respect their experience and watch your pace—not everyone can keep up with your 32 GB speed or energy.

Traditionalists at a Glance

Assets: Respectful, disciplined, and loyal
Stereotype: Close minded, rigid, inflexible, stubborn, and risk averse
Tagline: Duty over play; values and tradition rule

BABY BOOMERS (BORN 1946–1964)

Boomers! A name like that just screams for attention, and at 79 million strong, the baby boomers rightfully deserve serious consideration. You may manage some baby boomers, but it's more likely that you have a

---

*A watch is a device that tells you the time of day if you don't have your smart phone with you.

boomer boss or that boomers dominate your senior leadership team. You also may have boomer parents.

Now, why are they called the baby boomer generation? After almost four years of being overseas, the boys came home from fighting in World War II, and there were a lot of babies! You likely have seen the iconic photo of the blissful sailor kissing a nurse soon after returning from the war. That was the emblem of the time. The birth rate rose fairly consistently year over year for 18 years. As a result, there was a tremendous focus in this period on children, families, and babies.

Let's think about life in America during the 1950s. Television shows like *Leave it to Beaver*, *Ozzie and Harriet*, and *Father Knows Best* were popular, and they pretty much captured what the times were like. Dad went to work, and Mom stayed at home. The kids would go to school, mom would clean the house, and she would have a beautiful dinner waiting when Dad got home from work at 5:15 PM. He was wearing a suit and tie, and Mom greeted him at the door when he arrived. She was decked out in a dress, an apron, high heels, and a beautiful string of pearls. As Dad walked in, she had a martini in one hand and a pair of slippers in the other. Little Bobby was wearing a sweater vest with his hair slicked back, and sweet Cindy was wearing a pretty yellow dress with a bow in her hair. The entire family sat around the dining room table together and enjoyed a nice, relaxing multicourse meal, and the biggest problem of the day was that Bobby got in a "tussle" at school. Sound familiar? I didn't think so. When was the last time your entire family sat at the dining room table and shared a formal meal on a week day?

Levittown, New York, and other "planned" communities exploded in popularity during this time period. Suddenly, everyone wanted to get out of the city and into the suburbs. They craved the four-bedroom house with the white-picket fence and the two-car garage for their three kids. The focus clearly was on family, children, and community. That was the era in which boomers lived. They were idealistic, and they wanted to save the world—and the workplace.

Interestingly, to boomers, work is more than just work. Work is life. Boomers are much more defined by their work than other generations. They enjoy working hard and moving up the corporate ladder is important to them. Boomers have a wealth of knowledge, and they're connected to their job—and their job title. As they have evolved in their careers, they became the first generation of workaholics—those most attached to their jobs. As a millennial, you have probably heard a boomer tell you once or twice that you have to "pay your dues" and that you have to gain experience. Boomers follow a chain of command, and they feel that they paid their dues, worked their way up, and learned valuable experiences from doing so. As managers, boomers expect the best from you, and they want you to care as much as they do. If they're going to drop everything to finish a project, they expect you to *want* to do the same.

Boomers may be leading your organization—and retiring from your organization. They are overflowing with experience and insight, and as you are an emerging leader, they are excellent mentors for you. At first brush, you may think you don't have much in common with your boomer boss or direct reports, but they often enjoy sharing their experience and expertise—if you ask. This will help prevent the great "brain drain" as more and more boomers retire, and it can give you a leg up and some insight for your future.

Baby Boomers at a Glance

Assets: Optimistic, competitive, and collaborative
Stereotype: Egotistical, stuck in their ways, and power-hungry workaholics
Tagline: Good things come to those who work hard

GENERATION X (BORN 1965–1980)

Then generation X comes along and things change significantly. Let's start with the birth rate. For 15 years, the birth rate goes down, down, down—fairly consistently year after year. Let's think about why. What were the big issues in the late 1960s and early 1970s—the formative years of gen X? Vietnam, Hippies, Civil Rights, the Women's Movement, the birth control pill, *Roe vs. Wade*. How many of these issues scream big ol' family? Life focus had clearly shifted from children and families to broad sweeping social issues.

The latchkey kid was invented in this generation. Little, 13-year-old Melanie wears her house key around her neck when she goes to school so she can let herself in when she comes home. Why? Because dad AND mom are at the office, and they have to go to a big rally after work.

Remember the boomer kid? She was coming home to a mom who had spent the day roasting a turkey and baking a pie. The Xer kid comes home to an empty house and plops on the couch with a couple of Twinkies to hunker down for two hours of *Speed Racer.*

Since they often had to fend for themselves while growing up, gen X is a very independent generation. Mom and dad were at work focusing on the issues of the day, and Melanie could take care of herself for the most part. Because of the decline in the birth rate, families were smaller, and chances are Melanie was an only child.

Xers are fiercely independent and are accustomed to doing things on their own. I bet the light bulb just went off that your gen X employee doesn't despise you, he just despises "collaborating" and always working in teams!

In the workplace, more entrepreneurs come from this generation, as they are accustomed to working independently. They're not as afraid to strike out on their own or see what a new opportunity holds. This generation is more likely to leave a company to go somewhere else just for a 10 percent raise.

As managers, gen Xers typically are independent and hands off. Millennials—who love collaboration, constant structure, and feedback —can struggle with a Xer manager. If you are managing Xers, it's best to give them some leeway and refrain from micromanaging. Give them a project, and then leave them alone to do their job. Focus your collaborative energies on the next generation—your generation—the millennials.

Generation X at a Glance

Assets: Independent, creative, entrepreneurial, and pragmatic
Stereotype: Slackers, wannabes, cold, and cynical
Tagline: Work to live; too cool for school

MILLENNIALS (BORN 1981–2000)

Then, the tables turn again as millennials—you!—are born. The birth rate goes back up, and there is a tremendous focus on community, families, and—importantly—babies, babies, and more babies. The emblem of the millennial generation is a yellow, diamond-shaped sign we began placing in our automobiles in the 1980s and 1990s that says "Baby on Board." Parents were declaring, *I have a baby in here! The most precious, special, amazing thing in the world is a baby, and I have one. And you, bad man, stay away from my car, because I have a baby on board!*

We began placing these signs in a new breed of automobile we invented, just for our babies, called the minivan. We then created an entire store just for babies, named Babies "R" Us, of course. Have you ever been into a Babies "R" Us? Unbelievable. Fifty thousand products created just for babies—and most of these products didn't even exist in the 1960s and 1970s. (I'm not sure my parents would have invested in a baby wipe warmer, but now you're considered to be a monster if you subject your newborn to room temperature baby wipes.)

It was important that everyone had a baby. We created a new type of clinic in the 1980s and 1990s. Fertility clinics became the rage because EVERYONE had to have a baby. If you couldn't have one, all you needed were a few shots or a couple of pills and bam!—you have yourself a baby. Just look at the numbers. The birth rate of twins rose more than 70 percent from 1980 to 2009, and the triplet/+ birth rate rose more than 400 percent during the 1980s and 1990s.[5] The message of the millennials' time period is that life is not complete without a baby.

The attention for the babies never stopped. When I grew up, there was an expression: *Children should be seen, but not heard.* For millennials, that sentiment is long gone. You grew up in a time when as children, you were not only seen and heard, but you were given a big voice in family decisions. Life tended to revolve around you.

You grew up in a world where you were the most special, precious, and extraordinary being. What did your parents tell you that you could be?—Anything you wanted to be! You were told from day one that you were born perfect, and it wasn't just your parents and family telling you this. Songs have been written about millennials and how special you are. Lady Gaga—a millennial herself—wrote what I consider to be the anthem of your generation. Just take a couple minutes to think through the lyrics of *Born This Way.*

In this song, Lady Gaga sings about how her mom told her that each and every one of us is born special and beautiful and perfect. You basically are an all-star at birth because God doesn't make any mistakes — we are all perfect!

Think about that for a second. From the moment you come out of the womb, you're a perfect, beautiful superstar. Had they written a song about boomers and Xers it probably would have been:

My mama told me when I was young
We were all born mediocre
And if you work real hard
Catch a few breaks, maybe, at some point,
You could be slightly above average,
But I doubt it.

It certainly doesn't flow as nicely as Lady Gaga's version, but you can see the different messages that the generations were given as they were growing up and learning how they function in the world. Courtney was born a superstar, and I was born completely and absolutely average.

In addition to the idea that children are the single, most important part of a family's life, you also grew up in a time where philosophies on parenting shifted. Boosting self-esteem among kids became a powerful notion in the 1980s. Parents, schools, and organizations believed that the best thing to do for children was to make them feel good about themselves, and the way to do that was through constant praise and reward. Thus, the term "trophy generation" was born.

Now answer honestly, did you ever receive a ribbon or a trophy in a sport, activity, or educational event even if you didn't win? I am fairly certain your room growing up was filled with 13th-place ribbons and at least one last-place trophy. The message you were taught was at least you *tried* and simply showing up was enough. I'm not saying this is better or worse; it's just different.

When it comes to the workplace, your generation doesn't abide by a strict chain of command. Your respect for authority must be earned, and you rely more on your network than a hierarchal ladder. You love working in teams, and you're a very hopeful and optimistic generation. You want to change the world, and you want to make a difference. In this respect, millennials and boomers relate, and they both clash with a more cynical gen X. On the other hand, gen X and millennials are bound together by their love for technology and high-tech advances.

Millennials at a Glance

Assets: Hopeful, tech-savvy, fast paced, and collaborative
Stereotype: Impatient, entitled, spoiled, and disrespectful
Tagline: Follow your dreams; do what you love; work together

Here's a quick overview. We have the traditionalists and boomers who think in terms of hierarchy while the millennial generation is all about the network. Generation X is more independent, and millennials are more collaborative. Boomers want to work until they die, and Xers want to make a lot of money and get out. In the midst of all of this, all generations despise the music of the other generations. You can see how the workplace can be a difficult space to navigate if there isn't a strong foundation of understanding.

Sharla Ortega-Avila, Team Leader of Employment, Southwest Airlines, knows that millennials "can bring a wealth of energy and creativity to an established leadership team." Avila goes on to say that it's imperative that we all learn to understand, adapt, engage, and tap into the talents of each generation. "If that creative talent and energy is strategically utilized, our teams will soar to new heights," ensures Avila.

As a millennial manager, you can lead this charge. You can recognize and understand the differences and capitalize on the benefits that a diverse team brings. You can help bridge the gap. Each generation is molded and influenced by the society in which they were raised, and although everyone claims they are a member of the "best generation," there are no bests. When you're working across the generations, just think, "They're not better. They're not worse. They're just different." Maybe even VERY different, but that's okay.

Talkin' 'Bout Your Generation
◁ Telltale Tweets ▷

1. Each generation is shaped by society, culture, and the world in which they were raised. #bornthisway

2. Understand the driving forces and styles of each generation to better manage your team. #adjust #openyourmind

3. The generations at work—Traditionalists, Boomers, Xers, Millennials. Not better, not worse—just different. #verydifferent

2

MILLENNIALS DEFINED

"The ones who are crazy enough to think they can change the world are the ones that do.
—Apple Inc.

Millennials, Generation Y, Generation Me, Echo Boomers, Net Generation, and Trophy Generation. Your generation has quite a few terms of endearment, and you rightfully deserve a lot of attention. According to the Bureau of Labor Statistics, by 2015, there will be more millennials than boomers in the workplace. Watch out, the millennials are coming!

Undoubtedly, as a manager, you will oversee fellow millennials at some point in your career. First, this chapter will help you understand the driving forces, assets, and liabilities of millennials so you can better manage them. Second, it will give you great insight on how other generations view your generation and how you can successfully bridge the gap between the hierarchal management style of senior executives and the more casual, collaborative approach of your peers.

The millennial generation is comprised of more than 75 million Americans born between 1981 and 2000. As said earlier, it is hard to speak on behalf of more than 75 million people. Certainly, there will be exceptions. If you already are a millennial manager, then you may be on the "older" end of the generation. You are what we call a "cusper"—an individual on the edge of two different generations. You may find that you relate to some attributes of millennials and some characteristics of Xers. If you're a cusper, you probably are mad that the Lady Gaga song is stuck in your head!

Neil Howe and William Strauss, authors of *Millennials Rising,* use seven distinct terms to describe your generation—"conventional, sheltered, team-oriented, achieving, pressured, confident, and special."[1] Let's take a closer look at each adjective because they all shape how you manage and lead. It's important to know what you're all about, and it's important to know what drives the millennials you manage.

NIRVANA VS. BACKSTREET BOYS

This characteristic surprises older generations. "No way! They're defiant little punks always looking to buck the system!," they protest. However, if you think about it, your generation is quite conventional[2]— especially when compared to other generations at the same age. Music can help tell the story.

In the early 1990s, gen X—my generation—influenced musical popularity and taste. What type of music became popular? Grunge. Pearl Jam, Nirvana, Nine Inch Nails, Smashing Pumpkins, Alice in Chains, and scores of others that burst onto the scene. Let's think about Grunge as a genre. Was that a "conventional" form of music? No way. First of all, the word is a dirty word. Just think about what grunge means.

Now picture the band members. Are you convinced those band members even showered every day? Doubtful. And what were they singing about? If you could understand the words, you would learn that the world was horrible, unfair, and desolate. Here are a few words found in the lyrics of grunge music, brought to you by the letter D: *die, destructive, defaced, disgraced, dead, dusty, drowning,* and *doomsday.* Just take a look at some of the song titles from this era:

Downer, Nirvana
Doomsday Clock, Smashing Pumpkins
The Man Who Sold the World, Nirvana
March of the Pigs, Nine Inch Nails
Sea of Sorrow, Alice In Chains
Black, Pearl Jam

The Day the World Went Away, Nine Inch Nails
We Die Young, Alice in Chains

My word: depressing.

Fast forward ten years. In the late 1990s and early 2000s, millennials start to define musical taste. What type of music becomes popular? What were you listening to in those days? Pop! And especially, BOY BANDS! 'NSync, Backstreet Boys, 98 Degrees, Boyz II Men, New Kids on the Block! Now let's think about boy bands for a second. You had four or five *boys,* all dressed alike or each with his own unique style—the preppy one, the cool one, the sporty one, and the *rough* one. They all had coordinated dance moves and gestured in-sync as they belted out tunes of falling in love and finding that perfect girl. All of the songs basically follow the line of "Girl, I love you so, Girl, you are so sweet."

It's all about falling in love, treating a girl right, and going anywhere for her. Basically, these boys would do anything for just *one simple kiss.* What's more, girlfriends aren't the only special ones; moms also receive a few serenades. In the Backstreet Boys song, *Perfect Fan,* and Boyz II Men, *Mama,* these boys give a shot out to the greatest woman in their life—MOM! Let's take a quick look at the song titles from this era:

Anywhere for You, Backstreet Boys
God Must Have Spent a Little More Time on You, 'NSync
A Song for Mama, Boyz II Men
As Long as You Love Me, Backstreet Boys
I Do, 98 Degrees
I'll Be Loving You Forever, New Kids on the Block
I'll Never Break Your Heart, Backstreet Boys

Can you imagine Nirvana putting out a holiday album? Are millennials more conventional? Nirvana vs. Backstreet Boys! I think that says it all.

Furthermore, millennials are more likely to follow the rules, and they say family and values are important to them. In the millennial generation, violent crime and drug-related crime are all down. Older generations tend to take your casual and inquisitive nature as defiance. It's not that you want to break the rules or cause trouble; you simply want to know the reasoning behind the rules.

LAWNMOWER PARENTS

You have led a very sheltered[3] life thanks to your helicopter parents. Helicopter parents are moms and dads who hover over their children and are ready to swoop in if anything goes wrong. While that's a popular term to define millennial parents, I actually don't like it. Why? Because it's not strong enough! I like to say the parents of millennials are more like lawnmower parents. Instead of hovering, they are right there on the ground in the weeds with the kids. If anything gets in their kid's way, they will mow it right over. Parents tried to protect their kids from everything while growing up.

When I was growing up, I could jump around the backseat of the car or sleep on the floor during road trips. Now, kids are strapped into car seats with a dozen buckles and safety straps—sometimes until they're ten years old. Kids can't play in the dirt because there are too many germs, and parents face the bully, the tough teacher, or the coach at school. Forget about drinking from the hose, riding a skateboard without a helmet, or heaven forbid, eating a sandwich made by someone not wearing plastic gloves! I'm certainly not advocating reckless behavior. It's just that the definition of what's considered reckless has changed dramatically for millennials.

If boomers received a poor grade in school, their parents punished them and blamed them, not the teacher. If Xers faced a bully at school, they stood up to him, got beat up, or figured out a solution; mom swooping into help wasn't an option. Your generation grew up being protected from difficult situations, so you entered the workplace a little sheltered. Of course, these are generalizations, and there are always exceptions and people who were raised differently. A refrain that I will repeat time and time again is: It's not better; it's not worse; it's just different. It's also up to us to mind those differences.

LET'S GET TOGETHER

You are all about working in teams and being collaborative.[4] Millennials have played on more sports teams, been involved in more activities, and worked on more school group projects. As described in the introduction, when you ask millennials if they had a leader of a group project, the majority say that they all worked together without any real leader. You enjoy the social experience of connecting and working in groups. For millennials, it's very much about teams, working together, and collaboration. This can be a great asset for you as you begin leading a team and I will talk more about collaboration in future chapters.

LOOKS GOOD ON YOUR RESUME

You are part of a high-achieving[5] generation. The prevalence of As in grade schools and colleges has gone up. It's not that kids are smarter; there is just more and more pressure on students, teachers, and schools to give As. As a result, you're used to doing well, succeeding, and getting good grades.

Millennials are also pressured.[6] It may sound crazy, but some of you had to interview to get into nursery school! By the way, you *better* get into the best nursery school, because otherwise, you may be doomed to that mediocre kindergarten, which won't get you into the best grade school, so you'll be stuck with the average high school, forever losing hopes of landing the Ivy League education and hot-shot job.

In our workshops, I ask millennials when people started talking to them about college. As in, "Katy, it might not be a bad idea to learn Mandarin now, it will help you with college," or "Why don't you start that service project now, it will look good on your college application." The answer we typically receive is that parents begin talking about college when their children are in middle school. You're being pressured about college eight years before you go. In my day, most of us started thinking about college junior or senior year of high school.

You have taken on leaderships roles, volunteered on the weekends, and studied Latin all in the name of building a great resume. When millennials get to the workplace, they want to do well from day one. You are accustomed to excelling.

YOU CAN DO ANYTHING

Your entire lives, you have been told how special you are. You can be anything you want to be. Your parents told you, your family told you, and your teachers, coaches, tutors, and mentors too. As mentioned, even Lady Gaga told you how great you are. These messages were all around you.

A couple of years ago *The New York Times* sent a reporter to listen to college commencement addresses to gauge what advice graduates were getting before entering the workforce. Here are a few phrases gleaned from these speeches:

> "**You** can be anything **you** want to be."
> "March to the beat of **your** own drummer."
> "Chart **your** own course."
> "Follow **your** dreams and find **yourself**."
> "Follow **your** passions."[7]

Let's think about this for a moment. Think about the new hires at your company. Do you really want them "marching to the beat of their own drummer"? I'm sure many of you are shaking your heads no. These are very hopeful messages, but they also all center on—**YOU!** Just look at how many times "you" or "your" were mentioned.

Your generation is "conventional, sheltered, team oriented, achieving, pressured, confident, and special."[8] Maybe you don't identify with all of these adjectives, but some of them may hit home for you or the millennials you manage. If there are any negative references in these assessments, I am sure you are starting to see whom you can blame—your parents!

To highlight some of the main points, here is a quick look at the assets and liabilities of your generation. It's important to know the "perception" of you as a manager, and it's also significant as you manage other millennials.

Assets	Liabilities[9]
Goal oriented	Distaste for menial work
Positive attitude	Lack skills for dealing with difficult people
Tech-savvy	Lack of experience
Collaborative	Confidence beyond ability
Multicultural awareness	Impatient

With a better understanding of what makes everyone tick, you can work more effectively with your bosses, colleagues, and direct reports. As your generation enters management roles, you undoubtedly will shake up the way business is done and how managers manage. You will bring your personality and strengths to the role. Having a firm foundation of understanding on all of the generations—including yours—gives you the leg up when it comes to building a strong and cohesive team.

Millennials Defined
◁ Telltale Tweets ▷

1. Millennials Defined—Conventional, sheltered, team oriented, achieving, pressured, confident and special. #millennialsrising

2. Millennials are more conventional, sheltered, and team oriented. #backstreetboys #blameyourparents #goteam #noleaderhere

3. Millennials are confident and special. You were told you can be ANYTHING you want to be. #babyonboard #haveatrophy

4. Understanding the negative and positive perceptions of millennials gives you a leg up as a leader. #nowIknow #worktogether

3

⊙

FROM INDIVIDUAL
CONTRIBUTOR TO MANAGER

*"Millennials have a great opportunity to change the way leaders
lead, from the old school of command and control
to the new school of trust and track."*

Paul Spiegelman, CEO of The Beryl Companies
and author of *Why Is Everyone Smiling?*

Now in the red corner, we have the millennials at more than 75 million strong; in the blue corner, we have a tag team of Xers and Boomers weighing over 15 billion pounds!

Although it's not a battle and I'm not pitting people against one another, I often see the quick, verbal jabs among the generations. I have worked with tens of thousands of senior leaders across the country, and they express a little—okay, a lot of frustration—with the millennial perspective. As you become a manager, you will begin thinking less about your individual performance and more about the performance of your team. Admittedly, millennial manager Cheryl Ryan was surprised with how difficult this transition was. "It's a big shift to go from *knowing* the work to *leading* the work," shared Ryan, Director, Human Resources at Centro. "It took several months to feel comfortable delegating and taking a step back. It's hard to let go and no longer own what you were truly great at."

To help you make this transition, we're going to look at what I hear from your elders as being a dichotomy in viewpoints. This review of **"millennials vs. older generations"** will help you see where some of the struggles come into play as you go from individual contributor to manager. It's important to note that these are just perceptions, but as a manager, perceptions make a big difference. Additionally, as a millennial manager, you probably still have a boss and your own job responsibilities. This information will give you insights on how your boss may see you and how you can manage up and be an even better employee.

Our team has even written "manifestos" that capture the viewpoint of a millennial just starting work and that of older generations with more work experience. This way you can understand each perspective and where they're coming from. Let's take a look.

MILLENNIAL MANIFESTO

I am a millennial. Hear me roar.

Hear me roar. Seriously, will you listen up? I have big ideas. I have big aspirations, and I am ready to put them to work. I have prepared my whole life for this job, for this chance. My entire life, everyone has told me that I can do whatever I want to do and be whoever I want to be. "The sky is the limit. If you put your mind to it, you can change the world," everyone said. "You are special."

Well, here I am, a part of your company. I want to be a part of something great—and to contribute to something special—every day. I want to make a contribution, and I want to move up.

But I don't feel like I fit in your system. It's hard for me to get inspired by climbing the corporate ladder and increasing shareholder value. It's not even my job duties really—it's all those things that surround the job. Working with my boss, having to prove myself, and understanding all those unwritten rules that just don't make sense to me—it's all so different.

What can I do to succeed? How do I navigate this career path? How do I make my mark? I like to achieve. So what can I do? What can we do? It wasn't so long ago that you were in my position.

Let's figure this out together. Let's work together. I am ready to listen. I am a millennial.

Xer/BOOMER MANIFESTO

I am your manager. I am tired of hearing you roar.

Listen up. I am trying to understand you—really, I am. I am trying to be patient, but we have so much to do. You are not in school anymore. Your parents can't solve your problems anymore. What you need to learn at work wasn't covered in your college textbooks.

Changing the world takes hard work. And it doesn't happen on your first day, your first month, or even your first year.

Here we are. I'm ready for you to contribute, but you have a lot to learn. Around here, if you want to be special, you have to earn it. Do you know anything about paying your dues?

I want to teach you, and I want you to succeed, but you've got to meet me halfway. It's hard to be understanding when you give off the air that you know it all. Don't you think that my experiences are valuable? I get it. You want it all—don't we all? But you can't have it all right away.

What can you do to succeed? You have to think less about "me, me, me" when it comes to your career. You'll make your mark by asking, "what can I do for you?"

Let's figure this out together. Let's work together. I am ready to talk. I am ready to listen.

I am your manager.

This gives you an inkling of the two perspectives that I will discuss—both well intended, but both coming from very different places. In many ways, based on much of what I have covered, the way that your generation has been raised and shaped by society, culture, technology, and parenting is fundamentally different from other generations. What I will address now is how on four separate measures the perspective of a millennial manager will be just the opposite of other generations. I'm not saying that once you're a manager, you have to "sell out" and go to the "other side," but it is helpful to see these ideas from different viewpoints.

Millennials Versus Older Generations

Entitlement vs. Duty

Equality vs. Hierarchy

Explanation vs. Action

Partnership vs. Ownership

ENTITLEMENT VERSUS DUTY

When I conduct our workshop and ask older generations about millennials, the number one issue that I hear is—*entitlement*. You want to get promoted instantly, or you believe you have a college degree so you shouldn't have to do any menial tasks. I hear that millennials complain that the computer they've been issued is two years old or the variety of beverage choices being provided for free at the meeting is not nearly diverse enough. "How dare they serve us simply Coke and Sprite. Would it kill them to offer some Dr. Pepper? What are we, heathens?" That's an extreme example, and you may have been raised very differently than what I'm describing, but it's important to recognize some of the *perceptions* of your generation.

The Downfall of Menial Summer Jobs

Now, let's talk about two specific things that contribute to the perceived entitlement in the millennial generation. First an interesting statistic: "Fewer than three in ten American teenagers now hold summer jobs— jobs such as running cash registers, mowing lawns or busing restaurant tables. The decline has been particularly sharp since 2000, with employment for 16-to-19-year olds falling to the lowest level since World War II."[1] Even though in recent years, there are more experienced workers taking jobs that teens would normally hold, there is an even more important reason for this phenomenon.

If most teenagers aren't working, what are they doing? Activities are a big one: You grew up with tennis camp, soccer camp, baseball camp, space adventure camp, LEGO camp, and more. You name it, and there's a camp for it. Teenagers are also taking more summer school classes or unpaid internships to help with college admissions. Perhaps you spent your summers playing video games or hanging out at the pool, or you may have been traveling. Possibly you and your family toured the great sites of Northern Europe. A couple of summers ago my 16-year-old niece went on a teen tour. A bunch of kids her age took a chaperoned trip to the Pacific Northwest where they went white water rafting, camping, and hiking for eight weeks.

Now what has permitted all of this? Because, let's be honest: The thought of a "teen tour" when I was 16 would have sounded pretty amazing. The fact is, money prevented those of us my age from doing all those great things. Millennials are part of the richest generation in the history of the world. Let's hand it to your parents!

The important thing is that many of you were not working. When I do my workshops, I ask for a show of hands to see who worked in fast food as a teenager. With older generations, 50 to 60 percent of people raise their hands. With millennials, that number is about 5 to 10 percent —and occasionally zero!

Let me tell you something. If you spend your summers pulling fries out of a vat of boiling oil, you learn a sense of duty. You don't learn a sense of duty touring the great sites of Northern Europe with your family. I'm not saying it's better or worse; it's just different.

Additionally, for many millennials, the first job they have out of college is the first "real" job they've ever held. If you spent four years working in a fry vat and you start a new job in which someone says, "Pull the numbers for the spreadsheet." you're likely to say, "Cool, I get to work on a spreadsheet instead of immersing myself in boiling oil, which runs the risk of scalding my body."

Conversely, if you've spent the previous few summers on a teen tour, at soccer camp, and visiting the Eiffel Tower, when someone says pull the numbers for the spreadsheet, your response may not be so positive.

Successful Business Icons Who Are . . . Young

There is another reason for a strong sense of entitlement among millennials, and it has to do with how business has changed on some profound levels. I graduated college in 1987. When I began my career and looked up in the corporate world at the titans of American industry, I saw folks like Warren Buffet, Lee Iacocca, Jack Welch, and Louis Gerstner. Let's think about these business icons. What do they all have in common—in addition to being rich, white, men (remember this is decades ago)? They were all *old!* At the time, they were in their 50s and 60s. When you're a 22-year-old who just started working, fifty and sixty seem old. I remember thinking, if I bust my butt, if I work incredibly hard, and if I'm in the right place at the right time, MAYBE in thirty-five or forty years, that can be me.

In the 1980s, did I know any 25-year-old, self-made *billionaires*? No. Nobody did. In those days, if you wanted to become a corporate icon, you had to work at it for decades. How about today? It's pretty different. We all know several self-made millionaires and billionaires who are incredibly young! The people who started Facebook, Napster, YouTube, and Twitter —many of them were in their twenties or early thirties when they made their millions. Now, I can see how you might be thinking:

"Mark Zuckerberg is smart. Mark Zuckerberg had a good idea. Mark Zuckerberg is young. Mark Zuckerberg is a billionaire."

"I am smart. I have good ideas. I am young. By the transitive property...."

Now, maybe you don't expect to be a billionaire, but why can't you be a vice president or at least run that big project? In your head you think, "People, the rules have changed. You don't need to be sixty to run the show." To some extent, you're right. However, in addition to all being young and being in the tech field, these modern-day corporate icons share another thing in common—they started their own companies. In other words, at age 22, GE didn't approach Mark Zuckerberg and ask him to run the company. Zuckerberg, and others like him, became 20-something CEOs by doing their own thing. While to some extent the rules have changed, you need to understand that there's still something to be said for experience.

Let's think about it this way. Fast-forward to 2037, Mark Zuckerberg is in his 50s, and he decides it's time to retire. Facebook is worth a trillion dollars, and he wants to hang out at the beach in his golden years. When Zuckerberg goes to select his successor, do you think he will pick a 22-year-old to run Facebook? I doubt it. Chances are his successor will have more work experience and be older, even though Mark was twenty when he started the company.

Based on the downfall of summer jobs as well as the business icons of the day, you can see how your generation might act more entitled than other generations. Many professionals say they have learned critical skills through their sense of duty—working their way up and gaining experiences along the way.

This section is not meant to squander your hopes, dreams, and goals, but it is a valuable reminder to be appreciative of the experiences of those around you and to learn from them. Instead of trying to skip steps one through five, focus on learning, growing, and developing during these beginning stages of management. As you become a more seasoned manager, this idea of "entitlement versus duty" is an important aspect to be aware of and monitor. When you're entitled and an individual contributor, you're very concerned about yourself and your future. As a manager, it's more about stepping outside of yourself and upholding your duty to your team to help them grow, succeed, and achieve results.

EQUALITY VERSUS HIERARCHY

Our next dichotomy in "millennials versus older generations" is equality versus hierarchy. As you take the first step into management, this one is important to understand. It can be difficult to wrap your head around, and it's especially hard for those new to the workforce. As a student, everyone is equal. You are all charged the same tuition. You start and end classes on the same day. You have the same academic requirements and follow the same rules. Think about growing up. As a kid, did you ever say "That's not fair!," as it related to a sibling? If your sister got a car when she was 16, you got a car when you were 16. If she stayed out until 10:30 PM, you could stay out until 10:30 PM. Everything was perfectly equal growing up.

Now, at work, there is hierarchy. You have a boss. Your boss's boss has a boss, and so it goes all the way up the line. There is a hierarchy; there is a leader; and everything isn't always equal.

This situation may sound familiar. Your boss tells you that you should practice your presentation at least three times. You always do your due diligence and practice the presentation out loud at least three times. The next time your boss has to deliver a presentation, he walks into the room and delivers it—seemingly without any practice at all. You say to yourself, "That's not fair!" You're right, it's not fair, but in your manager's mind, it's perfectly fine for him to do that. He has delivered so many presentations that he doesn't need to practice as diligently or specifically as you. As you enter the ranks of management, you may have done similar things—even though you probably hated that as you started your career.

It can be hard to understand that it is not fair up and down, but it's also not fair across. For example, a company may hire 100 entry-level employees on the same day. Are they all going to get promoted or receive raises on the same day? No. They may work different hours a week, at different locations, and for different types of people. Some people may get to travel while others are stuck at their desks all day; some get promoted quickly while others get a larger raise or an opportunity to work from home a couple days a month. All of these things can be absolutely fair even though they aren't equal. It may sound harsh, but in the working world, fair does not always mean equal. As you begin to manage a team, this idea may make more sense to you. Why shouldn't your high-performer who goes above and beyond get to work on that cool project or get a little extra perk? It's absolutely fair that your high performer is rewarded. It's fair but not equal.

EXPLANATION VERSUS ACTION

The next difference I would like to discuss is explanation versus action. To me, this is the biggest and most profound difference between the generations, and it's very important to recognize as you enter a management role.

No More "Because I Said So"

First, let's talk about the disappearance of the term "Because I said so." When my father gave me a menial task to do when I was growing up, he just said, "Bradley, go cut the grass." If I asked "Why?," what do you think he said? If you guessed, "Because I said so," you are correct. In fact, my father uttered that phrase to me a minimum of 5,000 times during my youth. At some point, once you've heard that 5,000 times, you stop asking and just do it. As a kid, when I looked up at an authority figure, it was my father. Then as an employee, when I looked up at an authority figure, it was my boss. When I got to work and my manager gave me a menial assignment to do, I never thought to ask why, assuming if I did, my boss would say, "Because I said so."

What I have learned is that the phrase, "Because I said so" is vanishing from the vernacular of the millennial parent. If you read a parenting book these days, there isn't a chapter on "The Power of Because I Said So." Parents are taught to answer their children with real explanations to their questions. When you asked your parents why you had to cut the grass, they likely gave you an elaborate answer. Dad might say, "Son, you are a part of this family, and everyone in this family has a responsibility. Your mom is at the office working, I'm cooking dinner, your sister is cleaning the kitchen, and it's your job to cut the grass." Interestingly, upon hearing that explanation, most millennials growing up would say, "Okay."

Now that millennial comes to work. His manager gives him a menial assignment to do—"Go pull the numbers for the spreadsheet." That millennial—accustomed to asking questions and getting real answers—asks, "Why?" How do you think his Xer or boomer boss takes that question? Not very well. The boss is thinking, "How dare you, you little punk, because I said so." In actuality, the millennial isn't asking "why" out of arrogance or distaste for the work but because he legitimately wants to know *why*. If you tell a millennial why he needs to pull the numbers for the spreadsheet, then he's usually okay with it. Your generation likes to see how your duties connect and contribute to meaningful work or a purpose.

Understanding why, having structure, and knowing the destination are all traits that millennials have grown up with. I serve as an executive coach to many millennials—helping them make the successful transition to the workplace and into management—and one of them said something quite profound to me. He said, "I deal much better with adversity than with uncertainty." When pointed in the right direction and given specific expectations and parameters, millennials work exceptionally hard. When unsure about what to do or how to do it, millennials often will resort to inactivity.

"I Heart Structure"

Let's look at another example. From generation X to millennials, free time—as a kid growing up—is down 37 percent.[2] That's big. The lives of young people are absolutely packed. They go from school to soccer practice to lacrosse practice to piano lessons to play date to math tutor to hip-hop class to bed.

Play dates are always a fun one to discuss. Essentially a play date is a 90-minute time period in which one child plays a supervised set of activities with another child, all the while supervised by an adult. Play dates are new. They didn't exist in my day. Here's how I "played." My mom would open up the front door, stick her foot in my back, and say, "Get out of the house!" In terms of structure, I always had two rules:

1. Be home by dinner.
2. Don't die.

Growing up, millennials had more activities, more sports, more clubs, and more of everything. It means that during their entire lives, millennials have looked up—at a coach, a teacher, an instructor, a volunteer, a tutor, a chaperone, a parent—and someone has told them EXACTLY what to do. As a result, when they come to work, they look up and they expect their boss to tell them exactly what to do. While that may sound just fine to you as a millennial manager, it is just the opposite of what older generations feel. Boomers and Xers dislike authority figures telling them what to do, and they have an extreme distaste for structure. Here's how I see it play out.

An older manager tells her millennial employee, "Here's a project, Ashley, and it's due in two weeks. I know you've never worked on anything like this before, but here's your chance to put your own stamp on the project. I'm not going to give you a lot of direction. Just figure it out and let me know what you come up with. See you in two weeks." Xer or boomer managers think they are the best bosses in the world, because to them, a direction-less assignment is the greatest gift ever! They get to work independently and figure it out on their own—with no one bothering them!

On the flip side, how would a millennial feel about this assignment? What would *you* do if your manager gave you that assignment?

You might freak out! In fact, that's the response I get from about four out of five millennials in my sessions. In two hours, Ashley is in her manager's office with twenty questions: *How long should the report be? Has this ever been done before? Can I look at last year's report? Where should I start? How in-depth should my research be? Should I write in bullet form or full sentences? Is it okay if I use Helvetica font and put it on light blue paper? Can we chat tomorrow if I have more questions?* The manager thinks, *I don't care! Just figure it out!*

You may be laughing right now because I am certain you have encountered this at some point during your career. The interesting thing is to understand both sides of the generational debate. First, here's what millennials say. In this particular case, here's Ashley's take:

"Fine, boss, I'll 'figure it out,' whatever that means," and then Ashley goes off and works on it for two weeks. She spends considerable time, gives it her best effort, and then hands it to her manager on the due date. Her manager looks at it and says, "This is not what I wanted." Millennials I work with make a pretty good point. They say, "Why do we play this game? Why do we play the game of 'guess what's going on in my boss's brain'? Wouldn't it be more efficient if my manager just told me what she wanted, and then I could go do it?"

In some ways, it's very difficult to argue that point. However, I do argue the point because there are a couple reasons bosses don't say exactly what they want. Reason one is that part of the process of figuring it out is part of the process of learning. However, this explanation is sometimes hard for millennials to grasp.

You are a high-achieving generation. You're used to getting good grades, you're used to succeeding. When your manager says, "This is not what I wanted," in your mind you haven't done a good job. You've failed. You got the bad grade. Truly, it's been a valuable learning experience. Xers and boomers were taught that if you face a barrier, you go around it, over it, or break through it. Millennials were taught that if you face a barrier, ask someone.

That's the first reason bosses don't tell you exactly what they want. The second reason is because they don't know exactly what they want. I understand at this point in your career that may make sense, but think back to your early years on the job. Before you started working, you spent virtually your entire life in school. At school you have someone above you—a teacher—who always knows the right answer. In fact, this teacher grades you on getting the right answer. When you start work-ing, the new person above you is a boss, and in your mind, they know the right answer. They're just not telling you what it is because they are mean!

This entire scenario of explanation versus action speaks to probably the biggest disconnect between the generations. This may sound coun-terintuitive, but due to the way you were raised, your generation almost needs to be *taught* to think on its own. As a millennial manager, you will have to think and act on your own, and you can teach your millennial employees to follow your lead. Having this insight on your generation will help you move toward looking internally to provide your own struc-ture for yourself instead of looking outside for someone else to provide it for you.

PARTNERSHIP VERSUS OWNERSHIP

The final difference in perspective between millennials and older gen-erations is partnership versus ownership. Remember our opening story about interviewing a candidate who worked on a group project with no leader? That's what this point is all about.

Due to all of the group work in school, the clubs you've been in-volved in, and the team sports you have played, the tendency is to think in terms of shared responsibility versus ownership.

In addition to corporate training, our company does a fair bit of indi-vidual coaching. We work with senior executives and newer employees, and we even help individuals or teams that are having trouble working together. We were engaged in one of those scenarios where a boomer was working with a millennial, and they were having some issues.

MILLENNIAL: I've been working at this company for a year and a half, and my manager won't let me send a single e-mail to the client without approving it first.

BRAD: That seems odd. At this point, you should be able to do that.

BOOMER: That's correct; Zach is not allowed to send anything to the cli-ent without my approval because every e-mail he sends to me, in-tended for the client, has at least one error in it.

MILLENNIAL: Well, there may be a typo somewhere, but since my boss is
   looking at it anyway, he'll catch it.
BRAD: Sticky.

That example may sound a bit simplistic, but it illustrates the partnership versus ownership issue. Remember mom proofreading that college paper?

Now, when you get to work, it's all about ownership. Of course, at
work, you're working on a team and you're partnering with colleagues,
clients, and bosses. Your boss will work with you to advise you and lend
support when needed, but the bottom line is, you have specific responsibilities. Success or failure is up to you. I often hear senior leaders complain that millennials don't see projects through from start to finish. The
perception is that millennials think their boss will make the final touches
and correct any problems. Of course, there will be collaboration, but
millennials also need to have ownership over their responsibilities.

From Individual Contributor to Manager

You can see the perceived dichotomy between the two perspectives. Especially as you enter a management role, you must start thinking more
in terms of *what can I do for my team and my company* instead of *what
can the company do for me*. I'm not saying that millennial managers
need to cast away their values or compromise their uniqueness to be just
like those managers who have come before them. I think you will bring
your own personality and breathe new life into the responsibility, but
you must also recognize that entitled managers who don't take ownership often don't make it very far.

Furthermore, if you look at the big picture, as a millennial manager,
you are somewhat of a "middle manager." You are a manager, but you
probably have a boss and your own job responsibilities. Being a millennial and understanding this perspective is also helpful when you think
of managing up and working more productively with your boss. I have
found that being a manager usually helps you be a better employee for
your manager as well. The first few months of management is likely
filled with thoughts similar to "Now, I understand why my boss always
says that" or "I see how frustrating it can be when an employee doesn't..."

or "Well, I get where my boss is coming from now." There is no need to leave what makes you, you, in the dust, but as you grow in your career, thinking on your own more and taking ownership of your responsibilities will help you bridge the gap among the generations and move from an individual contributor to a positive and influential manager.

From Individual Contributor to Manager
◁ Telltale Tweets ▷

1. Going from individual contributor to manager requires a mindset shift. From doing the work to leading the work. #majorchanges #hearmeroar?

2. Understand different viewpoints—Entitlement Versus Duty; Equality Versus Hierarchy; Explanation Versus Action; Partnership Versus Ownership. #bridgethegap

3. As you enter management, move away from your sense of entitlement. What can I do for YOU? Instead of what can YOU do for ME? #leader

4

DEFINING MANAGEMENT CHARACTERISTICS: SHAKING IT UP

"To be nobody but yourself in a world that's doing its best to make you somebody else, is to fight the hardest battle you are ever going to fight. Never stop fighting.

— e.e. cummings

How will you rewrite the rules of management? How will you lead your team as a millennial? What will be different, and importantly, what are the secrets to success? What legacy will you leave, and how can you ensure it is positive and powerful?

You have heard a lot about the different generations, and you are aware of the ways that your generation can be perceived. This background and knowledge base will help you immensely as you begin managing in a multigenerational workforce. Now let's take a glimpse at how *your* generation will manage.

Our team at JB Training Solutions interviewed and talked with hundreds of millennials, and we work with thousands of millennials every year. In our conversations, we heard a few themes that rang true for the majority of millennials. Although there always will be exceptions, there were a few adjectives and attributes that immediately came to the forefront during our interviews and conversations.

For millennial managers, work isn't just work—it's an extension of themselves. You bring your values to the workforce, and some of those principles fly in the face of the "way business has always been done." To make your mark, you are pushing for more collaboration, more technology, more fun, and more flexibility at work. Your values and principles will steer you, and you will bring these attributes to your management role to build a great team, solid relationships, and a rewarding environment.

After speaking with thousands of millennial managers, a few core principles jumped out. The main characteristics that will define your management style are *collaborative, flexible, transparent, casual, and balanced.* These concepts will drive your decisions, and they truly set your generation apart as managers.

To help you see how this plays out in your management role, this section will explore each concept individually. Although some of these attributes have been touched upon already, this chapter will discuss how they tie directly to being a manager. As you learn about each attribute, think how you can use these ideas and values to propel your path toward leadership.

COLLABORATIVE: WE'RE IN THIS TOGETHER

When interviewing millennial managers, we heard time and time again that you enjoy working together. Renee Oehlerking, a millennial manager at a public relations agency, said she wants to build a strong team environment where "we float together and sink together." For this millennial manager, her team could get through anything—the good and the bad—if everyone joined forces and stuck together. This quotation also capitalizes on the idea that millennials don't mind hardships if they're trucking through it as a team. Lessons can be learned and fun can even be had even when "sinking together." It's all about the team, and it's all about the people. Millennial managers want to like the people on their teams—and they want the people on their teams to like them as managers. "If I'm spending eight to ten hours with someone every day, I want to get along with that person," said Oehlerking.

Millennial managers enjoy hearing the opinions of their teams and working together to solve problems. It's about the partnership, collaboration, and relationships. You value relationships, and one of the things you take pride in is being able to build a relationship with your employees. Many millennial managers don't even like to call their direct reports their reports or subordinates because they want everyone to feel like equals. We heard numerous quotations about how millennial managers don't want to be leaders who just issue orders; they want every person's voice to be heard.

Maybe in an effort to distance yourself from older generations or to echo the way you were raised in a family where everyone had equal say, you have a fear of being seen as an authoritative figure who barks out commands. In our interviews, millennials said that they dislike when their managers do that to them, so they want to make sure they're not doing that with their teams. You like when your manager listens to your ideas and asks for your opinion, so you, in turn, want to provide that for your team. You appreciate when you have a voice, so you choose to give that to your team. You aim for everyone to feel like they have a say and a part. This is in sharp contrast to the "command-and-control" management style of previous generations.

"Building a relationship" with your team is one of the accomplishments millennial managers are most proud of. You take the time to get to know your employees and share advice, and you give everyone a voice. No one is better than anyone else, including yourself—the leader.

For millennials, the social and collaborative piece is one of the most rewarding aspects of work. Why work on something alone when you can have partners pooling ideas and resources? Can't a diverse group with an assortment of ideas come up with a better solution than the lone leader? Isn't it more rewarding if everyone is working together on projects? Millennial managers think so.

Here are a few anecdotes that we heard from millennial managers we interviewed:

I love the camaraderie.

There might be some rough days, but we pull together and power through it.

I'm less about making the decision from the top. I like to get all the opinions on the table.

We're in this together.

I don't want to make the decision for them.

I personally want a voice, so I want to give them a voice.

My favorite part of managing is watching people grow and be successful.

I take pride in the personal relationships I build. I feel people have more buy-in that way.

I enjoy creating a culture of sharing.

I'm very dialogue friendly. I like to consider everyone's ideas and incorporate them.

I genuinely care about the people on my team. I want to see them do well.

It has been proven that diverse groups working well together can develop more creative solutions than when individuals work on a problem solo. The book, *Multipliers: How the Best Leaders Make Everyone Smarter,* by Liz Wiseman, highlights the ineffectiveness of "Diminishers"—leaders who issue orders and stifle creativity by thinking their own ideas are best.[1] Millennials seem to have an innate predisposition toward being a "Multiplier"—a leader who encourages others' opinions, empowers people, and fosters the intelligence of those around them. Numerous millennial managers we interviewed showed wisdom beyond their years by saying that they know they have succeeded when someone on their team is promoted. Your generation carries a collaborative spirit and a willingness to foster the growth and development of your team members.

Now there can be a downside to any asset in extreme, and you will learn more about these ideas in our management section. I will cover some of the pitfalls of collaboration when there is a lack of ownership or a deferment in decision making. As a millennial manager, you should be aware that some of the Xers and boomers you manage likely won't be as excited about doing everything as a team. Of course, your millennial team members love this bias toward teamwork, but other generations are more accustomed to having a traditional leader and a hierarchy.

Your Xer employee may be thinking, "Please, please, just leave me alone to work! I can't take any more of this feel-good togetherness stuff!" When talking to Brian, a Xer working at a national retail store, he said his millennial manager struggles with moving from hearing opinions and ideas to making a decision and taking action. Brian recalls one meeting where the team talked and talked and talked, and the millennial manager encouraged a great conversation. However, the meeting wrapped up, and a decision had not been made. From Brian's perspective, the millennial manager was afraid to put her stick in the ground and make a decision; her fear of making the wrong decision or hurting people's feelings extended the discussion and situation much longer than it should have been. In upcoming chapters, you will learn how to walk this fine line and find a successful balance between collaboration and decision making.

On a whole, your collaborative spirit will serve you well to keep your people engaged and moving toward a common goal. Engaged employees are more productive, and employees are more likely to feel engaged if they feel like they are part of a team. In fact, take a look at these questions from Gallup's Employee Engagement Survey.[2] If you answer yes to its 12 questions, you likely are an engaged employee. Here are five of the twelve questions that tend to favor a manager who encourages collaboration:

▷ Does your supervisor, or someone at work, seem to care about you as a person?
▷ Is there someone at work who encourages your development?
▷ At work, do your opinions seem to count?
▷ Do you have a best friend at work?
▷ In the last year, have you had opportunities to learn and grow?

Your generation is known to care about your team members, encourage their growth, and hear their opinions. Even as you move through the ranks to take on larger leadership roles, you will uphold your value of teamwork and working together.

FLEXIBLE: OPEN TO HOW THE JOB GETS DONE

Millennials crave flexibility for themselves, and they are willing to give flexibility to employees. When talking with millennial managers, they stressed the importance of flexibility not only in work schedules, but also in what work is done and how it gets done.

You know that work can't be confined to 9:00 AM to 5:00 PM, so you're less concerned about the "where" or the "when" and more concerned about the quality of the final deliverable. Maybe an individual works better later in the day, or they have personal appointments, or they work from home because they have a long commute. Millennial managers are very open to these ideas. With technological advancements, you can tune into the office anytime or anywhere. If a millennial needs to leave early on Friday, he can just finish up his project Sunday evening. Millennials question, "If they know what the deliverables are, why should I regulate how they work best?"

Julie, a millennial manager at a global bank, sets the standard for flexibility by working out over her lunch break. She says that she knows that she works hard and is going above and beyond in her job. She often works late nights and puts in long weekends when there is a systems change. In this regard, she knows that it's okay to take an hour or even slightly over an hour running and lifting weights at lunch. She says this flexibility gives her the balance that she needs, and she trusts her direct report to do the same.

As an employee, millennials value flexibility, and they will instill this culture as managers. For millennials, there aren't hard and fast rules and policies for everything. There can always be an exception or a personal situation that warrants a targeted solution. Rules for the sake of rules are the bane of millennials' existence! Rules can and should be questioned, according to millennials. Now remember, millennials are more conventional, so if the rules make sense and if they stand up to a line of questions, then they will follow them.

Case in point, there is an upbeat Chicago office building that is full of millennial employees. Most of the companies represented in the building are young and entrepreneurial, and they attract tech-savvy millennials. The security guards in this building say that they find themselves constantly explaining the rules after a myriad of questions. "Why can't a group of us have an impromptu meeting in the hall? Why can't I play my guitar in the stairwell? Do I really have to put my friends on the security list? Can't you be a little more flexible?," millennial employees ask. The rigid nature of the experienced security guards contrasts with the flexible, go-with-the-flow approach of millennials. If a reasonable answer or solution can be reached, then millennials don't have a problem bending the rule or changing it, and now that millennials are in management positions, they have more authority to implement these ideas and instill this culture.

Trust goes hand in hand with this idea of flexibility, and millennial managers, as a generalization, are a trusting group. You believe that people will do what they say they will do, and you trust that employees are bright and committed enough to get the job done. Maybe because boomers and Xers didn't go through their career with as many flexible options, they struggle more with giving their employees flexibility. "Will they actually be working or just goofing around?," the boomer boss asks himself. Boomers also put a lot of emphasis on face time and coming into the office, so they're skeptical of this new idea of "working from home."

Lindsey Dortsen, a millennial manager at Discover Financial Services, talked about how flexible she is with her employee who also is teaching college business courses. This employee changes his schedule so that he works from 6:30 AM to 3:00 PM, which allows him to support his interest in teaching. Lindsey said she was happy to accommodate this flex schedule as often as the workload allows, which she says is 90 percent of the time. There is a genuine trust she is placing with this employee, so he can foster an outside activity. Millennial managers can help bridge the gap between the structured work style of senior leaders and the looser approach of their peers.

For example, Kate, a millennial manager at an HR consulting firm, stresses the importance of balance between working from home and being in the office. Kate shares, "I don't mind working from home from time to time when my schedule calls for it, but I do believe you should be in the office, face-to-face on a pretty regular basis. I think seeing people face-to-face makes a big difference and, sometimes, my millennial employees don't understand that." She goes on to say that working from home too much can delay individuals' career development; they can miss out on seeing how things are done and getting to know people. Kate has openness for new ways of doing business, yet she still respects the strengths of the more traditional management structures. Successful millennial managers will help bridge these gaps.

Millennials are also flexible in their management style—they can decide as they go along. Since your lives are always changing, you can "roll with the punches" as change hits your team and work environment. This adaptability seems to be ingrained in your hard drive and makes you more nimble and open to change. When it came to the idea of flexibility, here are a few anecdotes we heard from millennial managers:

I'm open to how the job gets done—as long as the deliverables are there.

Everyone on my team is smart and dedicated. We're incredibly tech driven, so people are always available wherever they are.

I use to be very concerned with a hard start time, but I realized how important flex hours were to my team, and I knew that wasn't where I needed to be wasting my energy.

Flexibility is incredibly important. Sometimes, it has been looked at as a benefit in the past. Now, it is more of the status quo.

I manage a team in a call center, so I don't have the privilege of being flexible with hours and those kinds of things, but I try to keep my expectations flexible and remain open to new ideas.

I think it's important to be flexible with different people and personalities, even with time and work styles.

Life happens. It's nice when I can show I get that. If appointments come up, no problem. I always tell them that I know they will get their work done.

When it comes to flexibility, you have to break people's stereotypes— being flexible is perceived as bending the rules. Sometimes, there is a sense or pressure to be there in person, and you feel that you have to justify yourself. If our company has flexible policies, then absolutely, we should use them!

Millennial managers are bringing trust paired with flexibility to their role. Again, these are two key attributes that foster highly engaged employees. This open mind toward flexibility will help millennials thrive and excel in a more diverse and virtual workplace and global economy.

TRANSPARENT: BEING "IN THE KNOW"

"What you see is what you get." The millennial manager is more transparent than previous generations. Millennials say that they feel like some senior leaders cloak the board room and executive decisions in secrecy, and they do not like the idea that the state of the company is shielded from employees. Millennials say, if you want my team to be part of the solution, then I think they deserve to know the full story. Millennials ask, "Wouldn't that help people make better decisions if they can see the whole picture?" They want companies and leaders to be transparent in their strategies and values; according to millennials, it helps build trust and respect.

This push for workplace transparency stems from their need to know "why?" and, importantly, the transparency that social media brings to the lives of millennials. From where they are vacationing to what they are having for breakfast, millennials are accustomed to letting the world know through the World Wide Web what they are doing. You tweet your updates and post pictures from your weekend, the family holiday, and your work trip. In the eyes of older generations, there doesn't seem to be much of a filter when it comes to putting things out there. In fact, 40 percent of millennials think that blogging about workplace issues is acceptable, compared to 28 percent of boomers.[3]

Millennials often take the view "I am who I am." This transparency in their personal lives has them in turn expecting that from their work life and from their employer. They look at senior leadership and think, *Why all the secrecy? Why all the "privacy settings"? Shouldn't you be proud to put who we are and what we stand for as a company out there?*

As managers, millennials will break through this facade and forge a more transparent path, but some millennial managers say they still need to know when to draw the line.

Christie Yerks, a millennial manager at a technology company, recognizes, "I feel the responsibility to be professional, so I try to live up to that level of 'there's a time and place to openly share information and your opinion' with trusted people. For me, that's my manager. But I don't know that it is okay for me to be 100 percent transparent with direct reports because I don't want to overly influence their experience." Millennial managers encourage transparency and try to bridge the gap between a more closed, senior C-suite and the overshare tendencies of their millennial peers. Here are a few anecdotes we heard from millennial managers:

I want my team to believe in the company and the end result.

A lot of the tools we grew up with make people more vocal about how they feel about things. Through things like Facebook and Twitter, we are much more open to share our feelings because it's not just work, it's our personal work too.

I want them to be proud of our product and know what they're supporting.

I'm comfortable with my employees and I tell them what I can, and if I can't, I tell them that too.

I feel like the relationship I have with my employees has never been authoritative. I've never believed in scaring your people into working. I give context as to why we are doing what we are doing and why expectations are what they are.

I know managers who work with me see transparency and not stand-offishness.

Being "in the know" helps people feel more connected.

As a millennial manager, you will share the full story with your team because *you* would want to know the full story. With the significant role of social media sites like Facebook, Twitter, and Pinterest and the 24-hour news cycle, millennials are receiving and sharing information, ideas, and perspectives throughout the day. They're accustomed to this constant flow of information and, at work, they think it should be no different.

A millennial manager who supervised twenty employees shared how she became more transparent as a manager and how that aids in her team's growth. She stated, "I think when I first stepped into the management role, I wasn't transparent enough because I was learning a lot of both roles. Now that I know what's going on, I like to relay business decisions that I think will be beneficial for them to know from a growth standpoint. Obviously, there's some confidentiality, but I do try to share information that I can with them, even if it's not directly related to their role."

Millennials think it's respectful and necessary to share. Share, share, share. Transparency can contribute to higher engagement by trusting employees with knowledge and allowing them the freedom to solve problems, knowing the entire challenge. In *Training + Development* magazine,[4] Stephanie Castellano writes, "Building trust is not merely the workplace trend du jour. High-trust organizations are full of engaged employees who help to drive bottom-line results." Castellano continues, "Trust in the workplace these days is all about transparency, predictability, consistency, and collaboration." Millennial managers can increase the feelings of trust, connection, and engagement and drive bottom-line results by serving as a transparent leader.

Of course, there is a flip-side of the "over-share" that could hurt teams. You will learn more about watching the "over-share" as a manager, but in general, millennials will forge a strong path toward transparent leadership.

CASUAL: JUST BE YOURSELF

Gone are the days of suits and ties and panty hose. It's time to get real and be casual. *Wahoo!* Millennials are taking a stand and not backing down on this one—*my work is not affected by my attire.* And the casual tone isn't simply limited to clothes; it extends to their attitude, the way they work, and the way they talk and interact as professionals.

A great story to showcase this phenomenon took place at a reception in Chicago, where Crain's Chicago Business was honoring "40 under 40"—the forty individuals who have achieved so much under the young age of forty. The banquet to honor these individuals was held at the Union League Club, one of Chicago's "oldest and finest establishments" —an establishment with a dress code that aligns more with traditionalists and boomers and where jeans are not allowed. A young award winner showed up to the banquet in jeans—and the Union League promptly gave him a pair of slacks to wear for the night. The honoree accepted his award in someone else's pants. The President of the Union League assured, "It's not that we're stodgy. We just have standards."[5]

Likewise, let's talk about the infamous hoodie recognized around the world. You know the one, it is faded black (or navy?), a little frumpy, and is touted by one of the world's richest and most notable millennials, Mark Zuckerberg. You can argue that Zuckerberg is extremely successful and that if he can build a network one billion people strong, who cares what he wears. However, you could see the clash among the generations and working styles that took over the headlines on blogs and news outlets as Facebook went public:

Zuckerberg's hoodie rankles Wall Street

Is Mark Zuckerberg in over his hoodie?

Zuckerberg's Hoodie a 'Mark of Immaturity,' Analyst Says

Mark Zuckerberg wears hoodie to Facebook investor meetings

Doubts Intensify About Zuckerberg's Role as Facebook CEO

You are witnessing the butting of heads by millennials and boomers firsthand! And what happened as soon as Facebook's stock began to plummet? Headlines read, *Experts call for inexperienced Zuckerberg to step down as Facebook's CEO.*[6] Investors and older generations start to think, well, Zuckerberg is giving me the perception that he is immature and, now, I have the business results to prove it. On the flip side, you can see Zuckerberg's perspective. I started this company in my dorm room with this little ol' hoodie, and I'm not going to put on a suit and try to be someone that I'm not. It's obvious that there is a lack of understanding on both sides.

Some people may find wearing jeans or hoodies disrespectful, but millennials hardly think twice about it. Millennials have a tough time understanding how attire affects the ideas coming from their heads or how it hinders getting their work done. Think about college again. If you showed up to take an exam in pink pajama pants, did it affect your grade on the test? No way. Millennials carry this perspective to the workplace where they want to hang on to their individuality and self-expression. As millennials become the majority in our workplaces, expect to see more and more casual environments. Especially as millennials enter management roles, they will instill a more casual and laid-back atmosphere.

In addition to attire, millennials are much more casual in the way that they do business. As mentioned, you don't adhere to a strict hierarchy, so business is conducted much more casually where ideas and strategies can come from anywhere. Business meetings start with how the weekend went instead of strictly following Six Sigma rules. You blur the lines, so work is not just work and play is not just play. Work and play come together to create a much more casual scene where it's okay to listen to your headphones, answer your cell phone, play Words With Friends during breaks, or chitchat with the CEO at work. Millennials aren't stiff and professional outside of work, so why should they be that way at work?

U get a bad rap 4 UR communication SKILLZ! Time and time again, I hear from senior leaders, "Please, please, help them write more professionally!" Millennials think, *I text my friends and parents, why can't I text my boss or our client? Does it really matter if I send off a quick e-mail with no capital letters? If I call my friend "dude," why can't I call my colleagues "dude"?*

Nell Madigan, Associate Dean, School of Labor and Employment Relations at the University of Illinois, asserts that millennials tend to be "very casual and candid and can improve their poise. Although some of that will come as they get older, millennials will always be less formal and more candid."

A millennial manager who oversees three millennials on a customer design team reveals how your generation is bridging the gap between the more traditional, formal management style and the casual approach of millennials. She explains, "I knew I needed to be more formal at the beginning to show people I was serious. There's this balance where at the beginning you are aware of the perceptions working against you, so I wasn't as laid-back. Once I earned the credibility, I was more casual. It was probably a month and a half into the process." Millennials will lead a more casual workplace, but they also are showing that they think there is a time, place, and audience for everything. Here are a few more ideas we heard from millennial managers:

Casual dress attire and pushing for jean Fridays is a passionate topic. To me, I understand that can be energizing to a workforce, but there is a time and a place.

Managers who are older are more likely to know the documented process and follow the rules more so. Millennials may be more apt to challenge, bend, or take a creative approach.

Millennial managers can be more casual in terms of appearance and language, but that doesn't translate to career outtake or how seriously we take our careers.

I think we are more casual in the sense of conversation, writing skills, and appearance. I find that recent graduates are even much more casual and less appropriate.

There's the tendency to feel like you always need to be working. I encourage her [my employee] to leave at reasonable hours. I encourage her to walk away from her desk if she's overwhelmed. I'll write her a card when I know she's stressed.

I try to keep open lines of communication like pulling people aside and having a relationship outside of the director/subordinate roles. If you can't have normal conversations, it is uncomfortable for everybody.

I think you should just be yourself at work. You shouldn't have to put on this fake or overly professional persona.

Millennial managers wanted to stress that the "casualness" of the generation isn't necessarily due to a lack of respect or interest. For millennials who text constantly, sending a "text-speak" e-mail doesn't seem like that serious of an issue. Millennials don't show as much reverence to authority because they view the workplace as more of a network rather than a hierarchy. Even though other generations would see this as far too casual, for millennials, "Hey!" is a perfectly polite and acceptable way to start an e-mail or greet an executive. It doesn't mean you don't care. Zuckerberg wearing a hoodie does not mean he doesn't take the situation seriously. He simply does not see his external apparel as a reflection of his internal mindset. With the blurring of work and life, millennials are bringing a more casual way of dressing, writing, communicating, and managing to the workspace.

BALANCED: SUCCESSFUL AT LIFE AS A WHOLE

"Work/life balance was always the elephant in the room. The reality is that now, we are talking about it and expect it," says millennial manager Amelia Forczak. Rare is the millennial who jumps at the opportunity to work from 8:00 AM to 8:00 PM. Millennials are not workaholics, and there is not a clear boundary between work and life. Leading a balanced life is not something that millennials aim for; rather, it's ingrained in them. Furthermore, for millennials, it's more of work/life integration and less about a balance. With a balance, work is on one side and life is on the other side. Millennials see work and life as more of a medley and integration that ebbs and flows in response to needs at work or needs outside of work from week to week.

In our interviews with millennial managers, we often heard that millennials want to succeed in work AND outside of work. One manager said that she wanted her legacy as a manager to be that she was "successful at life"—not that she was just an amazing manager. Millennials are much more likely to look at their lives as a whole. It's not as though work only happens between the hours of nine to five. Millennials may spend the first few minutes catching up on social media while they are at the office, but they may answer a few e-mails in the evening or over the weekend.

Friends, family, and extracurriculars are very important to your generation. As we have established, you grew up living a highly programmed life, and you enjoy the fulfillment and "busy-ness" that it brings. More and more, companies are incorporating these flexible practices to foster a balanced environment.

For example, Best Buy has instilled the ROWE (Results Only Work Environment) program, where work hours are more flexible and employees are graded only on results. Centro, a media logistics company, offers its employees "Ferris Bueller" days. In addition to vacation and holidays, each employee receives ten personal days with no questions asked. Centro even grants a three-week paid sabbatical after four years of service to give their employees some time to explore an interest, travel, or just relax and reinvigorate with family. With an employee population comprised mostly of millennials and numerous millennial managers, Centro is speaking the language of its employee base.

Furthermore, millennial managers encourage their people to lead balanced lives as well. You have seen what happened to your burnt-out parents and senior leaders. Your generation doesn't see work as your defining feature, and you have stated that you're not going to sacrifice everything for work. Here are a few anecdotes we hear from millennials:

I want to be known for working hard and playing hard.

I love that I have things outside of work that make me happy. I think it's sad when all you have is work.

I want work to be a place that I want to go to when I wake up.

I plan on getting married and having kids down the road, and that's what I want. I want to succeed at both work and life.

I genuinely care about the people on my team. I want them to have work/life balance.

It's unrealistic to expect anyone to put their job before their families or their own personal well-being. Of course it is important to do your best work, but if you get completely burnt out, it isn't healthy.

I would never ask for people to do anything that I found to be unreasonable—working on a Saturday or calling when they're off.

This made me think of the "get a lot, take a little" approach. You'll get more out of everyone if people are happy, and this is connected to flexibil-

ity. Sometimes, you need a break outside of work to be able to think the most clearly.

I offer work/life balance to my team by reiterating that I don't want them to work while they are on vacation. One of my colleagues was about to take a three-week honeymoon, and he told the team he was going to check his e-mail every day. We were like 'no, don't do that'!

This is where a lot of millennials and older generations hit heads. Boomers are a "work til you die" generation, and they believe in paying your dues and working your way up. Right now, millennials feel as though there is disconnect at some organizations with work/life balance. Companies have policies to help facilitate balance, but then no one follows them. A millennial at a consumer goods company says that they have "no meeting Fridays," but senior managers still set meetings on Friday. Few people are actually going to say no to a meeting called by their manager. A millennial manager will be more compelled to honor and uphold these policies.

Furthermore, flexible work schedules are offered, but millennials are looked down upon if they actually take advantage of the offerings. Again, there seems to be a disconnect that balance is okay if it's for taking care of children or older parents, but balance isn't okay if it's for hanging out with friends or catching an early yoga class. One millennial notes,

> Traditionally, work-life balance is driven by families and children, and things that are a no-brainer. For example, "My kid is sick, I'm leaving" or "Story time and homework are from 5 to 8 PM so work is blocked out," which is perceived to be legitimate. Our generation is getting married and starting later in life, and choosing to have "me" time doesn't seem to fit into "traditional" work/life balance. When you're single, the ways you may balance your life may seem luxurious or selfish. Leaving at 4:00 PM to go to spin class versus leaving at 4:00 PM to pick up the kids from daycare.

For boomers, paying your dues may mean that at first, you don't have that much work/life balance. That's something that you earn more of as you gain experience. Millennials will fight for this to change. Millennials say that as long as they are getting the work done, why should it matter how long they are working?

Millennials see how their managers stifle initiatives for flexibility by the way they run their teams, and millennials will be "enablers" when it comes to flexibility. A millennial manager asserts, "You don't always need to share the reason as to why you need to leave early. You can keep the reason to yourself. Younger people have a mental roadblock that balance looks different for different people." Millennial managers will make sure they are practicing what they preach and that they are running their team in a way that supports balance. It's a dynamic that undoubtedly will cause a little more turmoil as the millennials stick by their value for a balanced life for themselves and their team.

Shaking It Up

If you look at companies started by young professionals, they are little microcosms that reflect all of these millennial values. With millennials or young gen Xers as their founders and with millennials as most of their first employees, they could start from scratch with these new, fundamental principles. At Facebook, they host company-wide "Hackathons" with company-provided food, beer, and tunes and where any idea is up for grabs. They have gourmet chefs who whip up free food in their cafeteria, and video games, a ping-pong table, and an annual game day. Their motto is "to move fast and break things." That's collaborative, flexible, transparent, casual, and balanced.

Groupon's company culture is similar. Founder Andrew Mason told *Fast Company* in an interview, "The companies that I like to do business with are—even if you find them a bit strange—genuine and real."[7] The Groupon team is rich with improv actors and comedy writers, and just like its witty and lighthearted promotions, the company likes to keep its culture fun and collaborative. It even has a whimsical "Michael's room," where employees can retreat to take a break—or a nap.

At Twitter, employees have happy hour Fridays once a month and the company covers 100 percent of an employee's health insurance.[8] EventBrite has regular company outings and trips to a trampoline park.[9] However, it's not all about the perks of foosball tables and free food. It's the underlying principle that work is more than just work. It's a launching point for a collaborative team that fosters hard work but supports a balanced and healthy life and career of learning. And this perspective on work is working.

Millennials are attracted to companies that reflect their values, and companies are finding that if they want to attract the best talent, they need to make their workplaces more millennial friendly—which really boils down to being more friendly. Even for companies that have been around for centuries, millennial managers are spreading their influence and instilling these new values—collaborative, flexible, transparent, casual, and balanced—to build a more rewarding work environment.

Defining Management Characteristics: Shaking It Up
◁ Telltale Tweets ▷

1. Work isn't just work for millennials. You're bringing your personality, style, and values to your management role. #shakingitup

2. Millennials managers are building a rewarding work environment—collaborative, flexible, transparent, casual, and balanced. #soundsnice

3. Millennials are not afraid to shake it up. You are the next generation of leaders. More teamwork, more trust, more play! #andmoreflipflops

5

---◉---

REWRITING THE RULES
OF MANAGEMENT

"Here's to the crazy ones. The misfits. The rebels. The troublemakers.
The round pegs in the square holes. The ones who see
things differently. They're not fond of rules. And they
have no respect for the status quo. You can quote them,
disagree with them, glorify or vilify them. About the only thing
you can't do is ignore them. Because they change things."

—Apple Inc.

You are ready to shake things up. You don't mind rocking the boat, going against the grain, or charting your own course. The road less traveled—why not? The path *never* traveled—absolutely! A shortcut to any path or road (traveled or not)—well, that's more like it.

After speaking with many millennial managers, it is apparent you are not afraid to rewrite the traditional rules of management that you feel aren't working anymore. When you think through the traditional rules of management, it can be a bleak picture. You think about:

Command and control

Authority telling you what to do

People executing orders or demands

Rules, regulations, and policies

Hierarchy and a chain of command

Looking *up* to find out information

Organization and discipline rule

Ideas and initiatives coming from the top

Shunning eccentric ideas from people who want to change the world

Doing whatever the boss says to do

Millennial managers are not going to do something the way it's always been done just because it's always been done that way—especially if it doesn't make sense to them. When you think of modern-day management and the values that your generation is instilling, you think:

Consensus building and collaboration rule

Look *out* to find information

Ideas can come from anyone or anywhere—including the bottom

Being a leader people *want* to follow

Adjusting management styles to fit different people

Helping employees grow and develop

Engaging and empowering

Listening, understanding, and working together

Making mistakes is okay

Thinking differently is encouraged

Even the individual words used in this list are brighter, more positive, and more inviting. This is the language of millennial managers. You want your organization to make profits and progress, but you also put a priority on people and passions.

If there is a faster, quicker, easier, or more fun way to do something, the millennial manager will find it and take that route. You don't mind throwing tradition or process aside if you can improve efficiency. You are accustomed to having a lot of data at your fingertips at a moment's notice, and you don't mind offering a new, different, or unconventional idea if it will be beneficial—even if it shakes things up.

You grew up with change—in an environment where a six-month-old phone is outdated. Your generation has lived in a world that is ever-transforming itself, so you don't mind if your workplace reflects this "normal." On the other hand, for older generations that may be more comfortable with security or proven strategies, they may not mind going along with the flow to keep things steady and consistent. You can see how tension may arise between the "why don't we just try it" millennials and the "why don't we stick with the plan" elders.

Now you're not shaking things up in a negative or revolutionary way, but you will tweak the ideas and structures that you don't think work anymore.

TEARING DOWN THE LADDER

"Tear down this ladder!" I have talked about this theme before, but millennial managers will bring down the corporate ladder. Again, it's not all about looking up at a boss; it's more about working together as a group to solve problems.

This notion of connectedness greatly impacts how you perceive hierarchy in the workplace. With social networking, connections can be made like a spider web. In previous generations, a chain of command was just that—a chain. It started and ended at specific points, and movement up or down could only be made one link at a time. While fundamentally you don't have an issue with authority, you don't think about hierarchy the same way other generations do.

In a keynote address, Malcolm Gladwell, author of *The Tipping Point*,[1] compared and contrasted the idea of hierarchy versus the millennials' idea of the network. Millennials don't think in terms of hierarchy, as they are accustomed to looking "out" for information instead of looking "up." The Internet and social networks give you the information you need. Gladwell analyzed the traditional view of hierarchy through a couple of prominent social movements. When you think about the Civil Rights Movement of the 1960s and 1970s, that was a hierarchy. There was a clear leader—Martin Luther King Jr.—and there was a structure and order in the people below him. Now take a look at the two big millennial-driven movements of recent years—Occupy Wall Street and Arab Spring. Who was the leader? Who drove those initiatives? No one really. They were inspired by social media and the power of the collective. Again, a dramatic difference from other generations with a powerful impact on what you will be like as a leader.

For millennials, it's not about the hierarchy ladder. It's not about busting your tail and working countless hours to move up a rung on the ladder, to climb slowly toward the top. For millennials, that sounds exhausting and unfulfilling. You want to make a difference, and you want to do meaningful work. That doesn't mean you want to be tied to your desk and controlled by your job so you can *maybe* earn a few extra dollars one day. For millennials, it's not worth it. Millennials are turning this career ladder—where the only way is up—into career scaffolding. You can take the ladder up toward management, but you also can take the parallel route for a career transition. You can go up, around, or across to try out different jobs, and you can even take the walkway down for less responsibility. There are different options to fit different people at different points in their lives. It's not the "up-or-out" burn-out idea of the corporate ladder.

Companies such as Deloitte have embraced a similar idea, termed the "career lattice."[2] Not everyone wants to bust their tail and work up toward senior management. Maybe a dad wants to take a step back to a less time-intensive role while raising his kids, or maybe a salesperson would like to make a career change into human resources at the same company. More organizations are moving away from the "up-or-out" philosophy to retain and engage top talent. Millennial managers will support this idea of a career lattice as great employees are shirking from the idea of "climbing the corporate ladder." Tony Hsieh, CEO of Zappos and author of *Delivering Happiness*, shares, "A lot of people work hard at building a career so that one day down the road they think it will bring them happiness. And most of the time, when they finally accomplish their goal, they realize that it doesn't really end up bringing happiness or fulfillment for the long term."

Likewise, millennials aren't game for putting in five to ten years climbing up this corporate ladder to one day, maybe, possibly, hopefully, reach that point of happiness or success. Millennials want to have that all along the way. Your generation is more inspired by building relationships, having meaningful work, and making a difference. These are the ideas and values that inspire you, and these are the principles you will share to inspire your people.

BREAKING DOWN THE WALLS

Millennial managers are breaking down the walls—figuratively and literally. Millennials do not want obstacles that put "walls" in between levels or groups of employees. Your generation does not understand or see any benefit in bureaucracy. Why go through a ladder of people or jump through hoops to try and reach a decision? Millennial managers will just say come directly to me, and I will answer your question. Millennials see bureaucracy or gatekeepers as a waste of time. Productivity is all about accessibility. Millennial managers have an open-door policy because if their employees need information now, then they want to provide that. Millennials solve and handle problems as they come up—on the spur of the moment. Their team members can feel free to pop by their desk to ask questions or bounce ideas off of them because "closed doors" or bureaucracy hinders the free flow of information and stifles productivity.

I talked about transparency of information, and millennials want their physical work spaces to be transparent as well. Millennials are breaking down the mahogany desks and doors to the corner office, and they are creating open workspaces. No one has to wonder what happens at that big, executive meeting, because now the conference room is behind glass doors. The physical space is transparent just like the culture.

There are fewer cubicles to create artificial walls, and more companies have open floor plans to allow for the free exchange of ideas that can come from anywhere—the assistant account coordinator or the CEO sitting right next to him.

Young professionals who run or lead companies are making this statement that they are no better than their newest employee. The CEO of 37signals—Jason Fried—sits on the open floor next to his team. He doesn't shroud himself in secrecy behind closed doors.

Millennials are also breaking down the walls between people. According to the U.S. Census Bureau, in 2011, twenty percent of millennials are Hispanic, and millennials are more racially diverse than any generation before them. One of the most multiculturally aware generations, millennials see and connect with people first, and they are open to differences—gender, religion, age, culture, experiences, sexual orientation, and the list goes on. In general, millennials are tolerant and accepting, and they appreciate the richness that diversity brings.

Millennials embrace the new term of "Conversity®," which is the idea of finding similarities among people that open you up to the differences that surround you. Millennials grew up with diversity, so it's like second nature. Alexandra Levit, author of *They Don't Teach Corporate in College*, recalls poignant interchanges with two different millennial employees at two different companies. When talking to managers about diversity, millennials made a statement along the lines of, "Why do we have to have a special program for diversity? Diversity should be a given. You should be able to walk into the lobby and see all kinds of faces." For your generation, it's hard to understand that people need to be taught about diversity. You grew up with it, and you're accustomed to it.

In an ever-changing economy and world, the successful organizations and leaders will be those who can understand and work well with diverse teams and people. Millennials have grown up in a diverse world, and they expect their workplaces and teams to be that way as well. Your generation will continue to forge a path and break down the barriers to create an open, transparent, accepting, and diverse workplace.

COMMUNICATING ON THE FLY

Talk in person—what? Talk on the phone—why? Just e-mail, tweet, or text. Millennials are making business communication much more casual. Many millennials are of the opinion that long, four-sentence paragraphs in e-mails will never be read, and most important things can be said in 140 characters or less. According to a 2010 study by eMarketer, 43 percent of 18- to 24-year-olds say that texting is just as meaningful as an actual conversation with someone over the phone.[3] Do you text your employees, colleagues, or bosses about work on a regular basis? It's becoming more and more common.

At a national conference for HR professionals, a keynote speaker touched on how technology and the young generation are pushing us toward a new normal.[4] He posed the question that hinted at a new future for our business communications, "What about a real-time performance review via Twitter?" Instead of a formal, annual review where you sit down with your manager, what about a running chronicle of tweets that keep track of your employee's strengths and development areas throughout the year? That sounds more transparent, casual, and open for millennials. Your generation will continue to push the bounds and incorporate new technology into your work life, communications, and management role.

Technology will be the immovable force that millennials carry with them. In fact, 24 percent of millennials say that "Technology use" is what most makes their generation unique, the number one answer.[5] As a millennial, you have grown up with technology and the Internet. I would call you a "digital native." Xers and boomers—myself included—are "digital immigrants." Some of these technological advances are a little foreign to us, but technology is integral to your life. You can't imagine life without computers, smart phones, and techy gadgets. You lead a connected life with the help of social networks like Facebook and Twitter and 24/7 connection. Eighty-three percent of millennials either sleep with their smart phone or place it right next to the bed![6]

Since technology is so innate for your generation, millennial managers tend to communicate via technology rather than the old-fashioned face-to-face meetings. Technology will help you communicate, learn, and manage on the fly. You listen to a TED talk or an educational podcast on your way to work and make sure no important e-mails come through when you're hanging out with friends in the evening. You don't mind sending off an e-mail or text over the weekend or when you're out of the office because you are always connected. And the assumption is that everyone else is connected as well. As managers, your generation will communicate on the fly and expect your team to do the same. Communication—anytime, anywhere.

WORKING WHERE AND WHEN YOU WANT IT

Since you can reach someone anytime, anywhere, then why not work where and when you want? Millennials are all about flexibility. Life isn't solely about work for millennials, and they want work to work with their schedule. As stated, flexibility is one of the most important perks to millennials, and you can bet that they will pass that perk along to their teams. This way of thinking starkly contrasts to the ideas of the boomers who have a much stricter view of how and when work is done.

Again, work and life aren't on two different ends of the balance bar; it's not either work or life. They can happen at the same time and in the same spaces, so there isn't a clear dichotomy for millennials. There are no clear boundaries, so work and life integrate to be—just life. There will always be some jobs that are tied to a workplace, but more and more industries are being creative with how they can offer their employees flexibility, and millennials will champion this cause. Your generation is all about the final product. Are you getting great work done? If you are, then it doesn't matter when or where you do it. Work from the coffee shop, tune in at night, go for a run during lunch, or swing by the dentist in the morning. As long as you're all set to make a great presentation on Friday, then your millennial manager will not mind.

PLAYING AT WORK

Who said work shouldn't be fun? Your generation is not excited to trudge through a long work day or boring work just to get a nice pay-check. Simply consider this statistic from MTV's study "No Collar Work-force,"[7] which says 89 percent of millennials want their workplace to be social and fun (compared to only 60 percent of boomers). Furthermore, this same study shows that half of millennials would "rather have no job than a job they hate." That's pretty revealing.

Millennials are staking their claim in the workforce by saying there is no reason why work and play can't coexist. Millennials want work to be enjoyable, and this doesn't just mean pool tables and happy hours. It also means you want work to be rewarding, to be meaningful, and to contribute to something bigger than yourself. Partly due to your casual nature, your generation doesn't think work has to be stiff and profes-sional to get things done. You actually argue the opposite, which is if people are having fun and being themselves, then everyone will be more creative and productive.

As a manager, you will make sure your team is enjoying work. All work and no play is not a millennial mantra. Your mantra is to work hard and play hard. "Playing" ranges from spending time chatting with colleagues, celebrating someone's birthday in the break room, eating group lunches, and working on projects together. In fact, 93 percent of millennials want a job where they can be themselves.[8] Life is too short for work not to be fun.

For millennial managers, creating fun and keeping their employees engaged will be an important initiative. Many of the "Best Places to Work" honored by business magazines and newspapers have happy hours or beer carts that go around on Fridays. They have office Olympics and games—ping pong, foosball, and hula hoops—in the office. Isn't fifteen minutes of ping pong in the afternoon good for stress levels and creativity? Millennials think so.

Rewriting the Rules

These are just a few ways millennial managers will shake up the workplace and rewrite the rules of management. Paul Spiegelman, author of *Why is Everyone Smiling? The Secret Behind Passion, Productivity, and Profits*, shares "Millennials managing in business can have it all—a company that not only makes money, but makes a difference in the lives of all of its stakeholders."

You will make a difference. You will question the traditional rules of management and business and forge a path toward collaborative and open leadership. You know your values and your principles, but managing and leading a team is not easy and rewriting the rules of anything can be particularly trying. You will be tested, you will be questioned, and you will be doubted. At first, your times of frustration, confusion, or fear may outnumber your feelings of triumph and clarity.

Millennial manager and marketing professional Amanda aims to be "like a duck in the water." From the surface, she seems calm, cool, and collected, but beneath the surface, she's working ferociously and paddling like crazy. Because one thing is clear. You're not afraid of standing up for your values and charging fiercely toward a more open, diverse, flexible, and fun work environment. This book will help you get there. It will give you the insight, skills, and tactics to bridge the gap between the old and new and embrace a fresh dynamic of leadership.

Rewriting the Rules of Management
◁ Telltale Tweets ▷

1. From old school of command and control to the new school of trust and track, you're rewriting the rules of management. #watchout @paulspiegelman

2. Millennials are tearing down the ladders and breaking down the walls. It's all about working together to achieve your goals. #noboundaries

3. Work when and where you want and have some fun at work. Millennials are charting a course of flexibility and engagement. #getonboard

4. Millennials are rewriting the rules, bridging the gap, and embracing a new dynamic. Manager 3.0—the next generation of leadership. #today

6

---◉---

LEADING YOUR TEAM: CONNECT

> "A tribe is a group of people connected to one another, connected to a
> leader, and connected to an idea. For millions of years, human beings
> have been part of one tribe or another. A group needs only two things
> to be a tribe: a shared interest and a way to communicate."
>
> —Seth Godin, *Tribes: We Need You to Lead Us*

What do you want your legacy as a leader to be?

When our team posed this question to millennial managers, we received quite a few inspiring answers.

I want to be known for:

... empowering individuals

... helping my people find their passions and have a sense
of accomplishment

... shaping and developing their careers to help them move forward

... being someone who gets things done and listens to problems

... making the right decisions that were the most effective

... my hard work and fairness

... getting people to see what they couldn't see in themselves

One millennial manager, Amanda, shared a great analogy. Amanda said she wanted to "Float like a butterfly, and sting like a bee." Now, I don't think Amanda wants to knock the lights out of her employees like Muhammad Ali did to his opponents, but she does want to be a graceful and powerful leader. She wants to be nimble and quick, yet stand firm for the values and expectations she believes in. The millennial managers we spoke with were optimistic and ready to make a difference.

YOUR LEADERSHIP LEGACY

You want to be an amazing manager and a leader whom people *want* to follow. If you look back on your career and life, you probably have had a few key managers or mentors who were excellent role models and gave you that extra push you needed. Now, you want to be that person for someone else. You want to inspire, engage, and excite. You want to create a powerful team that can break through obstacles and make a difference at your company. As a millennial manager, you have pushed to achieve and excel all your life, and this new role is no different—you have high goals and expectations for yourself.

As a first-time manager, you might get those little butterflies in your stomach—a combination of excitement and nervousness. Will your team like you? What should you say during team meetings? How can you show confidence but not arrogance? How do you set expectations? Can you still go to team happy hours? These are just a few questions racing through your head.

In the following chapters, you will learn the answers to all of these questions and many more. Being a manager is not easy. Captain of *USS Benfold* and author of *It's Your Ship*, Mike Abrashoff says, "Leadership is the art of doing simple things really well."[1] Have you ever tried to lose weight? The recipe for success is so easy: Just exercise more and eat fewer calories. It's so simple! How has that worked for you? Likewise, leading a team involves easy steps, but when it comes down to implementing them, it can get tricky.

TAKING IT UP A NOTCH

Most individuals are promoted because they are high performers and excellent individual contributors. Often, the skill set that makes you a high-achieving individual contributor is very different from those that make you a great manager of people. Many new managers assume that if they apply the same skills and ideas that always helped them excel, they undoubtedly will do well as a manager. However, going from individual contributor to manager is a significant change and requires a fundamental shift in your mindset. In the past, maybe you gained job satisfaction from putting together winning proposals or being the go-to person for your boss. Nothing made you happier than marking things off your to-do list! Now, you may have to look for new sources of satisfaction—guiding an employee toward writing *his* first winning proposal or eliminating obstacles so your star employee can crank through *her* to-do list. This is actually a profound difference, and I have a story to help explain.

I recently was coaching a millennial manager named Colin at a manufacturing company. Colin is a real superstar who became a manager in his early 20s and is now a vice president—the only millennial to achieve that rank at his company. He was not feeling fulfilled at work, and we talked about why. He managed a division of thirty employees and he loved his team, but the issue was from above. Colin now reported to a very senior executive. His director worked on a different floor, had eight other vice presidents to manage, as well as clients to work with, and was responsible for executive board duties. In short, Colin's boss was busy and didn't have much time for Colin. He expected Colin to do his job, leave him alone, and continue to succeed. He talked to me about how he needed to "fill his tank" to achieve satisfaction at work. Traditionally, Colin's "tank" was filled with praise, recognition, and feedback from above—all traits consistent with your generation. Now that he was off on his own, with a distracted boss and in a position with no room for quick promotions, Colin was struggling.

He and I talked about how instead of looking up to gain job satisfaction, he would have to look down to earn a sense of accomplishment. In other words, he now would derive satisfaction from the growth of his team, from the successes its members achieved, and from seeing them enter the ranks of management. For the past thirty years of his life, Colin had been driven, inspired, and fulfilled from above, but now as a millennial manager, this would have to come from his team below. It's a pretty big shift.

Think about it. For many years, you excelled at managing yourself—a known quantity—and now you have to manage a team of others—unknown territory. I'm not here to say it will be easy; it will take time and energy. It will be hard work, but it *will* be worth it. Vince Lombardi, the legendary coach of the Green Bay Packers, said it best, "Leaders aren't born, they are made. And they are made just like anything else, through hard work. And that's the price we'll have to pay to achieve that goal, or any goal." Many good things in life come from hard work, and being a millennial manager is no different.

The big downfall in this whole process and transition from individual contributor to manager is that companies often reward individuals with a promotion and management role, and they say, "Congratulations Milo, you've been doing a great job, so we're promoting you to manager. You are now in charge of a team of four folks. Go gettum tiger!" with little to no direction or training. Does this sound familiar? Millennials are left repeating to themselves, "Don't freak out. Don't freak out. I can do this. I can figure it out. Don't freak out."

In the following chapters, you will learn everything you need to know to excel as a millennial manager. You already have a firm foundation for understanding how to work successfully across generations. Now, you will jump into the nitty-gritty of managing and running a team. From setting goals and expectations to giving feedback and showing recognition, you will learn it all.

CONNECT: YOU, YOUR PEOPLE, AND THE BIG PICTURE

To guide us through this beast of a topic, the advice has been grouped under seven key themes. One of the defining features of your generation is that you are all about connection—connecting to people, results, and the world. In our interactions with millennials, the word "connect" and the idea of connecting came up time and time again. Here is a snapshot of the words and phrases we heard from millennial managers:

I let them know how their task is connected.

Even if you're not in the office, you're still connected.

We work together to solve problems.

I want to connect to the big picture.

Everyone should be connected to our company and our products.

I connect with my team and understand them.

There seems to be a disconnect with senior leaders on flexibility

I love connecting with people, brands, and companies.

Through technology, we're always connected.

We feel connected to work.

I want them to feel connected to the success.

With my phone, I'm always connected.

Whether it's being connected through technology, relationships, or purpose, it is apparent that this idea of connection is integral to millennial managers. You tend to see the world as a network or spider web, where people, companies, and information all connect, support each other, and make each other stronger. Collaboration—one of your generation's strongest values—is based on and propelled by connecting. You're optimistic, and you want to change the world. Maybe it's just a small slice—making the difference as a manager—but you can see how that connects to the larger picture of making a difference in the world.

Your generation has the power to change the face of leadership, but there are some tips and skills that can give you the leg up and round you out as a knowledgeable, collaborative, and connected leader. In the following chapters, you will gain insights on connecting with your teams and direct reports, so you can be an inspirational leader. As a millennial manager, you want to make sure you CONNECT—Communicate, Own it, Navigate, Negotiate, Engage, Collaborate, and Teach.

Before you jump into these seven themes, let's talk a little more about this overarching idea of connecting. The first thing you want to do as a manager is connect with who you are as a leader. Now, I know that sounds like a boring, if not nebulous, start, but too many people hop into a management role plowing full-force ahead, and they never take a step back to think.

This is actually a criticism that I hear a lot from more experienced professionals. Some senior leaders say millennial managers have a propensity to jump in with a ton of energy and just start running ahead—without orienting themselves or clarifying where they're running or why. Have you thought to yourself, *What do I stand for? What are my principles and boundaries? Do I have mottos that drive me? What is my mission and goal?*

It's a good idea to pose these questions to yourself before plowing ahead. Think of a few great leaders throughout history who have inspired you. A few that come to mind are Martin Luther King, Jr., Gandhi, Amelia Earhart, Walt Disney, and Eleanor Roosevelt. They absolutely knew what they stood for. They had crystal-clear principles, and they had ideas and visions for a bright future that drove them and their people. You could probably rattle off a few strong adjectives right away that exemplify these great leaders. *Inspiring. Insightful. Daring. Creative. Visionary. Empathetic.* Of course, these examples and people are extraordinary. These individuals give us a high aspiration to follow. As a millennial manager, you can model the way of these great leaders by taking time to think through what you stand for and how you will lead moving forward.

CHALANT: PINPOINTING YOUR PRINCIPLES

To paint a picture of how this works on a team level, I will share JB Training Solutions' key principle or motto: CHALANT. What does chalant mean? It all starts with a story.

It was a beautiful, sunny day, and I was driving in Chicago, my hometown. I happen to be a pretty impatient driver, and you can imagine that I often get frustrated with Chicago's traffic. This one day, I was at a stop light, as impatient as ever and undoubtedly late for something. I sat there waiting as best I could for the light to change, with my hand restlessly tapping on the steering wheel. In Chicago, we now have these crosswalk signals that count down how long you have to cross the street. So I was looking across the intersection to see how long I was going to wait for the cars and pedestrians to cross in front of me. 6, 5, 4, 3. . . . I'm starting to get excited because soon I can go. At the moment the counter hit 1 and the light turned yellow, a pedestrian entered the cross walk in front of me and began to cross the street. Now I will admit, as a pedestrian, from time to time, I have done the same. But, if I do, I sprint across the intersection as fast as I can. It's not acceptable to make the cars wait. However, this particular pedestrian on that day was different. He didn't sprint. He sauntered—as slowly as he could, with no care in the world. Of course the light changed for me to go, but our friend was in the intersection. As my blood was boiling, I thought for a second I could teach him a good lesson and hit the accelerator. Then I thought a bit more rationally and realized that would not be a good call. Instead I sat there and seethed at this man's lackadaisical attitude and apparent disregard for all others. I thought, "How could he be so nonchalant?" And then it hit me. This is *exactly* the opposite of how we work at JB Training Solutions! We do things with purpose, direction, passion, and energy. So, if we are the opposite of nonchalant, what does that make us?—CHALANT. Obviously. If clients ask for something by Wednesday, we get it to them on Tuesday. We underpromise and overdeliver. We go above and beyond for each other and our clients. And we race across intersections if the light is about to turn green. We are chalant.

That's one example of a motto and value that drives our team. We have chatted with managers who have a "Happy Monday!" motto. They want to create such a rewarding, engaging, and fun place to work that employees just can't wait to return to the office on Monday.

Courtney's motto is to "Just crank...but keep fun in the tank." Courtney and her team have a bias toward action. They think through decisions and ideas, but their hallmark is their followthrough and results. They crank through their work, their to-do's, and their projects. But for a hard-driving atmosphere, Courtney tries to make sure everyone is enjoying themselves and *keeping fun in the tank.* If everyone is busting their tails and she looks around and morale is lagging on the team, she takes a group lunch, goes for an outing to Dairy Queen, or calls a board game break to rebuild morale. One, she wants her people to be happy and engaged, and two, she knows having fun is important to her millennial team. Courtney even schedules an action item on her to-do list every two weeks that simple says "What have you done to re-recruit your employees?" This simple reminder gets Courtney out of her "crank zone" and allows her to reflect on the morale and engagement of her team. One hundred percent crank isn't going to be sustainable, and her motto of "Just crank . . . but keep fun in the tank" keeps her balanced.

Now, take a few minutes to reflect on your ideals and principles. Think through words, phrases, or icons that can inspire you or keep you motivated and focused as your management responsibilities come into full swing. Maybe it's family, friends, hobbies, songs, quotes, places, or experiences. Have fun with this. You may feel like you have a strong grasp of who you are as a leader, but writing it down on paper or typing it out gives it a type of permanence and promise.

What drives you?

What inspires you?

What do you stand for?

How would you want your team to describe you?

What is your motto?

Doing some of this upfront work of connecting with your personal leadership values will help guide you as you face some of the tougher parts of managing. Once you understand and solidify your management ideals, you can focus on connecting to your organization and your people. As a leader, it's about staying connected with all of these entities—remaining true to yourself while staying in tune with your team and organization. Leaders who lose their influence or momentum are leaders who lose that connection with their people. To keep your team engaged and high performing, make sure you CONNECT—Communicate, Own It, Navigate, Negotiate, Engage, Collaborate, and Teach.

Leading Your Team: CONNECT
◁ Telltale Tweets ▷

1. Millennials are all about connecting as leaders—connecting to people, passions, and purpose. #powerful

2. Connect with who you are as a leader. What do I stand for? What are my principles, boundaries, mottos, and goals? #knowyourself #chalant

3. Millennial managers: You want to collaborate, empower, trust, engage, support, and push your people. You will connect. #yourlegacy

7

COMMUNICATE:
JUST SAY IT

"The single biggest problem with communication
is the illusion that it has taken place."
—George Bernard Shaw

"The less people know, the more they yell," marketing guru Seth Godin wisely states.[1] Lack of communication is the cause of 80 percent of workplace conflicts. Communicate, communicate, communicate. The foundation of any good working relationship—or any relationship for that matter—is built on trust and communication. You cannot have one without the other. The traditionalists' view of "no news is good news" is long gone with our hyperconnected workplaces. Robert Half International and Yahoo! HotJobs polled more than 1,000 millennials and found that more than 60 percent wanted to hear from managers at least once a day.[2] Millennials are all about communication and feedback. Communication is a key part of being transparent and collaborative—two core values of your generation. Here's the catch, the majority of the millennial managers we spoke with said "having difficult conversations" or "delivering tough feedback" is their main weakness. Senior leaders echo this sentiment and feel that millennials struggle in this crucial area. Anne Price, Global Marketing Capabilities Director, UPS, thinks that millennials need to boost their "managerial courage to have critical conversations and deliver difficult feedback." As you move through your career, holding people accountable through constructive conversations will become increasingly important. It's an essential skill that you can begin honing now.

Never underestimate the power of direct and sincere communication. Think about it. How many times after holding that dreaded critical conversation with a friend or family member have you thought or said, "I'm so glad we talked." How many times have you wished at work, "Well, if I had only known what was expected of me"? Likewise, when it comes to being in a relationship, have you said, "I wish you would have told me how you were feeling"? It's all about communication. The people on your team are not mind readers. As a millennial manager, you can set an example by having a conversation—listening, talking, and exchanging ideas—to set a foundation of trust and communication.

Communication is a hefty topic, and this chapter will cover two overarching themes when it comes to communication as a millennial manager. First, you need to communicate expectations, goals, and the structure in which your team will thrive. Second, you need to provide feedback. This is such an important section; the contents in this chapter alone could determine your fate and success as a leader.

ESTABLISHING YOUR EXPECTATIONS: THE BLUEPRINT

The first element to consider: don't assume anything. Establish your expectations right from the start. This is your blueprint for success. At work, there are the written rules, unwritten rules, and everything in between. For your team to be effective, you must have boundaries, direction, and something to shoot for. In the words of Yogi Berra, "You have to be careful if you don't know where you're going because you might not get there." If that was confusing to you, then you read it correctly!

You're not telling them *exactly* what to do; you're providing a structure in which they can operate. Bradley Aldrich, millennial manager and Of Counsel, Wolfe Law Group, says, "I now make sure that I am very clear with expectations and directions because I remember that was one of my main frustrations as a lawyer just starting out. It's tough when you are criticized for something you don't know."

I'm sure at this point in your career, you have been on teams that didn't seem to have clear goals, and the individual contributors all seemed to be on different pages—or maybe even in different books. As a member of a team, you know how that feels, and you don't want to create that disjointed dynamic for your team.

This reminds me of the "first day" for a teacher. The cardinal rule for teachers is to not start the school year off too easily because then it's very difficult to regain control and instill a stronger sense of discipline. Although it's not childhood discipline that you're instilling, it's a similar idea with your team. To begin, draw a hard line on what's acceptable and what's not. For example, if status reports are due by 5:00 PM on Friday, then set that hard rule. If you need to make an exception down the road for a dedicated employee, then you can choose to do that down the road. If you allow late reports from the start, it will be hard to reign that back in.

Let's look at an example from JB Training Solutions. We never miss a deadline (remember CHALANT?). If we tell a client that we will have something to them on Friday, then we send it to them on Thursday. Friday would be late to us. Even if we *know* we can have that proposal to them by Thursday, we tell them Friday, so that we can underpromise and overdeliver. It also helps with any unforeseen stalls in the project timeline, so we have some wiggle room and will never be put in the position where we can't meet—and even beat—a deadline. This is an expectation that I articulated to our team, and I drew a hard line. If you have your team live and breathe these ideas and expectations, then you soon won't have to talk about them. They will be ingrained in your people, and they will uphold them as their own personal values as individual contributors of the team.

Do you remember your self-reflection where you identified your principles, values, and motto? Communicate that with your team. It's a great way for them to gain insight into what you're all about and how everyone can best work together. Employees appreciate that glimpse into your mindset and your values. You're not micromanaging and telling them exactly what to do; you're just giving them the boundaries for how they can succeed.

ILLUMINATING THEIR ROLES: "SHOW ME THE LIGHT"

In laying out the expectations, one fundamental thing you can do is share the individual's job description and go through it together. Hopefully, you have job descriptions! If you don't, write down bullet points of their main job duties. Walking through the job description lets employees know *exactly* what is expected of them. Your millennial employees will especially love this information and structure—it's like a college syllabus or those infamous CliffsNotes. You are showing them the light!

When I started at Leo Burnett right out of college, I was hired to be on the media team. Quite honestly, I had no idea what that was or what I would be doing. My manager helped clue me into how the organization functioned and how our team fit into that structure.

You also need to be cognizant of client or customer names, senior leaders, acronyms, or insider lingo that you're throwing out to your employees, especially if they are new. It is extraordinary how quickly a company, division, or even an individual team develops its own internal language that no one else is able to speak. I remember sitting in my first meeting on the McDonald's account when I worked at Leo Burnett. Someone said, "Hey Brad, we need to work on that QPC EVM promotion for JFM. We're trying to reach the HCM SHUs, so get me your POV ASAP no later than COB." I quickly asked for an English translation:

QPC—Quarter Pounder with Cheese

EVM—Extra Value Menu

JFM—January, February, March

HCM—Hispanic Consumer Market

SHUs—Super Heavy Users

POV—Point of View

ASAP—As Soon As Possible

COB—Close of Business

Sure, your new employees would eventually figure it out on their own, but easing them into the transition goes a long way in getting them up and running.

When going through the job description, make it clear that a job description is the baseline—it's the minimum and a broad outline of what the employee is expected to do. I would tell my new employees that what is listed on the job description is roughly 50 percent of what they would be doing. The other half would be things that come up in the course of the business day. Explain that you know your employees can tackle these responsibilities, as well as look for other ways to go above and beyond in their position. Push them to bring their own personality and strengths to the position.

For example, at JB Training Solutions, Allison Lackey is our Manager of Communications. One of her responsibilities is to market our services and engage our clients and professionals. We didn't tell her how to do that. Outside of her Communications degree, Allison minored in theater, and two of her strengths are connecting with people and being on camera. To engage our audience, Allison ran a series of interviews and YouTube videos that gave viewers insight on workplace issues. It was a creative and interesting idea, and it was Allison who brought her unique strengths and ideas to that bullet on her job description.

Then, take your communication a step further by sharing the job description of the next level. Now the individual will know what they need to do to get ahead; they can push themselves to tackle stretch assignments that would prepare them for promotion. For example, Juan is an assistant account executive at an advertising agency, and he aspires to be an account executive. His manager shared how Juan will have to be a strong communicator and project manager to serve as the main contact with the client as the account executive. Juan set a personal goal to listen and learn from his boss on how he interacts with and works with the client. He even asked if he could sit in on some important meetings, just to be a sponge and begin learning how to lead a strong client–agency partnership. Juan's boss is giving him a leg up by showing him the skills he will need to make that next step. This may seem a little premature, but employees appreciate this insight and challenge for how to get ahead.

When coaching employees, a Senior Vice President of Human Resources at a logistics company advises, "Take a step up. You don't get promoted for keeping the lights on." Let your employees know that doing the bare minimum won't help them get ahead. Especially if you're managing other millennials, they value this straightforwardness and transparency. Maybe they won't ask for that promotion after just three months!

Millennials thrive with structure, and this fundamental acquaintance with the job and their responsibilities will go a long way in getting them started off right. Think of it as chalking the field and outlining the space in which your team can play.

You should also acquaint new team members to your company, clients or customers, and the industry. Of course, they can research it, but it's much more effective if you transfer some of your knowledge than having them struggle to pick things up during the first few weeks. Unless you tell them, your employees will find out the hard way that a particular client hates phone calls before 10:00 AM or that they shouldn't wear jeans on CEO-walk-through Thursdays. You will find that your employees' results also reflect on you as a manager. While waiting for meetings to begin, tell your employees about competitor X, and over lunch, fill them in on how the company direction has changed over the past five years.

This takes time, but again, your team will be up and running faster if you take a few extra moments on the front end. That's a theme that you will hear often. These tips and pieces of advice will take extra time. I recognize that millennial managers are often "middle managers." You have a team, but you also have individual responsibilities, and you have a boss as well. Sometimes, it can be hard to take a step back and sacrifice time to prepare, coach, and lead your team. However, it is worth it. If you have 37 things to do, you can complete all of them—and more—with an effective team. You have to keep thinking in terms of ROI—the return on investment—in your management. You can accomplish more as a team, so what you put into developing and building your team will pay off in business results—and likely job satisfaction for you.

Describe Their Duties and Responsibilities

After reviewing the higher-level job description, discuss and describe their upcoming duties and projects. If you have a new employee, give more information and provide more structure at the beginning. For all employees, go through a project list in priority order and determine specific deliverables and key dates. In the case of some employees—maybe an Xer or boomer—a deadline may be all the structure that they need. For millennials, you may need to establish a couple of key checkpoints to ensure the project is moving along smoothly.

With a running to-do list, it's helpful to your team to know what the priorities are. It's your job as a manager to keep your team focused on what matters most. As we all know, priorities often and quickly change. "A" list items can become "C" list items and vice versa after a short executive meeting. Do you take the time to communicate that to your team? Do you keep the team members in the loop on the goals of the larger organization? Again, the more they know, the better they can make decisions and solve problems.

I remember talking to a new hire—Lucas—during one of my workshops. He was working in marketing at a fast-paced consumer goods company. He talked about a project that he was cranking on and investing extra hours in. Lucas was so excited to present the finished product to his boss, and then his boss said, "Oh, I guess I forget to tell you, we decided that initiative didn't fit into our strategic plan." Lucas was devastated—all of that work for nothing. Likewise, your employees want to be working on and contributing to meaningful work, so tuning them into changing priorities will keep them engaged and connected.

As a millennial manager, this type of communication appeals to your values of building a relationship and fostering the growth of your people. However, you may be feeling skeptical and thinking—do I really need to take them through a job description? Shouldn't they already know what to do? Isn't this type of instruction coddling and similar to holding their hands? If so, then take a step back and orient yourself—this is just at the beginning of the partnership. At first, you will provide more direction. As you move forward, you can empower your team to create its own project list and deadlines. To keep things running smoothly at the start, you can put forth the projects and priorities with the goal of weaning your team off of this structure as the members get more acquainted with the business. One of our clients provides an agenda for its new employees the first week of work. Within a few months, those employees come to meetings with their own project lists and to-do's.

Pinpoint Check-Ins

Caitlin Harley, millennial manager and senior research analyst, has a "See one, do one, teach one" management approach. Harley said, "I've had 'sink-or-swim' managers in the past, and they expected me to get it after they told me just one time. These types of managers make me inclined to offer more support along the way for my team." I touched on this idea previously, but pinpoint specific check-ins for large projects and put those dates on the calendar.

For example, if you have a project that you would like Lisa to complete in two weeks, schedule a midway point to check in—especially if this is the first time she is working on the project. Managers often have this fear of being a micromanager. We hear things like, "I want to be a hands-off manager. I don't want to tell them what they have to do." Your gen X employees might appreciate this dynamic, but the truth is that millennials love more structure.

If you're a new manager, most team members like the check-in points to ensure they are completing the project to your expectations. When you have your meetings, don't tell them exactly what to do, but let them know if they're on the right track or if you're expecting something a little different. Ask more questions, and listen more than you talk. Courtney checks in with me when we are developing a large proposal. She will run through the big idea of how she thinks we can present the information. Once we're in agreement, she can throw herself into the details and ensure we have a fine-tuned, sharp offering. As a manager, it's tempting to instruct your team to do something exactly the way that you would do it, but great work can come from unique ideas and perspectives. Be careful that you are offering guidance and support and not being overly instructive during these check points.

SETTING PUSH GOALS: INFILTRATING FUN

It sounds obvious, but you would be surprised by how many new managers do not set strong personal or team goals. First, setting goals can be boring. Second, setting goals, especially team goals, can be difficult. What do you measure? How do you measure it? What constitutes success? And what are the priorities? You can set a successful path forward by developing what I call PUSH goals. At the heart of a push goal is a goal that pushes you past mediocre or pretty good into the realm of great and excellent. A PUSH goal is not easy to achieve. To break it down, a PUSH goal is **P**assionate, **U**rgent, **S**pecific, and **H**airy.

Passionate—You must have passion and excitement in your goals! If you don't, they're just goals—boring and lifeless on the wall, sticky note, or little black book tucked deep in your desk drawer. Passionate goals are ones that will make a difference on your team, to your people, and to your organization. Just reading it gets you fired up!

Urgent—Let's make it happen now! Let's set this in motion now! Goals should be timely and relevant. Is there a need here? Is it important and necessary? Likewise, can you give an important responsibility a sense of urgency?

Specific—This is the heart of a good goal. Can it be measured? How will you measure it? How will you achieve it? By making a goal specific, you paint a clearer picture and path toward achievement. A little upfront work on the details gives you the leg up on conquering it.

Hairy—It's HAIRY! It's not easy. It's a little difficult and will push you and challenge you. You will probably get a little messy wrestling around with such a big goal, but there is no way that you won't grow, develop, and learn just from tackling it.

Goal setting seems like one of those "duh" topics—everyone should know how to set good goals, right? At this point, you've experienced a couple decades of New Year's resolutions. How has that worked out for you? The fundamental error in the majority of goals is that they are not PUSH goals. Just consider the most popular New Year's resolutions from 2011 according to a study by Northwestern University's Kellogg School of Management.[3] The most popular resolution was "to lose weight" followed by "exercise more" and then "achieve professional growth and be a better person."

Let's break that down. "To lose weight" doesn't stand up to the test at all. I guess it's a hairy goal, but it's not passionate, urgent, or specific. Why do you want to lose weight? How will you lose weight, how much will you lose, and when will you lose it by? Think about how you can make that a PUSH goal. How about this?

To lose three pounds each month by working out three times a week and fitting into my skinny jeans by June 15th.

Is that a little more passionate (skinny jeans!), urgent (working out three times a week), and specific (by June 15th)? Put that all together and you have one hairy PUSH goal! It's easier to hold yourself accountable and stay excited about this second version of the same goal.

Let's take a look at a few weak management goals I have seen:

1. To be a better manager
2. To be more assertive
3. To have more fun at work

Boring! Even the goal that mentions fun is boring. How can we make these PUSH goals? For the first goal "to be a better manager," think about how you would like to improve in this vast category. Do you want to be more responsive to needs, challenge your team more, or provide more feedback? Choose a key area that you would like to focus on and bring passion, urgency, specifics, and some downright hairiness to it. Some examples could include:

1. To develop my team members by having a "Wise Up! Weekly" fun and educational session every week for the next six months
2. To enhance engagement by holding a 15-minute check-in with each employee every month, helping employees be amazing at what they do
3. To improve morale by incorporating a five-minute team-building activity at each weekly meeting this quarter, bringing a dose of inspiration for our mornings

What do you think? More passionate, urgent, specific, and hairy? Absolutely! These are great personal PUSH goals. Once you talk through these goals, write them down and plaster them wherever they would serve as a good reminder. When it comes to setting goals, the author of *Working Smart*, Michael Leboeuf, urges, "When you write down your ideas, you automatically focus your full attention on them. Few if any of us can write one thought and think another at the same time. Thus a pencil and paper make excellent concentration tools." Millennials, you can also type them out.

You also want to share these techniques with your team and encourage them to establish PUSH goals for themselves. In addition, you can set goals as a team. At JB Training Solutions, we set goals for the year, but we break those down into quarterly goals that keep us focused. This also makes our high aspirations and long-term goals more urgent. What happens when you set a goal that has a year-long time frame? You often lose sight of it and wait until the last two months to get started! The key for setting team goals is to set them—as a team. It's hard to be passionate about a goal that someone else gives you. Brainstorm ideas together and really push each other to arrive at goals that inspire, motivate, and focus everyone.

Now, when talking about PUSH, especially with your millennial employees, you will need to clarify the P—Passionate. Some people may be stumped right away when trying to think about a work goal they're passionate about. And, of course, you don't want them to be stumped right from the beginning. Think about it. For your employees, work could be "fine," but are they really passionate about increasing productivity, hitting quarterly goals, or boosting shareholder value?

Passion is a word you may tend to reserve for your extracurriculars, friends, or family—"I am so passionate about running!" or "I absolutely love international travel. I just can't get enough" or "I just love, love, love my niece and nephew. They are to die for." Does that parlay to running the logistics for an event your company has coming up? "I just love, love, love all this paperwork! I just can't get enough of these contracts. These spreadsheets are to die for!" There is a myth out there that you should absolutely love your job, every single day and every single minute, and your generation, especially, has bought in to this idea. I absolutely love what I do—traveling the country and training employees on how to become better leaders and managers, but there are some parts that I dislike—airline delays and missing dinner with my family, losing my voice, expense reports, and dealing with other logistics. But I still wouldn't change this job for the world.

Maybe your employees are not passionate about every single part of their job, but help them think about how they can bring their passions to their roles and their goals. Maybe they're passionate about people, building relationships, or supporting the company's values. Help your team and your millennials tie their goals to those things they're passionate about. I always found that SMART (specific, measurable, attainable, relevant, and timely) goals could get pretty cold and calculating: *To increase gross profits by 14 percent by December 31, 2013.* The passion in PUSH goals invigorates a normally cold and uninspiring goal.

Let's add some passion and purpose behind this cold SMART goal: *To increase gross profits by 14 percent by year end, helping more and more companies have stronger leaders and better managers.* This connects a monetary goal with a larger purpose or mission. This is especially important for millennials. Your generation may not be inspired by just making another sale or meeting a deadline, but you may be inspired by helping make a customer's life easier or being part of a successful team. For example, when writing this book, Courtney set goals for herself to keep her on track. One of her PUSH goals was "To write 15,000 words by July 20th, infiltrating fun anecdotes and personality to create a book that I am truly proud of." You could see how that's more exciting and inspiring (and thus more likely to be accomplished) than "To write 15,000 words by July 20th." That's just downright depressing.

Furthermore, one of my favorite aspects of goal-setting is celebrating once they are achieved. Goal setting and achieving can be incredibly inspiring. Celebrations include team lunches, outings, or surprises. One of my favorite celebrations was after a particularly successful and hard-working quarter. I hid spot bonuses around the office—there is nothing better than stumbling across a few greenbacks to keep everyone laughing and energized! Now, maybe you don't have the budget or resources for bonuses, but there are countless creative ways to celebrate. Have a lunch potluck, "early dismissal," or a recognition round-up of sorts.

At JB Training Solutions, a lot of work goes into gaining a new client. When we began working with Kraft, we celebrated with a Mac 'n' Cheese, Oreos, and Crystal Light party. It was inexpensive, a ton of fun, and it made us feel even more connected to the brand and our new client. Make sure you take time to celebrate and enjoy before jumping to the next challenge. "Celebrate what you've accomplished, but raise the bar a little higher each time you succeed," suggests Olympic soccer player Mia Hamm. Keep challenging yourself and your team members to PUSH when it comes to your goals.

COMMUNICATION STYLES: MEETING IN THE MIDDLE

Communicate expectations, communicate responsibilities, and communicate goals. Now, let's talk about more talking—this time about communication styles. Chat openly and candidly with your employees about how you like to work. Are you more of an analyzer who likes to think through decisions after reading the fifty-page report or do you like to receive an executive summary and make a quick decision? Do you prefer *writing* the presentation or *delivering* the presentation? You have your unique style, and your employees appreciate having insight into the way you like to work and your expectations. However, good managers learn the style of each of their employees and adjust their style accordingly. In Chapter 9, "Navigate: Managing Through the Unknown," you will learn more about adjusting your style and navigating different personalities on your team. Ideally, you and your employees will meet in the middle—you each will adjust your style a little to form a great partnership.

Case in point, Courtney and I are nearly complete opposites when it comes to our communication style. This dynamic is either a complete disaster or a raging success. If you understand each other and recognize differences, it's a great working relationship because one person's weaknesses are often the other's strengths. By talking about our differences, we are able to compromise. For example, Courtney gives me the topline information on projects, and she leads with conclusions and recommendations. She knows she will lose me the second she gets in the weeds with too many details. Likewise, when I give Courtney a project, I debrief her and then give her time to think, process, and brainstorm on her own before we talk through it. I talk to think; she thinks to talk. Talking about these preferences and communication styles with your employees is important and goes a long way in building a strong relationship. After talking, you likely will find—just like the generations—they're not better, they're not worse, they're just different.

GIVING FEEDBACK:
THE GOOD, THE BAD, AND THE UGLY

The second overarching theme under "Communicate" is feedback. Business consultant Ken Blanchard says, "Feedback is the breakfast of champions." Just like those Wheaties, feedback and constructive criticism are critical for the growth and development of your team.

Feedback, constructive criticism, and critical conversations. I have a feeling that a little anxiety is setting in just reading those words. In all of our interviews, we discovered that millennial managers think the hardest part of their job is "having difficult conversations."

You want to build strong, close relationships with members of your team, so you might struggle when it comes time to give constructive criticism. You may have thoughts or questions like, Will they take it okay? Will I hurt their feelings or discourage them? Will they be mad at me? We heard from numerous millennial managers that drawing the line between being someone's friend and being someone's boss is difficult. You don't want to be the big, bad authority figure who is too far removed from your employees, but on the flipside, you need to maintain a level of influence. I think that's a shift in verbiage that could work for you: As a millennial manager, you want to have influence over your team instead of having authority over your team. The bottom line is, if you want the best for your employees and if you want them to excel, then you have to give them direct and sincere feedback.

To help put this tough topic into perspective, I will tell you the infamous spinach story. The fundamental truth of feedback lies in the form of a spinach salad. Have you ever had the unfortunate experience of getting a little morsel of spinach from a salad wedged between your teeth? Now, we ask: If you had spinach stuck in your teeth, would you like someone to tell you about it? Or would you like to go the ENTIRE day smiling and carrying on with spinach stuck in your teeth, just to go home, look in the mirror, and discover that you have looked like a fool for the better half of the day? Would you want someone to tell you? Of course, you would want to know!

Now, think about the other side. Isn't it a little difficult or awkward to tell someone they have spinach in their teeth? You're not sure what to say or how to say it. A CareerBuilder survey reveals that professionals have a tough time being direct and forthright with colleagues and managers when it comes to having something stuck in your teeth:[4]

▷   66% of colleagues at your same level say they would tell you.
▷   60% say they would alert a lower-level worker.
▷   Only 49% would tell a higher-up.

It's not easy. Seeing the spinach in someone's teeth can bring on a plethora of questions. Should you tell them in the middle of the meeting and direct everyone's attention to their green culprit? Or should you let them continue grinning that green grin and tell them individually after the meeting? Or should you make little hand motions when no one is looking, hinting that they have something in their teeth? The fact is, it doesn't really matter. The person with the spinach just wants to know! This is like feedback! It may seem a little awkward or difficult to deliver, but *people want to know.*

If your employees are making mistakes or could be doing something better, they want to know sooner rather than later. One of our clients shared a story about a tough time delivering feedback to a new employee—Willie—who was wearing a hoodie. Hoodies were not allowed at this company. The human resources department didn't know what to do, so for a while nothing was done. Every day, HR showed up hoping that Willie wouldn't be wearing another hoodie. Another hoodie! Day after day, Willie showed up in a hoodie—Purdue hoodie, Wisconsin hoodie, Illinois hoodie. HR stalled—Willie couldn't possibly have any more hoodies left to wear! Indiana hoodie, Ohio State hoodie. HR was scared—it looked like Willie had a reservoir of hoodies that included the entire Big Ten conference. If he moved into the SEC conference, HR knew they were in trouble. Finally, a brave HR representative talked with Willie and told him that hoodies were not acceptable at the office. Do you know what Willie's response was? He was mad! Why was he frustrated? Because he had been wearing hoodies for two whole weeks and no one told him it wasn't acceptable! Why didn't someone tell him on day one to save him the embarrassment of walking around for two weeks breaking the policy? He wanted to know!

As millennial managers, it can be tough to get in the habit of delivering constructive criticism. You may be afraid that the person will take it the wrong way or get emotional, defensive, or discouraged. You must ingrain this idea in your mind—feedback is for the employee's own good. Again, "Feedback is the breakfast of champions."

Think about your favorite teacher, mentor, or coach. Was that person a pushover? Did any of them let you get away with everything, or did they hold you accountable and challenge you? Did they expect great results, and let you know when you weren't cutting it? I'm guessing so. Most memorable mentors are those who really pushed us and didn't let us get by. Often, we learn the most from the people who are the toughest on us or expect the most from us. Be that manager. Don't settle for mediocrity. "Good is the enemy of great," says Jim Collins, author of *Good to Great*.[5] You don't want to fall into the trap of saying, "Oh, Trevor is pretty good, and he's doing just fine. I would hate to say anything to mess things up."

Courtney will never forget her middle school English teacher—Mrs. Stanley. Mrs. Stanley was tough. She didn't let anything slide. You better mind your split infinitives, comma splices, and dangling participles or the red pen would adorn your paper. She even had a penny jar, and you would have to pay up for using incorrect grammar, such as "Can I go to the bathroom?" instead of "May I go to the bathroom?" "I don't know, CAN you?" Mrs. Stanley would ask. Courtney says she thanks Mrs. Stanley practically every day (not every day) for being tough and ingraining such discipline when it comes to writing and grammar. I have Mrs. Stanley to thank as well; I never send off an important e-mail or proposal without having Courtney check and proofread it. Indeed, Courtney is the one responsible for all the commas (and more!) in this book because I never had a Mrs. Stanley. Mrs. Stanley gave constructive criticism all the time because she wanted her students to be great. She knew being easy on her students would not prepare them for high school or college. She wouldn't be doing anyone any favors. She challenged students, pushed them, and even had them believe they could be authors one day. That is the type of manager you want to be.

I hope the spinach story, the hoodie hindrance, and the Mrs. Stanley message are hitting home and helping reframe how you think about the topic of feedback. To prevent you from fearing feedback or avoiding it altogether, I have very specific tips for millennial managers. From our interviews, I know this is an area in which millennial managers really struggle. Do you remember that liability of the millennial generation of "lacks skills for dealing with difficult people"? Although it isn't the case for all millennials, in general, you had protective parents who often swooped in to rescue you from difficult situations or people. Now that you're managing a team, you probably realize there are difficult people everywhere! "Mom!" Fortunately, you will gain the skills and tangible tips to deal with even the stickiest situation. First, I will cover the different types of feedback, and then I will share advice for delivering each type of message.

There are three different types of feedback that you will deliver to your employees:

1. Day-to-day feedback
2. Informal, regularly scheduled feedback
3. Formal review

Day-to-Day Feedback

Day-to-day feedback happens—you guessed it—daily. This is the best enforcer of behaviors—to let someone know how they did right after the fact. Think of it as on-the-spot coaching. Often, we associate feedback with an annual review. Feedback should be day-to-day, and it doesn't have to be formal, written, or have any numbers assigned to it.

For example, if you notice that Gus is consistently speaking out of turn at meetings, pull him aside and mention it to him privately, and let him know how his behavior is being perceived. Likewise, if Milo did a great job on a sales call, let him know right after the call and point out specific instances that were impressive.

Feedback really loses its luster when you mention it a few weeks down the road. "Hey Milo, do you remember that sales call you made about three weeks ago? No, not that one. No, not that one. Maybe it was with ATAD Payroll? Yes, right, so you think you remember? Well, I thought the way you handled it was really good. Nice job." To increase your effectiveness, try to get into the habit of giving immediate feedback. Your millennial employees will especially appreciate it. This establishes a firm foundation of trust and communication that you want to build as a millennial manager.

Although day-to-day feedback is informal, you still want to be very specific. If your direct report did a good job at the meeting, let her know—specifically. How many of you would say, "Good job at the meeting, Brittany!"? Sure, that's fine, but Brittany doesn't really know why or how she did well. Instead, tell Brittany after the meeting, "I was really impressed with you in the meeting today. You had a great idea, and you supported your perspective with two different data points. Our department really focuses on the numbers, so I know our department head appreciated your insights and could relate well." Now isn't that better? Doesn't Brittany know what she should try and do again next time? Being specific is the key to good feedback.

Now what if Brittany didn't do well at the meeting? That's a little tougher, right? Remember the spinach. She wants to know! As a millennial manager, you want your team members to grow, develop, and be the best that they can be. Well, they won't get there if you hold back all of your constructive criticism and shield them from the areas they need to improve.

You want to make sure you deliver the feedback in private and in person, especially if you're offering constructive thoughts. As tempting as it may be to hide behind e-mail, all constructive feedback should be delivered face-to-face. You *never* want to give feedback via e-mail. You can't be sure how Brittany will read it, and it's too easy for the message to be misconstrued. For those of you who manage remote employees and you can't talk in person, you can use the phone or a video conference.

Be Direct and Specific

When delivering constructive feedback, be direct and specific. If you're too vague or general, Brittany doesn't know how to improve. For example, "Brittany, I was disappointed in your presentation today. I expect better next time." Brittany is left with, what did I do wrong? What could I do better? Was it my intro? Did I talk for too long? Was it too short? Was I like saying *um* and *like* too much? Did I have poor body language?

It's much more constructive if you say something like, "Brittany, I wanted to talk about your performance at the meeting today. You had to present ten minutes on your area, and I felt as though you were ill prepared. You were fumbling for the necessary materials, you couldn't read your notes, and it reflected poorly to the client. I expect everyone on the team to be prepared. What was going on today?"

During feedback, you want to create a dialogue. It's not one-way direction and reprimand; you want to try and ask questions to get at the root of the problem and see what is going on. Sometimes, our instinct is to jump to the worst conclusion, but you always want to give your employees the benefit of the doubt—until they prove they don't deserve it! You could be so frustrated at Brittany's performance at the meeting that you jump to thoughts of "I just can't believe Brittany blew off this meeting. She didn't even prepare one bit! She must not respect me, and she doesn't even care about our client." Instead of jumping to these hasty conclusions, think, "Why would a reasonable, rational person do this?" Maybe Brittany has been swamped working on other projects; maybe she wasn't clear on directions; or maybe she's just having a tough week. Now, we're not saying excuses are okay. Excuses do not legitimize poor performance. However, asking these questions helps you approach the conversation without the hostility or about-to-explode frustration. You may be amazed that many times situations like this come from a lack of clear expectations. Your rational perspective sets the stage for a much more productive conversation.

The bottom line is you must have the conversation. Now, I know what you're thinking. Of course, I'll give Brittany the benefit of the doubt and just assume she will never do that again. You follow that line of thinking and say to yourself, "Oh, Brittany is having a tough day, and her performance at the meeting was poor. But I'm sure she's swamped, and I'm sure it won't happen again. I would hate to tell her something to demotivate her." That does you no favors and Brittany no favors. One of the best things you can do as a leader is to hold your team accountable.

Hold your team accountable. You are the person who helps people do the things they said they were going to do, and you are the person who helps people do the things they didn't even think they could do.

The other critical point is that the more you give feedback, the less awkward it feels—for both parties. The first few times may be a bit uncomfortable, but once you do this on a consistent basis, it's smooth, effective, and much easier. The discussions become much more conversational and much less dictatorial.

Millennials especially LOVE feedback, so day-to-day feedback is exactly what your generation craves. Keep communication levels high, and make sure you're recognizing employees for the good things they're doing and holding them accountable for the things they can improve.

Informal, Regularly Scheduled Feedback

Outside of day-to-day feedback, you want to take about fifteen to twenty minutes every month to sit down and chat with each of your direct reports. If you have a new employee, sit down with that individual once a week for a month and then move to monthly meetings. I know you don't have any time! But if you have a high-performing team, you will have more time, and regular feedback is one of the best ways to get your team there.

This is exactly what I did when Courtney joined JB Training Solutions. We chatted every Friday for the first month. Since then, not a month or two goes by where we don't sit down and have an informal feedback session.

Importantly these meetings are about your direct reports and how they are doing at work. These are not status meetings or get-togethers to discuss projects. It's not, "How are things going on Project Thunder?" but instead, "How are things going for you at work?".

This type of feedback is a two-way conversation, and as a manager, you should be asking a lot of questions and doing a lot of listening. You should also let your employee know how he or she is doing and offer any support for development. Here is a sample outline for the meeting:

I.   Ask how everything is going. You may need to ask a few probing questions:
    a. What's going well?
    b. What can be improved?
    c. What do you enjoy doing?
    d. Are there any blockers getting in your way right now?
    e. Is there anything I can be doing to be a better manager?
II. Give a few examples of things that your employee is doing well.
III. Give two or three examples of things that your employee could work on.
IV. Offer development opportunities and any coaching advice.

This structure will give you a solid guideline for these monthly meetings. Try not to let a month go by without chatting one-on-one with your employees. The truth is that when the fifteen minutes are done, you will be so glad you talked. In these short conversations, you can dispel small problems before they become bigger issues for your team. Conflicts often stem from misunderstandings or differences in communication style, and a simple conversation can get you through that.

The quotation from the book, *Crucial Confrontations,* captures this idea, "Rare is the sudden and unexpected emotional explosion that wasn't preceded by a lengthy period of tortured silence."[6] If you don't talk about problems, they build up, build up, build up, and EXPLODE!

After you have this short talk, you're usually reminded that this team member isn't evil; she's just different and she may do things a little differently than you. She walks away thinking you're not so bad after all as well. By talking about issues as they come up, everyone can keep problems away from the explosive stage. To uphold a value of millennial managers, these routine, honest conversations go a long way in building a great working relationship.

Formal Review

We won't spend too much time on the formal review because you likely have a certain form or process for your company—this is where the numbers often come in! Most companies have a formal annual or semi-annual review. The most important point is to not wait until the annual review to deliver your feedback. There should be no surprises at the annual review. The worst thing you can do for the individual and your team is to recognize improvement areas in June and just say, *"Oh, I'll tell Edwin in December at his annual review."*

Putting together formal reviews takes time and preparation. It's an investment in your people to give them a clear picture of their performance. You have to spend time writing, preparing, and practicing what you will say and how you will say it. In the formal review, you want to include a summary of strengths and areas of improvement. You also want to set a development and action plan. How will your employees develop over the year? What are their career plans? What do they see as their goals and challenges? You also want to ask check-in questions, such as "How can we keep you happy and fulfilled here?" This will give you valuable insight into keeping your all-stars engaged and contributing.

It's the little things that count when it comes to evaluation day. On the day of the review, give your employees some time to read the review on their own so the information can be digested. Then, talk through the review in a private room. Your employees are likely a little nervous as they have been thinking about this day for a while. To show how important you think the session is, eliminate interruptions. As a manager, you don't want your employee to think that the person on the phone or the person e-mailing you is more important. Hold your calls and meetings for a few minutes, and dedicate your full attention to your employee.

If you have a poor performer, you can't be afraid to reflect that in the review. Even just for legal reasons, poor performance needs to be documented. One of our clients told us about a poor performer and aggressive employee that the company wanted to fire. Management put together its case, but when they looked at the employee's evaluations from his manager, they all said "meets expectations." None of the written documents supported the fact that this employee deserved to be terminated. In this case, the company might be at risk because the evaluations seemed fairly glowing.

Phillip Schreiber, partner in the labor and employment practice at the global law firm Holland & Knight LLP, says that there are two main reasons you should document an employee's poor performance. Schreiber says, "First, you must have documentation because of legal reasons. If you need to terminate an employee for performance reasons, but there is no formal documentation of poor performance, then you are putting yourself at risk of being sued by that employee. Second, the documentation is a guide that the employee can refer to and use to help him or her improve and meet the employer's expectations. After a few weeks, the details and specifics of verbal constructive criticism tend to fade, but the employee can reference a written document as often as needed."

Remember the spinach. You're doing no one any favors by sugarcoating performance. Make sure you're forthright and frank; glossing over poor performance will only put you and the company in a tough predicament. Schreiber adds, "The documentation need not be overly formal in tone. Managers may use informal language in conveying, with specificity, what the manager's expectations of the employee are, how the employee is not meeting those expectations, what the employee needs to do to meet those expectations, and a reasonable time frame in which the manager would like to see those expectations met." Be direct and sincere, and you may be surprised with how receptive employees can be.

I found myself in this exact situation with an intern—let's call him Anthony—who was working at JB Training Solutions. This intern was goofing around, heading out early, and producing average work—all in the first week. My initial thought was to fire him. This guy seemed like a lost cause. I talked about it with Courtney, and she convinced me I should talk to him. She said we probably shouldn't be the company known for firing interns. Sound advice.

However, I was dreading having this conversation with Anthony. You know which one I'm talking about—the Dad conversation, "Son, you need to show up earlier, have a good attitude, proofread your work, etc." So I took him to a popular workshop that we deliver called "The Right Start." It's for interns and new hires about how to make a successful transition from college to work and covers critical topics like communication styles, time management, initiative, and business etiquette—perfect for my slacker intern! The entire time I was delivering the workshop, I kept looking at Anthony and thinking, *Yes, this point is for you! I hope you're taking notes!*

On the ride home, I knew I had to have the conversation with him. I couldn't avoid it any longer. I proceeded to tell Anthony about how his performance was poor—he's missing deadlines, showing up late, and not taking initiative. We had a heart-to-heart conversation, and he ended up thanking me! He said, "Thank you so much, Brad, I had no idea. I really appreciate this feedback." From that point on, Anthony was a new intern. He took the extra effort, pitched in on all projects, and produced creative work. At the end of the summer, when I asked him about his favorite part of the internship, he said it was that conversation we had on the way home from the workshop! I couldn't believe it! I had been so worried about that conversation. I had stalled and pushed it off, and I was worried about how he would take it. I almost fired him because I didn't want to have the talk. Then, I found out that was the most memorable part of his internship.

I hope these examples give you the courage to say what you need to say or address a tough topic that needs to be addressed. Your employees want and need to know.

Now when it comes to giving any type of feedback, there are certain things you want to keep in mind. These tips are relevant for day-to-day, informal regularly scheduled feedback, and formal reviews.

Let your positive intentions be known. Let your employees know that this is all for their benefit. You want them to learn, grow, and excel.

Focus on the issue, not the person. By focusing on the issue or the behavior, you decrease the chances of the individual taking your comments personally. For example, say "Production is poor" instead of "You are slow." Focus on the issue by stating, "I've noticed your business writing often contains a lot of typos" instead of "You are sloppy."

Own what you say. Use "I" statements to own what you say. You don't want to say "Everyone agrees that you have a bad attitude" or offer hearsay, such as "I've heard through the grapevine that you really haven't been working when you're working from home." Instead, consider this,

"I've noticed at meetings that you don't participate as much, and when you do, you're sharp and curt with your responses. Is anything going on here?" Focus on "I" statements by saying something like, "Alex, I have noticed that during your work-from-home days you're difficult to reach. I've also noticed that you don't finish the projects that were assigned for that day. I know this perk is important to you, so help me better understand what's going on here."

You want to provide observations not interpretations. For example, "I've noticed you now only make ten sales call a day when you were previously making 35 a day." Instead of "It seems like you've been procrastinating and getting a little lazy with your calls lately."

Be direct and be sincere. Millennials, especially, will listen if they know your intentions are true. Furthermore, there is no good in tiptoeing around the issue—just say it. An example of tiptoeing would be: "Well, Ben, I've noticed that maybe, you've sort of been slacking, er, not performing that well when it comes to updating your reports. I mean, you're doing a great job in the majority of areas, but I feel like your performance has maybe, just a little bit, possibly slowed down when it comes to this reporting thing, do you know what I mean?" No, Ben has no idea what you mean.

That wishy-washy, indirect feedback doesn't help anyone. Be direct and assertive. Use powerful talk to own what you say, and try to eliminate those filler words, such as maybe, kinda, sort of, possibly, um, ah, like, you know. In addition, be careful with words that might make the person defensive. "Always" and "never"—seemingly innocent words— fall into this category. What happens when you tell your significant other, "You never do nice things for me anymore"? The person is on guard! The defenses shoot up as the offended party tries to rattle off a few instances when he or she did nice things for you, and your entire point that you haven't felt valued or appreciated lately is lost. That's the same reaction you likely will get if you use "always" or "never" with an employee. "Tommy, you never show up on time" or "Jeanne, you always cut me off in meetings." These are hot-button words that will not get your message across effectively. Thinking through the actual words that come out of your mouth is an important step in preparing for the best.

Be prepared with specifics. Take the guesswork out of feedback by giving employees specific examples of their opportunity areas. What is the first question you ask when someone gives you constructive criticism? Naturally, it is, "Can you give me an example?"

For instance, one of our clients wanted to give a new hire feedback on being more detail oriented when it comes to business communications. Her feedback went something like this, "Taylor, I have noticed that your e-mails to our clients aren't as polished as they can be. For instance, last week you copied me on a couple e-mails that didn't have subject lines or your signature. I also noticed that you forgot to send the attachment. I know these seem like small things, but we want to be buttoned up and polished in all of our communications with our customers." In this example, the manager told Taylor about the issue and gave two examples to support that statement. Always be prepared with evidence. Your feedback really loses your thunder if you can't think of examples, "Well, Taylor, er, well, I can't really think of any examples right now, er, when you weren't detail oriented, but believe me, you haven't been focusing on the details. Trust me on this one." That's not very effective.

Specific examples also help for those finer feedback points that may be tougher to explain. "Landon, I would like to see you take more ownership of your responsibilities." Landon is thinking, "Huh? Ownership? What does that mean? I think I own my stuff—unless it's not mine. I don't own that. Am I supposed to? Huh? What?" To elaborate, you can say, "For example, let's talk about the proposal you wrote this week. We had to go through four rounds of revisions, and I feel as though you rely on me to perfect the proposal or catch any inaccuracies. When you give me your final draft, I want you to be 100 percent confident that it is perfect and the absolute best it can be. Taking that kind of ownership is an example of something I would like to see more of. Does that make sense?"

Try to have three examples to support your statements when delivering feedback. In a particularly tough session when our client—Chanda—was delivering some direct feedback to a poor-performing employee, she knew she had to be armed with a lot of examples. She was communicating that the employee needed to take more initiative in his position, and she didn't want him to get hung up on some of the buzz words. What would taking more initiative look like? What would "going above and beyond" look like? Sometimes, managers can throw around words and phrases like "upping your game" and "taking it to the next level," and employees can walk away not really knowing what needs to improve and how they can get there. For the poor performer, Chanda gave examples for his position. "One example of taking more initiative would be to create a marketing plan to tell our clients about our new workshops. Another example would be to update our media list as those names change so quickly. Taking initiative means anticipating needs such as these without me telling you to do it."

Avoid the Feedback Sandwich

You also don't want to communicate through the infamous feedback sandwich. "Garrett, great job at the meeting today! I'm concerned that there is $20,000 missing from your budget. By the way, nice pinstripes." Now that's a little exaggerated, but I'm sure you have found yourself in the position of "softening" your feedback. You get worried, and you want to couch it and make it come off a little easier. However, that likely won't change any behavior, and your direct report may never even realize you were trying to squeeze in some constructive criticism. Garrett walks out thinking, *Yeah, these are pretty nice pinstripes.*

Our advice is to not give *meaningful* positive feedback and *meaningful* negative feedback at the same time—unless it's the annual review. Because what does everyone typically remember when you hear both good and bad? Everything after the "but."

"Lisa, you've been doing an amazing job with us this year. You blew us out of the water with your creative idea for achieving third-quarter goals. Then you delivered an impressive and information-packed presentation to our clients. Our clients even commented on your job well done. *But* I did want to talk about how your attitude is hurting team morale..."

Do you think Lisa will remember anything before the "but"? No. You can have a soft, short buffer, such as "Lisa, overall, we're really pleased with your work here. Today, I wanted to talk about your teamwork skills and the influence of your attitude on the team."

As a millennial manager, you have to remember that **you can be assertive AND nice.** You can be assertive and nice. Are you doing more of a service to tell your employees the truth or shield them from the truth? It's best for their professional development if you tell them how it is—sincerely. Anne Price called it "managerial courage." If you show the courage to address difficult conversations, you will be respected. Remember the spinach, recall the hoodie story, and please don't forget Mrs. Stanley. Thinking of these examples reinforces the point that employees and managers alike want to know about their performance—the good, the bad, and the ugly. Awareness is the only way for employees to grow and *develop*.

Just Listen—Receiving Feedback Openly

You have learned at great length about giving feedback, but there is another side to this form of communication—listening. You also want to receive feedback openly. Typically, we think of feedback going from a manager to a direct report, but it is important that employees also have an opportunity to give their manager feedback. As we said throughout, feedback is really a dialogue, so listening is a key skill for managers. And as a millennial manager, I know you want to know!

When receiving feedback, listen openly and try to embrace it. Ask probing questions to try and get your employees to open up. When Courtney started working for JB Training Solutions, she was very hesitant to give me (the boss!) feedback, so I would ask her a lot of questions. *How can I be a better manager? How is the work environment? What projects do you like working on? Is there anything I can be doing to challenge you more? Is there anything I can be doing better? What else? What else?* One time, I even had Courtney come with three specific things that I could do to improve. I let her think about it in advance, and I said she could have no less than three things. Again, it's tough to give your boss feedback, so the easier you can make it for them, the more likely they are to tell you the feedback you need to improve.

Furthermore, since this is so difficult for employees, it's much more important that you do not act defensively or negatively. If you do, you can guarantee, your employee will not utter another word again. Hear them out, and soak it in. If you receive feedback, then you have to act on it. You're an obstacle remover, a problem solver, and a dutiful messenger. If you can't act on the feedback, you follow up with that employee and tell them why you can't. If you don't act or respond, then there is no reason why your team would give you feedback down the road. In the words of Colin Powell, "Leadership is solving problems. The day soldiers stop bringing you their problems is the day you have stopped leading them. They have either lost confidence that you can help or concluded you do not care. Either case is a failure of leadership."[7] Listening and acting upon feedback is just as important as delivering feedback. It's a two-way dialogue that builds trust and breaks down challenges.

Just Say It

Communicate. There's a lot to think about in this chapter, but trust and communication are the foundation to a strong relationship. Communicate expectations, communicate goals, and give and receive feedback. I know as a millennial manager, it's easier to avoid and push back tough decisions or conversations. *Oh, I'll talk to Viola tomorrow,* or, *Oh, it's a Monday; I don't want to taint the rest of the week. Or Oh, it's Friday, and everyone is in the office; it will be awkward to have a one-on-one. I guess I'll have to wait until next week.* Yes, I have played that game way too many times.

Patti Grace, U.S. Director of Learning and Development for OmnicomMediaGroup, says "Genuinely open yourself up and ask for feedback and advice often from senior leaders, and embrace this as a huge learning opportunity. Constantly work on fine-tuning and communicating expectations and delivering feedback . . . people *will* look to you for advice. You are in a position to make a lasting impact." Just do it. Talk. Communicate. Listen. It's never as bad as you think. Communicate, communicate, communicate.

Communicate: Just Say It
◁ Telltale Tweets ▷

1. Communication can make or break you as a manager. Communicate early and often. #justsayit

2. Talk about roles, responsibilities, expectations, and PUSH goals. Don't assume anything. #loudandclear #hairy

3. Deliver feedback—the good, bad, and ugly—to help your people grow and develop. Be direct and sincere. #youcandoit

8

OWN IT: TAKING—AND GIVING— RESPONSIBILITY

"The ancient Romans had a tradition: whenever one of their engineers constructed an arch, as the capstone was hoisted into place, the engineer assumed accountability for his work in the most profound way possible: he stood under the arch."

—C. Michael Armstrong, former Chairman of AT&T

Ownership. Outside of the term "business casual," ownership might be one of the most nebulous terms in business for millennials. It all became apparent to me after hearing Captain Mike Abrashoff speak at Leo Burnett, where he shared his turnaround story of how he took a ship—the *USS Benfold*—from being one of the worst ships in the Navy to winning the Spokane trophy for combat readiness. One of the first things that Abrashoff did was instill a slogan on board the *USS Benfold,* "It's your ship." He put the future, the results, and power in the hands of each and every sailor—"It's YOUR Ship." Abrashoff said, "Show me an organization in which employees take ownership, and I will show you one that beats competitors." Abrashoff shifted the focus from the typical "chain of command" to a focus on *purpose.* He made it about performance not obedience, and I remember how he told stories of "aggressively listening" to his crew members, trying out their ideas, and rewarding them for taking risks. Abrashoff took ownership of the success of his ship, but he also instilled responsibility and ownership within each and every crew member. In this chapter, you will learn about these two sides of ownership and how to empower your people just like the captain.[1]

You likely have heard the term "ownership" thrown around a lot. Ownership is holding yourself accountable for what you do and how you do your job. Since your job is manager, your ownership goes a step further. You are the leader of the team, so you must hold yourself accountable for how the team performs. You are personally invested because the results and outcomes from your team reflect on you, the manager.

This is a great area of opportunity for millennial managers to grow. Take ownership of the success—or duress—of your team. Some negative feedback we hear about millennials is that they don't take ownership of their position. Senior leaders tell us that they think millennials struggle to see their responsibilities as solely their own. Millennials often seek permission when it comes to incorporating new ideas, or they miss a few steps when "seeing a project through from start to finish." With your collaborative nature, you tend to see things as more of a shared responsibility rather than ownership. You think of shared success and shared responsibility, and your generation likes consensus.

According to a Mr. Youth survey, 70 percent of millennials say they prefer consensus, especially when they're with their peers.[2] Scott Adams, the creator of Dilbert, makes the analogy, "Few things in life are less efficient than a group of people trying to write a sentence. The advantage of this method is that you end up with something for which you will not be personally blamed." By making decisions as a team, millennials can try and sidestep the ownership of that decision. "It was everyone's decision, so it's everyone's responsibility," you might say.

For example, it is Frank's responsibility to compile the report after the site visit. He sends the report to his colleagues who visited the site to see if they have any input, but the final deliverable is the main responsibility of Frank. Now, Frank sends out the report, and his manager finds a significant discrepancy. As a millennial, Frank likely thinks, "Oh, our site visit team really messed up on that one. We should have caught that," instead of "I messed that up." Frank could also think, "Well, that's why my manager is there—to double-check and make sure everything is perfect before we send this out." Senior leaders and Frank's manager are really looking to him to be the final stop and ultimately the one responsible for his report. Now that you have stepped into a management role, this idea of ownership is even more important. You must have the responsibility, and you must instill it in your team.

HOLDING YOURSELF ACCOUNTABLE

Julian Rotter conducted a study that hints at the underlying drivers and the fundamental reasons your generation may have a hard time with this idea of ownership as a manager. Rotter studied the "locus of control," which is a psychology theory that determines how much you think *external* forces impact your life.[3] Do you think you can control the events that affect you? If you have an internal focus, you're more likely to hold *yourself* responsible for the results of your situation. If you have an external focus, you're more likely to look at the *world* as responsible for your state of affairs. With internal locus, you look *within* to hold yourself accountable, and with external locus, you look *out* to hold people and forces around you accountable.

Some studies have shown that Rotter's idea of locus of control varies across the generations. A study by Twenge, Zhang, & Im discovered that younger generations are more likely to put greater emphasis on external forces.[4] This insight supports anecdotes we have heard from senior leaders who wish millennial managers would take more responsibility for their teams and really own the opportunities and challenges.

With an external locus of control, millennial managers may be more inclined to blame the poor performance of their team on the poor economy, new company policies, or a difficult client. If they have a poor performer, then the millennial manager may see the individual as the problem. It may take some time for the millennial manager to look within and question himself—Am I motivating this employee? Am I equipping this employee with the skills he needs to do the job? Am I adjusting my style and doing what I can to make sure this employee thrives? As a millennial manager, you may look at those external forces that impact "the situation" before taking a closer look at the causes of those external forces or what you can do to impact or change them.

When you played sports, was it often the ref's bad calls that made you lose the game? Or, was it because you missed several important shots? When you received a "C" on your literature paper, was it because the guidelines for the paper were misleading? Or, was it because you waited until the night before to write it and it wasn't as good as it could have been? In the workplace, did you get passed over for the new business team because the team lead didn't like you? Or, was it because you never took that presentation skills training, and you wouldn't have been the most qualified person to deliver the new business pitches?

As a leader, you must be open to looking internally for the answers. In Jim Collins's *Good to Great*, he cites one attribute as the differentiating characteristic between effective leaders (Level 4) and truly *great* leaders (Level 5).[5] Level 5 leaders, as defined by Collins, are ambitious and driven leaders who seek success for their team and organization, not their own, personal glory. Collins states that Level 5 leaders are the first to accept blame for poor results, and they are the first to share credit for a job well done.

The main difference between a Level 5 leader and a Level 4 leader is one unsuspecting characteristic. What characteristic separates good leaders from great? Take a moment to guess. Vision? Charisma? Integrity? Intuition? Intelligence? Creativity? The one defining characteristic of a Level 5 leader is *humility*. Collins noted that it was humility and the leader's ability to accept responsibility when things went wrong that defined them as truly great and a step above all those *pretty good* leaders. These great leaders weren't looking *out* for someone to blame; they were looking *in* for ways they could improve and change their circumstances. The Level 5 leaders often led companies in industries that were failing and getting hammered by outside forces, but the companies with Level 5 leaders at the helm realized they could look within and focus on the things that they could control.[6]

There will always be excuses. There will always be a world out there that impacts your business and team. But what do you do and where do you turn when hit by an unexpected jolt? Do you throw up your hands in the air and wave 'em like you just don't care, millennials? Do you play the "why me?" card? Or do you buckle down and try to figure out how you and your team can *change* these events?

In 2008, when companies were getting hit hard by the economy, our training and development business suffered. Training and development is often the first line item to get cut when a company is struggling. Admittedly, at first, we complained about the difficulties we were going through, but then, we rose above the fray and had a laser-like focus on building our client base in spite of the downturn. We could be victims, we could worry and complain, or we could figure out what to do about it. We stopped blaming all the forces trying to crush us, and we looked internally to what each of us could do to keep our business growing. We made it through 2008, and because of our grassroots efforts, we enjoyed a bright 2009.

Do You Own Results Through the Good and the Bad?

Do you have more of an internal or external locus of control? Admittedly, it's more difficult to have an internal locus of control when you're going through hardship. It's especially hard to maintain an internal focus if you're a Type A personality, and the individuals on your team aren't performing well. It can be hard to own the results of *their* mistakes or poor performance. It's their fault, right? There will always be some downright bad hires, and we aren't saying you have to own their idiocy. Frequently, there is something you could have done better or differently. "It's funny how often the problem is you," asserts Captain Mike Abrashoff.[7] Level 5 leaders would look internally and see what they could be doing better or differently to help the situation.

I recognize this is a significant change from being an individual contributor. Previously, you were responsible for your work and yourself for the most part. You felt like you had control over your performance. Now, you're responsible for the work of an entire team, and there seems to be quite a few things out of your control. To bring this important idea to life, think through real-life work obstacles you have encountered and consider the internal and external forces affecting them. Specifically, think through five examples of mistakes, obstacles, or poor results that you have experienced lately. I'm not saying you should accept all blame for your employees' mistakes. They, too, need to take ownership, but this exercise will give you a good awareness of your mindset. First, list the external forces that could have affected that situation, then list all of the reasons how you affected the situation (see the chart on the next page). The chart provides an example of an individual responsibility and a managerial responsibility.

Have you heard of Charles Coffin of GE, Bill Allen of Boeing, or Darwin Smith of Kimberly-Clark? Probably not. Jim Collins asserts they are Level 5 leaders and a few of the greatest CEOs of all time.[8] They were driven yet humble. They weren't afraid to hire people smarter than themselves, and they pursued success and glory for their teams and organizations—not themselves. That's why their names may not be familiar to you. It was less about them, although their companies were wildly successful.

Mistake/Obstacle/ Poor Results	External Forces	Internal Forces
Did not win a request for proposal	Potential client didn't really know what he wanted; design team didn't make final deliverable that eye-catching; potential client is *obviously* not very smart	I could have asked more questions up front to get at what the client really wanted; I should have set clearer and higher expectations with the design team; I didn't effectively show why we are the absolute best company for the project
Your employee sent a sloppy report to the senior team	Your employee is an idiot; your employee is really stressed with work and personal matters; your senior team is too critical	I could take more time to show what high-quality work looks like; I should have had her read a couple of my past reports; I could have established check-ins; I could have shared details about the quality of work the senior team expects
1. Your example:		
2. Your example:		
3. Your example:		
4. Your example		
5. Your example:		

As a manager, you will find that it is less and less about you. If you recall the way you were raised, it was all about you and your specialness. Now, as a manager, you have to take a step back from this mindset. Truly great leaders are not narcissistic; they are concerned with values and ideals greater than themselves. To "own" your management position, you must put your team members and the success of your team first. Lao Tzu offers, "As for the best leaders, the people do not notice their existence. . . . When the best leader's work is done the people say, we did it ourselves!"

Before you became a manager, you were likely a star employee, so you were accustomed to receiving accolades and appreciation. Now you want to focus on making your team stand out. I know what you're thinking, "So Brad, you're telling me that when things go wrong, I need to step forward and take ownership, and when things go right, I need to step back and let my team take credit? Where is the fun in that?" The fun is in watching your team learn, grow, and excel. And, your boss knows. Your boss knows that if your team is high performing, it's due to your leadership. As you are beginning to see, "owning it" might be a tough skill to master as a millennial manager. Throughout this chapter, you will gain tips and techniques for taking on leadership responsibilities and truly owning your management role.

There are a few elements to think about when it comes to owning your role as manager:

▷ Failure is on the road to succeeding.
▷ Do what you say you're going to do.
▷ Be your own CEO, and ask others to be their own CEOs.
▷ Orchestrate success and ownership.

FAILURE IS ON THE ROAD TO SUCCEEDING

The sticky part about "owning" your role is that you will find that there isn't always a "right answer." Or, the best answer might not be the best answer three months down the road. For the most part, in school, there is a right answer and a wrong answer, but in the workplace, the answers can be far more nebulous. Real-world problems are complex, multifaceted, and ever changing. It can be difficult leading through a situation where the answers and elements are always transforming, but that's what management requires. It requires flexibility to adapt and own the good and bad through the good and bad.

One thing I often hear from senior leaders is that millennial managers don't seem to own a decision as a leader. From the perspective of Brian, a gen X employee, millennial managers struggle with owning that final decision and answer in part because they are searching for the right answer. Brian says you are all about collecting more and more data, working together, hearing opinions, and thinking it through.

The next step, which is deciding and owning it, is scary. Just knowing that there won't always be a right answer puts you one step ahead. It actually makes you more agile and poised for success if you are working under the never-changing foundation that nothing will ever stay the same.

If there are no are right answers, then you're bound to make a couple mistakes, right? You are such a high-achieving generation that you have a hard time seeing that mistakes are okay. Millennials didn't want to earn an A- or a B, much less a failing grade. At work, failing is part of learning. Owning your mistakes and learning from them can be one of the most beneficial things you do as a leader.

A Look at Great Failures

Let's look at all of the great people who experienced great failures. They include Thomas Edison, Michael Jordan, Colonel Sanders, and Oprah Winfrey. You may see people at the top of their game, and you think, now that is the perfect leader who did everything right. Thomas Edison is famous for "proving that those 10,000 ways *will not* work."[9] Michael Jordan "missed more than 9,000 shots . . . lost more than 300 games . . . and missed twenty-six game-winning shots."[10] Colonel Sanders was rejected from 1,000 restaurants before someone finally accepted his secret recipe, and it took numerous rejections before a television station took a risk on Oprah Winfrey.[11] It was not the absence of failure that made these leaders great; it was their reaction to the presence of failure and their resilience to the abundance of failure.

The executive vice president of a financial services firm, Marc, has a unique view on failure. He requires it. Marc requires his team members to have a failure because he says if they haven't failed then they haven't really pushed themselves or taken a risk. He tells his employees,

"If you can look back over the last six months and you haven't failed, then you haven't been doing a great job—you haven't challenged yourself or tried anything new. Go out and fail."

Marc's view on failure also gives his team the confidence and empowerment it needs; it releases that fear of messing up. There is a beautiful quote by Theodore Roosevelt that speaks to this idea of failing along the road toward greatness. Roosevelt said, "Far better is it to dare mighty things, to win glorious triumphs, even though checkered by failure... than to rank with those poor spirits who neither enjoy nor suffer much, because they live in a gray twilight that knows not victory nor defeat." The hundreds and thousands of millennial managers I have talked to all had an element of a bright will and optimism that would never want to settle for a "gray twilight."

Exploring and making mistakes is good for learning. It's like when Courtney was trying to learn the public transportation system when she moved to Chicago. She was at first perplexed by all the different-colored lines, the "el," and the subway. It was so easy to go the wrong way around the loop. To speed up the learning curve, she bought an unlimited day pass, and she spent the whole day hopping on and off trains and buses. She got it! It just took a little exploration and going in the wrong direction a few times to understand.

As a manager, you will fail here and there. Own it, learn from it, and move ahead.

BEING YOUR OWN CEO

Leah Busque, the CEO of TaskRabbit, says, "I wake up every morning and think to myself, how far can I push the company forward in the next twenty-four hours?"[12] Leah owns her role and knows that her day-to-day actions have the power to move the company forward. Think about it this way—what if your team was a small business and you were the business owner? Although the term seems nebulous, "taking ownership" means acting like you're the CEO of your job and your team. If you mess up or an employee messes up, at the end of the day, it's your responsibility. What can you do in the next 24 hours to push your team forward?

The author of A *Thousand Joys*, Byron Katie, says, "Anything you want to ask a teacher, *ask yourself*, and wait for the answer in silence."

Your generation grew up with everyone telling you that no question is a bad question. You also were encouraged to ask "why?," and you were accustomed to receiving a real answer. You are comfortable with looking *out* for the answer. You can ask your parents, ask your boss, and ask your friends, and if you're still not sure, you can just Google it. You're not as comfortable looking *within* for the answer. Before asking or looking out, challenge yourself to look in and ask yourself.

Admittedly, it can be difficult to trust your decision making at the start. One thing that Courtney did to hone her decision making skills would be to guess what I would say or how I would answer questions in business meetings. Instead of being just a passive attendee at the meeting, Courtney was quizzing herself. She was formulating opinions and decisions in her head, and she was able to compare them side-by-side with my actual answers and decisions. As she stepped in a client relationship role, Courtney listened in on a lot of my calls. For example, a client asks us, "Can you customize your management workshop to include goal setting and motivating virtual employees?" Courtney thinks, yes, we can include goal setting in our first module, and we can customize the motivation section to encompass managing remote employees. Then she gets to hear me say, "Absolutely, we have a module on PUSH goals that fits nicely into our first section on laying out expectations. Then we wrap up the day talking about how to spark engagement and motivate employees, and we can give some tangible tips for working with employees who are remote in that portion. We could even write a role-play situation that covers this issue." Courtney, thinks "yes!" She just passed a no-risk decision-making test. Taking ownership and making decisions go hand-in-hand.

Do What You Say You're Going to Do

"Lead by example. There's nothing more discouraging than the opposite: seeing your manager circumventing responsibilities and possessing low morale," says Lin, millennial manager at a not-for-profit organization. As a leader, you have to own what you say. It's extremely frustrating to employees when a leader says one thing and does another—or does nothing at all. "Hold yourself accountable for keeping your commitments. No one respects someone who doesn't keep their word, no matter what excuse they give," offers Garry Tackett, Global Director, Learning and Employee Services at CareerBuilder. "Even if you absolutely hate what you're doing at the time, if you made a commitment—keep it. Learn from the experience and don't make or accept that commitment again in the future." Do what you say you're going to do. Own your words and actions, and honor your commitments to be the CEO of your position.

ASKING OTHERS TO BE THEIR OWN CEOs

Now, if you're taking ownership over the success—or duress—of your team, how do you make sure there is more success? You inspire your employees to take ownership as well. As you feel more comfortable being the CEO of your position, you can begin teaching your team members how to take ownership of their responsibilities as well. Teach them how to be CEOs of their positions. My favorite quote from Captain Mike Abrashoff is, "The key to being a successful skipper is to see the ship through the eyes of the crew. Only then can you find out what's wrong and help the sailors *empower themselves* to fix it."[13] He didn't say he would fix the problems for them; he would *empower the sailors* to fix it. It's a notable difference.

When it comes to empowering your people, your Xer and boomer employees are craving ownership and autonomy. For millennials, you may have to teach them how to think on their own and not always look to you and others for answers.

For example, Courtney was giving creative and entrepreneurial projects to one of her direct reports. The employee would think about it and then come back with an idea—*one* idea. Courtney had to explain that with creative and new projects, resourcefulness and big thinking are required. In most creative exercises, the first idea isn't always the best idea. It's the idea that comes after rooting yourself in the information, brainstorming different ideas, and processing and analyzing the pros and cons of implementation. To get the employee to embrace the project fully and take ownership, Courtney gave specific ideas of how it would play out.

She said, "When thinking through a new business opportunity like this, you really want to immerse yourself in the material. This topic is new to you, so you may spend a few hours researching and learning more. Then when it comes to idea generation, you want to go a little wild. Think outside the box. You came to me with one idea that would work. Can you fill up an entire page or two with ideas? Challenge yourself, and have fun with it." Walking through examples of what taking ownership looks like is helpful for millennials, and it's incredibly empowering.

Having them take more ownership does mean that you have to let go of some of the control. You may be waiting until they can prove that they can take ownership and produce high-quality work, but often, if you let go a little and give that freedom, then they step up and take it.

You Step Back; They Step Up

For example, I was coaching an executive creative director (ECD) at an advertising agency who had a brilliant, creative mind. Before becoming the ECD in charge of the entire department, he served as a group creative director in charge of a team of six. Quite frankly, the team he managed wasn't very strong, and he became very disappointed and frustrated. He would receive work that was absolutely not acceptable to give to the client, and he would have to enhance or fundamentally change it to bring it up to standards time and time again. Nothing left the agency without him having to put his stamp on it to make it the quality the client demanded.

Then he was promoted to ECD, and no one was brought in to replace him as direct manager of his former team of six. Spending more time with his new senior duties left his former team members on their own. He was no longer available to look at the work and improve the quality before it went to the client. He was petrified that left unattended his team would disappoint the client and ultimately lead to his agency losing the business. In actuality, just the opposite occurred.

Without him reviewing the work, it actually got better. He couldn't figure out why at first, but then it sunk in: they finally felt a sense of ownership. When the creative team didn't have the crutch of the creative director, the employees stepped up their game. Previously, they knew their work would just get changed and overhauled, so why put in the extra effort? At some point, when you know someone is going to go over everything you do with a fine-toothed comb, you just sort of give up. It took the creative director giving them more freedom to have them accept the ownership. It sounds counterintuitive. Often, when things aren't going well, we have a tendency to tighten control. Sometimes, those are the times you need to loosen your control and allow your employees to step up.

It has been found that in countries where there are fewer traffic signals and signs, there often are fewer accidents. People must be alert and aware. They must show up to drive every day, or they just might not survive. In the United States, where you can have four instructional signs or traffic lights on one corner, there are a lot of accidents. You can almost drive on autopilot—from your house to work without even thinking. You don't really have to bring your brain to the driving experience. In countries like India, there is more freedom on the road, which empowers drivers to take more ownership of their actions. With all of the outside rules and regulations in the United States, you're not as alert because there are so many outside factors protecting you. You assume that others will follow the rules—stop at red lights, go pretty close to the speed limit, and yield the right of way. One way you could look at this is that Americans don't have that much ownership in the driving experience and therefore leave the responsibilities to others. Everyone assumes everyone else is taking responsibility and a lot of accidents ensue. Those "defensive" drivers who take more ownership and are always alert skirt by with fewer incidents.

If we parlay that to work, it means that by giving more freedom and asking employees to take ownership, you create an environment where every day is "bring your brain to work" day.[14] Employees who have the freedom to make their own decisions make better decisions because they are more alert and connected. They have more ownership.

Think about a couple companies that give their employees a big sense of autonomy and freedom to do their job. Zappos and Southwest Airlines come to mind. At Zappos, the customer service representatives are empowered to do whatever they need to do to make a customer happy. They don't have to float their idea past two levels of bureaucracy and finally get back to the customer in five days. Right then and there on the phone, they can do what is in their power to wow their customers and "deliver happiness"—a Zappos motto and principle. They don't follow a script; they simply ask questions and listen to the customer. This is just one of the many reasons that Zappos has outstanding customer service reviews. They train their employees on how to do their jobs, but then trust that they are smart and resourceful enough to work without a script. They give them this freedom, and Zappos is rewarded with amazing customer service.

Similarly, at Southwest Airlines, employees have the autonomy to do what they need to do to serve their customers. All employees are empowered and tied to the company values. For example, if pilots see the baggage handlers struggling to turn the gateway bags around quickly, they pitch in to help out. If cockpit employees recognize that a customer has a question and the flight attendant is helping someone else, they offer to help. People step up when they have autonomy, freedom, and ownership. As you are beginning to see, freedom and empowerment go hand in hand with ownership. Overabundant rules and regulations and micromanaging bosses can stifle creativity and solutions. Give autonomy and ownership to your team members, and trust that they have the skills and tools to do a great job. Just as you can take ownership in your management role, your employees can take ownership in their jobs. Everyone can bring their personality and strengths to their position and complete projects the best they see fit. Be the CEO of your position and empower your employees to do the same. Gregory Tall, Director of Human Capital Management at Robert Morris University Illinois, sums it up, "The best way to lead by example is to take total accountability for everything you do. If those you lead do that too, there is no limit to what you will accomplish."

ORCHESTRATING SUCCESS AND OWNERSHIP

Say what? Orchestrate? Is this an "O" word I'm throwing in here to stick with our C-O-N-N-E-C-T theme? This idea of "orchestration" supports the theme of ownership because as you are learning "ownership" as a manager, you are helping your employees take ownership. It doesn't mean take control of everything; it means leading and guiding your team toward success. You're the conductor.

Let's think about the conductor of an orchestra for a moment. The conductor knows all the cues, understands everyone's parts, and leads the show. That's you, the millennial manager.

Unifying Your Team

I will talk more about this point in Chapter 11, "Engage: Connecting to the Big Picture," but as you grow into a leader, you will be the one who fosters engagement, keeps morale up, and rallies the team. Your millennial employees, in particular, want to be a part of a strong team. A millennial manager said, "If I'm spending eight to ten hours with someone every day, I want to get along with that person." As the leader of the group, you are guiding the group and ensuring everyone is working together to accomplish great things. "The way a team plays as a whole determines its success. You may have the greatest bunch of individual stars in the world, but if they don't play together, the club won't be worth a dime."

To parallel this quotation by Babe Ruth, you can have the smartest, most creative person on your team, but if she's aggressive and a poor team player, then the entire efforts and morale of your team will suffer. You will have ups and downs as a team, no doubt, but as the leader, you help unify the group through it all. You recognize that everyone brings different strengths to the table, and you can help your team members play to their strengths and complement other members of the team.

With a unified and strong team, employees feel more connected and take more ownership of their responsibilities. They know if they slack off, they let down their team. When talking about his millennial manager, Jorge said that his energetic manager was so supportive and engaging, that she made the entire team *want* to do a good job and *want* to go the extra mile. If you lead everyone to have a solid sense of teamwork, then they will be stronger individual players who take individual ownership to better serve their team.

Setting the Tempo

This is a really important part of being a millennial manager. You're used to multitasking and working at a fast pace. People can get burned out by the workplaces and teams that operate under an "everything is urgent" mindset. I find that especially in client-serving industries, everything is urgent, go-go-go, and a fire drill! When you step into the office that has an "everything is urgent" culture, you can almost feel the tension, anxiety, and frenzy in the air.

In environments like this, when there are so many urgent matters that pop up, the important projects tend to slip through the cracks. You may be familiar with the 80:20 Principle. It's the idea that 80 percent of what we do yields 20 percent of our results, and 20 percent of what we do yields 80 percent of our results. It all comes down to urgent versus important.

For instance, you receive thirty e-mails from your clients, and you spend the entire day rushing around, trying to find the information you need to address these urgent matters. You do this even though you were planning on making some quiet time to tackle and work through your important ideas for being more strategic with client partnerships. It's a project that would impact the entire company. However, it's not urgent, so it gets lost in the "everything is an emergency" atmosphere.

Teams are driving, pushing, working hard, and this breakneck tempo goes on and on and on. It's not sustainable. At the Wisdom 2.0 conference, Stuart Crabb, Head of Learning at Facebook, talked about this idea of a sprint and the importance of taking pauses—breathers—at work.[15] In a high-growth environments, such as Facebook, Crabb expresses, "Everyone needs to know the difference between sprinting and pausing.... It doesn't resonate if you try to tell them [employees] that they're running a marathon, not a sprint, because at this rate they'll be sprinting for a while. What we can teach them is the value of the pause. They have to break up their sprint into sprints."

If I sprinted a marathon, I most likely would die. However, I could sprint a marathon if I was able to insert some pauses. Okay, maybe I couldn't, but Courtney absolutely could. Even at highly energized and stimulating workplaces like Facebook, the "sprint marathon" and piercing tempo of work is not sustainable.

Unifying the team and setting the tempo are ways that managers can regulate the environment to create an atmosphere where employees are more likely to take ownership. You can set the tempo by encouraging your employees to take breathers between sprints. If you've been hard-charging for a while, trying to hit deadlines and finish projects, and you feel the energy waning, take a break.

At JB Training Solutions, we take a Boggle break. When more mindless breaks are needed, we complete a small jigsaw puzzle or even color. The color break usually takes place when I'm out of the office, but my team promises it's invigorating. Any time I return to the office and see colorful Crayola butterflies and pictures on the wall, I know my team has been working hard! After a short, 15-minute break, it's amazing how refreshed you are when you get back to your desk. It's that breather between sprints, the rest between sets in the gym when weightlifting, and the 15-minute power nap that gives you twice the energy.

The pause is a moment of mindfulness, a moment to allow the brain to relax and rejuvenate. It's true that most great ideas come in the shower, while you're running, or listening to music. Your brain needs the alpha waves of relaxation to shut down the logical left brain and allow the more creative right brain to have a chance to say hello. Creativity hates logic. Have you ever pressured yourself to try and think of something creative? It can't happen. The pressure and tension suppresses the right side of the brain that thinks creatively. That's why you always hear about the author who has writer's block after writing her first best seller. *"I have to write another best seller; this book has to be better than the last one."* This pressure shuts down the right brain and, therefore, creativity.

Encouraging your team to take pauses and monitoring the tempo of work allows everyone to center themselves, refresh, and be more productive. Nonstop sprinting pushes you toward burnout and an idea shortage.

Fortunately, your generation gets this idea. This is just another way that you're shaking up the workforce. Although the science and results are there, older generations can get stuck in this mindset of "all work and no play." As millennial managers, you can stand firm and lead the way that a little play or a few breaks at work is much more productive.

I find that older generations feel guilty about this break. "We're at work to work, so I must be working every single second," they seem to be saying. Your generation truly seems to embrace and get this way of thinking, and workplaces are listening. What are the "coolest places" to work equipped with? Most have fun spaces, so employees can take a break between sprints. At Google, employees zip around on scooters; at Red Frog Events, employees can have a conference meeting in the office tree house—just take the rope bridge there and the slide down. You can jam out to rock band at SilverTech in their "MTV Cribs Room," or you can climb the rock wall at Clif Bar's office.

Just 15 minutes of fun or relaxation to let your mind run free. More and more companies are realizing that it's easier to be creative, open, happy, and productive in an environment that physically represents these ideas with bright colors, open spaces, and innovative designs. How inspiring are those gray cubicles and heavy, mahogany walls? They practically are saying be boring and follow all the rules. This change in workspace is just another way to show that people recognize that work is more than just a fast sprint or place where you go to earn a paycheck. It's an inviting place with a dynamic tempo of go-getting high achievements and refreshing breathers.

As a millennial manager, help set this tempo. Constant high speeds will burn your team out, but on the flipside, a slow, long, arduous jog that goes on and on and on is just tiresome—especially for your millennial employees. Everything can't be "now, now, now," but everything can't be laid-back and "we'll get to it tomorrow." Employees appreciate a little of both. As the leader, you help set the pace and tempo to provide an environment where people are most likely to take ownership of their work. Be in tune with your team so you know when they can handle more and when they need a breather.

Executing Clear Preparations and Beats, Listening Critically, and Shaping the Sound of the Ensemble

You are setting the bounds in which your team can play; you are creating a stimulating yet stable environment in which employees are likely to take ownership. As the leader, you're always one step ahead. You are prepared. You know what's coming up; you plan.

Then, there's that "listen critically" cue again. Listening is not framed as a passive activity. Listening done right is aggressive and critical and analytical. It's discovering what's there, what's not there, and what needs to be done. Listening critically gives you the information you need to act and "shape" the results of your team.

I was working with a global energy company, and one of its departments was struggling because the rest of the company saw its members as "the police," who always said "no" to everything. The leader of the department listened to the comments from the company at large to pinpoint the best course of action. He set the stage for improvement by telling his people that "we need to be unfailingly self-critical." He knew his department first needed to look internally to see what type of perception and message it was sending to other employees. The leader—conductor—listened critically and shaped the direction of his department on the road to improvement.

In the orchestra, it's not about the conductor. Many people in the audience actually close their eyes, so all of their senses focus on the sound. The conductor, although in the front, takes a back seat to the power of his orchestra. It's about the beautiful piece of music that is created. It's about leading the way to empower your team to perform.

Take ownership of the success of your team by releasing a little control and giving your employees more responsibility. Trust and empower your people. You will make some mistakes along the way, and there won't always be a "right" answer. Look internally to see how you can impact the people around you positively. Because as a millennial manager, it's not about you. It's not about you; it's about them. It's not about you doing it for them—that would never work. It's about you owning the success of your team by leading, empowering, and guiding them toward greatness.

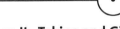

Own It : Taking and Giving Responsibility
◁ Telltale Tweets ▷

1. Hold yourself accountable for your work and your team's performance. What can YOU do to improve results? #level5leader #ownership

2. Have the confidence to make decisions. Don't be afraid of mistakes. Failure is on the road to succeeding. #dontstopbelieving #zappos

3. Do what you say you're going to do. #seriously

4. Orchestrate success for your team. Unify your group, set the tempo, execute, and shape. Lead the way. #sprints #boggle #listen

9

NAVIGATE: MANAGING THROUGH THE UNKNOWN

*Twenty years from now you will more be disappointed by the things
you didn't do than by the ones you did. So throw off the bowlines.
Sail away from the safe harbor. Catch the trade winds in your sails.
Explore. Dream. Discover.*

—Mark Twain

Think of a few of our great navigators. There was Lewis, Clark, and Sacagawea, who navigated their way down the mighty Mississippi River. Then, there was the fearless Jessica Watson, who at the age of 16 became the youngest person to circumnavigate the world—solo, unassisted, and nonstop. Finally, there is Bear Grylls, who navigates the wild, wild, wilderness. We could also mention Ferdinand Magellan and Christopher Columbus, as the foremost examples of the great explorers. What words come to mind when thinking about these great navigators and explorers? Daring, brave, determined, hopeful, stupid?

When you're "navigating," there is always an element of unknown. The unknown makes it exciting—yet scary. As a millennial manager, you have to navigate quite a few things—changes in business needs, personality style of your team members, ups and downs of work flow, and much, much more. I am sure you have seen that the workday and workflow are always dynamic and changing. If only you could know *exactly* what to do *all* the time!

Sara Blakely, the founder of Spanx and the youngest self-made female to join the Forbes Billionaire Club, hit a lot of unknowns as an entrepreneur, and she offers, "Embrace what you don't know, especially in the beginning because what you don't know can become your greatest assets. It ensures that you will be doing things absolutely differently from everyone else."[1] Although it's easier said than done, use your first years as a manager to learn and grow as much as you can. Instead of fearing the unknown and skirting away from it, seek it out, run toward it, and embrace it. Business consultant Margaret Wheatley says, "The things we fear most in organizations—fluctuations, disturbances, imbalances—are the primary sources of creativity." Navigate, learn, and grow as you go.

MAPPING OUT YOUR TIME

Now that you're a manager with unchartered territory before you, where will you focus your energies? I don't have a secret formula that determines exactly how much time you should spend focused on your people. For instance, if you have five direct reports, then you should spend 11.43 hours a week focused on managing them. Unfortunately, there is no secret to success here. I will say that dedicating at least 20 percent of your time to developing and managing your team is a solid baseline. One of the hardest parts about being a millennial manager is that you still have a boss to answer to and individual job responsibilities. It can be easy to crank through your individual work and just hope that your team is doing what it needs to be doing. If you're particularly busy, you push off your monthly feedback sessions or check-ins with your employees. Navigating your schedule and priorities will take a little practice.

I know that "management" doesn't fit nicely into a 9:00 AM to 11:00 AM time slot, but try blocking out time for management. It knocks you out of your individual contributor zone and back into the manager mindset. As I mentioned, management takes time, and you will be sacrificing some of the time that you would normally spend working on one of your important projects. As Maya Angelou said, "I've learned that you shouldn't go through life with a catcher's mitt on both hands; you need to be able to throw something back." You've learned a lot from others, gained experiences, and received advice and mentorship, and that prepared you to take the step into management. Now, it's your turn to share your experience with your team. It's time to throw a little something back.

Courtney blocks out time for managing because she recognizes that she easily gets caught up in the hustle and bustle of the day. She uses these blocks on her calendar to check the pulse of her team. The processing and questions she is asking go along these lines: *How is morale? Is Allison progressing on the goals that she set? Have I given her everything she needs to be successful? I have a meeting coming up with a client; I should have her come along, so she can hold these meetings down the road. How is Nicole doing? I know she was frustrated with a couple technology snafus; I should see how that's going. Have we done anything as a team lately? Boggle break this week!* These reflections help Courtney navigate the often uncertain job of managing.

Courtney also schedules a block of time at the end of each month to chat with her employees. It's on the calendar, so it's more likely to happen. It's a tried-and-true time management tip. If it's on the calendar, it's less likely to get squeezed out and pushed until the next day and the next day and the next day.

Although they don't put it on the calendar, we work with a client that has a team meeting at 9:00 AM every day. Now, the client misses a day every now and then if there are important deadlines to hit, but it's a time where the entire team gets together to ensure that everyone is on the right track and working on the highest priority items. Since the meeting is at 9:00 AM, everyone has about an hour or so to get settled in and put together their action items for the day.

Navigating your time as a manager isn't easy. You may find that you get a lot more interruptions and questions throughout the day. Determine how you and your team work best, and see if any adjustments need to be made. As a millennial manager, you likely welcome questions and ideas and maintain an open-door policy. On the flipside, interruptions can be one of the biggest time wasters and productivity killers. Now an interruption is not a "pause amid the sprints" to be sure.

Think about when you're working on a big project—let's say a competitive analysis. You're on a roll! You're writing, and the ideas are flowing. You do a little research, and then you write to summarize your findings. This is really coming along! You are in the zone. Then someone pops their head in your office, you look up, and the person starts asking you a question. More than likely you will ask to have the question repeated because your mind was so engrossed in what you were doing that it can't switch to processing the question fast enough.

Your employee wanted to know what should be done about an e-mail from the marketing department. You talk through it for a few minutes, your employee leaves, and you look back at your computer. Do you know that feeling of just staring at your screen for a while thinking, okay, what was I doing, where was I? It takes a little while to get back in. Now imagine if that happens every ten minutes. You can have an "open-door policy" and be very open with information, but you can also encourage your employees to hold some of their questions or try to figure it out on their own. Sometimes, in the name of being helpful, millennial managers are too hands-on. "I want to help my people, and be there when I can," you say. Absolutely, but helping them sometimes means challenging them to take on a few things themselves.

I know a manager who only checks e-mail three times a day. Now, not everyone can do that, but this manager finds that it keeps her focused on tasks that are most important. Being a manager requires a lot of discipline. Simply think about all of the things that come across your desk that need to be reviewed. Then there are check-ins, follow-up, meetings, feedback sessions, and e-mails, e-mails, e-mails! You have to determine how you get your stuff done and how you review projects in a timely manner, so your employees have the tools and the feedback to do a great job. Although being engaging and helpful is part of being a good leader, that's only part of it. Organization and time management are a big part as well. "If you have a sense of purpose and a sense of direction, I believe people will follow you." Just as Margaret Thatcher said, if your employees are going to look up to you, then they want to see a leader who has his stuff together and who models the way.

Now, how can you make sure you stay on top of the day-to-day tasks as well as plan for the future? How do you gain a vision for your team? Navigating is easier if you constantly check in with yourself and your surroundings. Here are a few questions you can ask yourself to keep you and your team on track and moving in the right direction:

▷ What's next? What's new?
▷ How can we do things better, faster, or bolder?
▷ What hasn't been working and how can we improve?

▷ If I were a consultant looking in, what would I say we should or shouldn't be doing?

▷ How do the dots connect?

▷ How can I look at this from another perspective?

▷ How would the CEO view this challenge or opportunity?

▷ What can I immerse myself in to gain better understanding?

▷ Are there any industries or teams that are similar to ours that I can learn from?

▷ How would my customer or end user view this?

These are great reflection points and check-in questions to test your navigating skills and steer clear of troubles.

FINDING YOUR WAY AS A TRANSPARENT LEADER

When the weather gets stormy, sailors look to their captain. When athletes are stuck in a rut, they look to their coach. When students have a problem, they turn to their teacher. In times of turmoil, stress, confusion, or frustration, people turn to their leader. They want to see the reaction of their leader to garner how they should feel about the situation.

Think about the last time you saw a small child fall down. Before the child starts to cry, he will look at mom or dad to see their reaction. Most of the time, if mom and dad are smiling and saying, "You're okay," the child understands the cue, picks himself up, and starts running around again. On the other hand, if mom and dad have worried looks on their faces and start sprinting to the child, the child understands that he must be hurt and starts bawling. Same fall—but the child learns the social cues from his parents. As the leader, your employees look to you for cues on how they should act and react. Anne Price, Global Marketing Capabilities Director, said that people will "look to the boss for reaction, and millennials must have the maturity to have a game face."

This is where maturity, attitude, and transparency come into play. First, as a manager, you now have a larger responsibility to support your senior leaders and your company's initiatives positively. Before you became manager, you probably didn't think twice about chatting with coworkers about HR's new benefits policy and how you think it kind of stinks. At team happy hours, you would have partaken in light-hearted yet pointed humor about your crazy client. Now that you're a manager, you have to be careful about how you're acting and being perceived. I know millennials might have a tough time here. It's not that you have to be someone you're not or that you can't have fun anymore. Your perspective simply changes a little. You have your team, but you're also on the management team, so you have to represent those views and perspectives as well. If you don't agree with some decisions of upper management, you have to be careful with how that comes off. As a millennial manager, I know you want to stay true to both of your teams. Maybe it sounds something like this.

> *I wanted to talk to everyone about our new HR policy. I know if you're like me, you were a little surprised with the changes. I, too, was taken aback at first. But I also wanted to share what my manager told me, and it makes a lot of sense. As we all know, these last two quarters have been slow. One of the biggest things that I took away is that the company has to make some cuts and, instead of having to lay off anyone, they're pulling back some of our benefits. Now, I know it's still hard to swallow, but our senior leaders considered quite a few options, and I think we can all agree that we can't afford to have less people around here.*

This doesn't change the fact that the new policy stinks a little, but as the manager, you can clue your team into how it connects to the big picture. I think you would agree that in this scenario, you are still being incredibly transparent.

When talking with millennial managers, we heard both sides about this idea of transparency and leading the way as manager. Your generation appreciates transparency, but sometimes a tough or resilient mindset is needed even when the prospects look bleak. I am reminded of one of my favorite people—Winston Churchill. At the time of the battle of France in World War II, the circumstances were grim. London was getting bombed every night. Did Churchill feel worry, anxiety, and sadness in his heart? There is no doubt. Did he reveal that to his country? No. Did he sugar-coat anything? No. He said it was going to be hard and that there would be a lot of fighting. He had to instill hope and encourage a relentless strength and heartfelt, patriotic pride. He sent out inspiring messages day after day. In one of his most famous speeches, Churchill said,

We shall go on to the end. We shall fight in France, we shall fight on the seas and oceans, we shall fight with growing confidence and growing strength in the air, we shall defend our island, whatever the cost may be. We shall fight on the beaches, we shall fight on the landing grounds, we shall fight in the fields and in the streets, we shall fight in the hills; we shall never surrender.

Do you have chills? That's leadership. That's inspirational. That's navigating the environment and delivering what your people need. There is an ambitious transparency that encompasses this speech. As a leader, sometimes you have to rise above your own fears or concerns and be the person that your people need you to be. In England, they needed their leader to tell them that they could make it through all the fighting. They needed someone to say that they would survive.

Now, I'm not comparing your company to a battleground or a world war. Hopefully, you don't see too many comparisons in your work environment. This is a great—an extraordinary—example of the type of leader you need to be when you're leading your team through a tough situation.

Let's take a closer look at this "ambitious transparency." Maybe your transparency focuses on "what is to be" rather than what currently is. You can be incredibly direct and upfront with your team but still focus on a more uplifting angle. Jason Houze, a millennial manager at Energy BBDO, admits that if a situation is unclear or unknown, he is upfront with his team. In these instances, Houze says, "My approach is that I am 100 percent transparent. A lot of times I say 'I don't know the right answer, but we'll find the right answer.' I don't lead them down any rabbit holes of inefficient work, which really helps. That way they don't waste time trying to figure it out on their own." Houze is transparent as he navigates an unknown situation, but he leads with confidence by saying, "We will find the right answer."

TAKING THE HELM AND INSTILLING HOPE

A great example of a leader who navigated through tough times is the former CEO of Southwest Airlines, Herb Kelleher. In the early 1970s, Southwest was struggling to meet payroll and Kelleher had a tough decision to make.² Should he lay off employees or find another way to cut costs? Kelleher found another way; he sold a plane to get the cash that was needed to keep the company where it needed to be and to avoid firing people. He made a statement to his people and let them know the gravity of the situation. Now, not all leaders and companies can do that. Honestly, great leaders and great companies have to let people go, but how is it communicated? How does the leader help the remaining employees adjust and transition smoothly?

During the economic downfall of 2008, JB Training Solutions coached a lot of leaders and companies on how to "keep up morale in a down economy." We advised managers on how to pilot the storm and navigate through tough times. In this training, I talked a lot about communication and transparency as a leader and when to know what angle to strike. In Kelleher's case, he was very transparent with his employees, and he let them know about the tough decisions he was facing. He also let them know that he specifically chose to protect jobs and people. This type of transparency yields a great sense of loyalty and appreciation.

In Churchill's case, raw transparency probably wasn't the way to go. Everyone knew the cold, hard realities, and what they needed was hope and inspiration. Churchill could have briefed them on the behind-the-scenes negotiations, considerations, and wartime tactics, but that wasn't what they needed to hear. They wanted to know that although it would be tough, it would get better. Neither Churchill nor Kelleher read a book about what to do in those exact situations. They couldn't even google it. They had to own the circumstances, navigate the situation, and communicate a targeted message. You can see how the themes of CONNECT are starting to connect.

Now I know what you're thinking. World wars, layoffs, bankrupt companies—isn't that a little extreme for advising a first-time manager? If I know anything about millennials, it is that you have the resolve to change the face of leadership and chart a new course for the way business—and therefore our world—works. Although you're just on the first step and you may have a small team, I have no doubt that you're headed for greatness. As a millennial manager, you have that within you.

Part of navigating is instilling hope. People want to believe. They want to contribute to a cause bigger than themselves. Millennials especially want to have challenging and meaningful work. Work isn't just work. They want to make a difference on their team, at their company, and in the world.

How can you communicate messages that instill hope and connect your team to the big picture? Instill hope and inspiration—that you will reach your quarterly goals, that you will land that new client, that you will make a difference in the lives of your customers. This doesn't have to be about noble and lofty speeches. This can be about your attitude and your actions. You can be that extraordinary leader in ordinary circumstances. I will continue to share extraordinary examples and then ground these examples in tangible management techniques that you can use in the field.

DISCOVERING DIFFERENT COMMUNICATION STYLES

You are learning as you go. You navigate your schedule to make time for management responsibilities, and you navigate both bright and bleak situations to determine your level or angle of transparency. The next big task as navigator is getting to know the personality and communication styles of each member of your team and adjusting your management style accordingly. Abraham Maslow, author of *The Theory of Human Motivation,* wrote, "If the only tool you have is a hammer, you tend to see every problem as a nail."[3] As a millennial manager, you're up for this challenge of adaptability.

You're accustomed to changing, adapting, gaining new skills, and understanding different perspectives, and this attribute gives you a leg up when it comes to working with different members of a team. Alexandra Levit, author of *They Don't Teach Corporate in College,* asked a millennial manager, "How would you describe your management style?" The manager responded, "I don't have one management style. I don't like having one style—it varies by the individual. It is all customized." This is an insightful quote and reveals that "adjusting your style" may come a little easier for your generation.

For older generations framed within the hierarchy, they sometimes think it is up to subordinates to adapt to *their* style. The boss is the boss, and he's not changing his style for some "underling." It's not that extreme, but I definitely hear inklings of this perspective in my management workshops. Some Xers and boomers get a little ruffled when I say they should alter their style for their employees. "No one did that for me!" they think. Well, they are starting to see that if their end goal is a more productive and high-achieving team, then they may need to change their perspective a little bit.

There will be more and more millennials entering the workforce, and the dynamic of work and management is changing. If Xers and boomers want to thrive in this new workplace, then they need to be open to these shifting perspectives. In the book, *Mastering People Management,* a 60-something worker reflected, "We wanted what they want. We just felt we couldn't ask. Herein lies the truth: what young workers want isn't so different from what everyone else wants. However, young workers are asking for it."[4]

When it comes to customizing and adjusting your management style, your generation gets this idea right away. You live in a world of customization. You can buy any product customized for your tastes or personality. Courtney remembers when her first, fire-red Cingular cell phone was considered a little wild. The choices were black, silver, blue, or RED! Now you can get purple spotted cow covers, bejeweled covers, and camouflage covers.

Millennial managers get it. Everyone is different and wants different things, so it absolutely makes sense that different people excel under different management styles. To be straightforward with the skeptical Xers and boomers, I say that it's not the sole responsibility of the manager to adapt her style and cater to her direct reports. It really should be a meeting in the middle. Remember how I said Courtney and I are nearly complete opposites? Well, we meet in the middle. She adapts her style a little, and I adapt my style a little.

Let's talk specifically about how you can adjust your style as a manager. First, you have to get to know your employees and understand how they like to work, communicate, and act. If you are managing employees with various experience levels—some millennials, Xers, and boomers —you need to look even deeper than the generalizations of their generation. Although we talked about how individuals in each generation typically act, you still have to get to know each employee. Even though many boomers prefer to communicate face-to-face, I know a lot of tech-savvy boomers who don't mind just e-mailing or texting. I know millennials who prefer to work independently, and Xers who enjoy collaborating on projects. You simply can't put someone in a box because of their age. As a manager, you should do your due diligence to get to know each employee individually.

I deliver a workshop on pinpointing behavioral styles in the workplace, and it's one of the most enlightening sessions for managers. If you've ever taken a Myers–Briggs personality test, a DISC profile, or Insights, then you're familiar with this idea of falling into one of four quadrants when it comes to personality style. No educational book or program is complete without a quadrant analysis!

The fundamental principle of all the models asserts that there are four types of personalities—expressive, analytical, social, and driven. Any good team has representation from each quadrant. Even if you think about television shows, you must have each type of personality to hold it all together.

Think about *Seinfeld*. Kramer is the expressive, light-your-hair-on-fire, burst-into-rooms, big personality. Then there is analyzing George who knows all the best bathroom locations in the city and ponders why bald men can't get more women. Elaine is the driven, assertive personality who can never find a guy handsome enough, smart enough, or rich enough. Finally, Jerry is the social, amiable one who brings the entire group together. The dynamic of the four personalities makes the show work. While each character is funny in his or her own right, it's the four working in concert that leads to a hilarious show.

It's the same thing with the characters in *The Simpsons, Sex in the City,* and *Friends*. In fact, you can take almost any show or movie with an ensemble cast of at least four and find this dynamic. In *Friends*, Phoebe and Joey are the expressive, slightly off-kilter ones. Ross is the analyzing scientist who likes to be right and know the details. Monica is the driven, assertive, and no-nonsense friend who makes the plans and the menu—well in advance. Finally, Rachel and Chandler are the social, amiable ones who help bring the group together.

Just like these television shows, successful companies and teams have a diverse group of personality and communication styles. What if you had a team of nothing but expressive Phoebes? The members would talk and talk and talk about the project (and a variety of other topics), but when it came down to doing the work, they would want to skip a few steps and jump to presenting it. The presentation of the project might be dynamic and engaging, but you could blow holes in the research and strategic plan. On the flipside, if you have a team of analyzing Rosses, the members would spend the majority of their time gathering data and trying to determine the right answer. They would run out of time and put together an algorithm to decide who had to present the material. Their presentation would be pretty lifeless—just like their bored audience. In both of these cases, major fail!

Although the analyzing type might butt heads with the expressive personality—the fact is, they need each other, and they're a great complement—IF they can learn to work together. Just like with the four generations, when it comes to understanding behavioral styles, it's important to note that no one is better or worse—they're just different.

ADJUSTING YOUR MANAGEMENT APPROACH

What is a great way to get to know your employees and their styles? Talk to them. Talking about communication styles upfront helps you and your employees get on the same page right away—without suffering through as many "learn as you go" challenges. You could even formulate a few fun and easy questions for your team to answer. Recognizing that people adapt to different styles at home, at work, and in different situations, it's nice to know what they prefer or how they feel they excel.

Here are a few questions to share with your team. You can answer them first and then have a dialogue with each individual about their answers. See how it plays out in day-to-day situations.

Make sure you tell your employees that there are no right or wrong answers. This isn't a test! You want them to be honest and forthright. (You don't want them to think the question about "obeying the rules" is a trap!) Finally, these should be answered from how you think you are *at work*.

1. Would you prefer to do 15 things adequately or 9 things perfectly?
2. In meetings, do you like it when other topics come up even if it means running long?
3. With business issues, is it usually obvious to you what should be done?
4. Is it easy to tell when you are disturbed, pleased, disappointed, or excited at work?
5. Do you feel that rules, policies, and procedures should be followed with few exceptions?

6. When the scope of work expands unexpectedly or deadlines are shortened, do you feel more anxious or more annoyed?
7. Do you take pride in your organizational skills and getting things done on time?
8. Do you tend to take charge in groups, or are you less forceful?
9. Do you talk more than you listen? Or do you prefer to ask questions?
10. Do you tend to be more restless and impatient, or do you take things as they come?
11. Are you comfortable taking risks, or do you like to stick to the plan?
12. Do you form opinions, or do you like to hear what others have to say first?

The answers to these questions will give you insight into how your employees work and how they view work. There is no right, wrong, or better way. Isn't it nice if you have some people on your team who like to take risks and some who like to stick to the plan? That will ensure that any risky decision that is implemented has been thought through completely. Don't you think it would make for a less intense meeting if you have some people who are forceful and some who don't mind sitting back a little? You must have talkers and listeners—take it from a guy who loves to talk! There can't be too many of us.

A good team has diverse people who have different ways of thinking and operating; you need to understand these idiosyncrasies to get the most out of your team. Nelson Mandela speaks to this point, "If you talk to a man in a language he understands, that goes to his head. If you talk to him in his language, that goes to his heart."[5]

You can never underestimate how you communicate information and treat your employees. When talking with one direct report of a millennial manager, she said that she likes that her manager "just gets me." If you speak on the individual's terms and in a person's language, you're going to get more buy-in.

Follow the Business Golden Rule

Do you know the golden rule that you were taught while growing up? "Do unto others as you would have them do unto you." Although the root of this rule is noble, it breaks down when it comes to the workplace and management. People need to be managed differently based on their experience level, attitude, motivation level, and personality style. The business golden rule is to "Do unto others as *they* would have you do unto *them.*"

Let's see how this plays out in the workforce. Everyone responds to conflict and pressure differently. If your workplace is reflective of the majority, then you often find yourself in the midst of conflict and pressure. If you have a tight deadline and you need an employee to put together an analysis quickly, you need to think about the individual's style, experience, and motivation level when communicating this responsibility. Maybe you know that Muriel is a regulator who thrives in a fast-paced environment and who just loves getting things done and scratching things off her to-do list. For Muriel, this assignment is perfect! When delivering it, you need to communicate the urgency and the importance, and she is on it. This is where she thrives!

On the other hand, if you're giving this assignment to Joe, you may need to change your approach. Joe is all about relationship building, helping people, and connecting them with the answers. For Joe, you tell him how this urgent assignment will impact the team and provide the insight that the team needs to make decisions that will benefit Joe's clients. Maybe you can even have Joe present his findings since he loves presenting and connecting with the group. Same assignment, two different people, and two different approaches.

Furthermore, maybe you know that Shanna only has a couple months of experience and that she likes structure. At this point, she has a high energy level, but her confidence and experience level are low. When she's working on a new project, you might set up more structure for her. Maybe you have a few check points, and you give her a lot of positive feedback to boost her confidence. On the other hand, you may have Richard who is a high achiever and go-getter, and he seems to like working on his own. Maybe you give him more autonomy with the project with only one review point. You know he is inspired by achievement, so you recognize his good work publicly at the next meeting.

Understanding your team and adjusting your style accordingly goes a long way in building a productive team. As a millennial manager, you should really thrive in this area. When we talked to senior leaders, they commended you and felt that you were very open to different styles and ways of doing things. Furthermore, one millennial manager we spoke to said, "I try to find out what someone likes doing, so I can give them more of that."

In addition, when we talked about "unifying your team," you should also be aware of the dynamic on your team and how everyone is working together. In the words of Albert Einstein, "Everybody is a genius. But if you judge a fish by its ability to climb a tree, it will live its whole life believing that it is stupid." Help your team members see their strengths and different personalities and how they too can adapt their styles to make their working relationships more productive and fun. Remember, no one is better or worse—they're just different.

Navigate your team toward success. Make and take time to manage, and work your way through new situations as a transparent and hopeful leader. Understand the different personalities on your team, and adjust your style to "do unto others as they would have you do unto them." Tony Hsieh, CEO of Zappos and author of *Delivering Happiness,* says, "Be true to yourself. If you follow that principle, a lot of decisions are actually pretty easy." Navigate the unknown, and learn and grow as you go.

Navigate: Managing Through the Unknown
◁ Telltale Tweets ▷

1. Management is a whole new world. Explore, discover, and try out new things. Lead your team toward success. #belikesacagawea

2. Work your way through tough situations by serving as an open and hopeful leader. Know what level of transparency is needed. #churchill

3. Understand the unique communication styles on your team. Do unto others as they would have you do unto them. #businessgoldenrule #seinfeld

10

NEGOTIATE: WORKING THROUGH DIFFERENT PERSPECTIVES

A good leader can engage in a debate frankly and thoroughly, knowing that at the end, he and the other side must be closer, and thus emerge stronger.

—Nelson Mandela

Negotiating. Just the mention of this word may make you squirm. It often conjures up images of sleazy used-car salespeople, awkward conversations about salary, or the fearless Priceline negotiator! Negotiating doesn't have to be sleazy, awkward, or combative. Negotiating isn't bad; it's just that most of the negotiating you see in the movies is negotiating *gone bad*. Negotiating—in and of itself—is actually positive and essential in business. While working at Leo Burnett in account management, I was constantly negotiating. I would negotiate the timeline with the client, and then I negotiated how quickly the creative team could deliver. I would negotiate who is responsible for what among our team members, and then I negotiated what the priorities were with my boss. Sometimes, our team meetings were just one, big negotiation— *What route should we go? What idea is best? How can we deliver?* Now, did I think I was "negotiating" in all of those scenarios? Probably not.

One thing I want to do is reframe your thinking around negotiating. Done right, there isn't a winner and loser, and it doesn't always revolve around money. I also think the topic is important enough to deserve its own chapter. Many people think that negotiation training is for more senior leaders, but I think it's especially helpful for millennials because you tend to shirk from this responsibility.

THE STORY BEHIND NEGOTIATING WOES

Let's take a closer look at your mindset. There are two main reasons you may fear negotiating, working with someone who has a different perspective than you, or dealing with a difficult person. The first is that someone has typically done it for you and that someone is your mother or father. One of the most fascinating generational differences I have found is the relationship that millennials have with their parents. In our workshops for older generations and for millennials, I kick off the sessions the same way. During a round of introductions, everyone tells the group who their role model is—either personal or professional. When I have a group of boomers and Xers, here's what I typically receive as role models:

My first boss

An old college professor

My dad

The person who founded our company

Abraham Lincoln

Now, when I do a session for millennials, here are the standard responses:

Mom

Dad

Mom

Mom

Dad

Abraham Lincoln (you always get Abraham Lincoln)

Without question, a minimum of 80 percent of millennials I work with consider their parents to be their role model. I then follow that exercise by asking how many millennials consider their parents not only to be their role models but also their best friends. An astonishing 30 to 40 percent of the hands go up. Now, do I love my mom and dad? Of course. Best friend? Eww. Seriously, eww.

It's not better or worse; it's just different.

Let's think about it. When boomers and Xers were in college, how frequently did they communicate with their parents in any way, shape, or form over the course of a given week? The average was *one* time. Sunday afternoon, the bells would toll around 4:30 PM, and most of the campus would descend upon their dorm rooms for the parent-calling ritual. We would spend about four minutes on the pay phone chatting with mom. The call went like this:

STEVE: Hey, Mom.
MOM: Hi honey, how are you?
STEVE: Fine.
MOM: How are your classes?
STEVE: Good.
MOM: Are you having fun?
STEVE: Yup.
STEVE: Oh, I'm a bit short on money.
MOM: Okay. I'll write you a check and mail it off this week.
STEVE: Oh and mom, is Grandma still alive?
MOM: Yes, honey.
STEVE: Oh good. Talk to you next week. Say hi to Dad and Debbie.
MOM: Bye.

Let's compare and contrast to your generation. The average millennial communicated with their parents two to five times a DAY when they were in college. Just think about cell phones, texting, social media, and Skype, and you can understand how. Here is a millennial's scenario.

Amber just found out she got a "C" on her history paper. She walks out of class, and the first thing she does is call her mom.

AMBER: Mom, I just got a "C" on my history paper.
MOM: What do you mean you got a "C" on that paper? That was a good paper. I believe I proofread that one, didn't I?
AMBER: Yes, you did. I couldn't believe it either.
MOM: What's the professor's phone number? I want to talk to her.

Of course that doesn't happen all the time, but it does happen, and it NEVER happened with older generations. The college I attended, like many others, now has an "Office of Parent Relations" to deal with all the lawnmower millennial parents.

Don't think it ends at college. I recall getting a very interesting phone call during my last year as Recruiting Director at Leo Burnett. A parent called me to negotiate a job offer on behalf of her daughter. Parents have even been caught phoning managers to protest job evaluations: "My Lacey doesn't *meet* expectations. My Lacey *exceeds* expectations!"

It's extraordinary and the impact—not intended by parents—is that their children are often not prepared to fight their own battles and deal with difficult people appropriately.

The second reason you haven't negotiated a lot or dealt with many difficult people—technology! Instead of dealing with people face-to-face, you can avoid them and just send off a good ol' text or e-mail.

Be honest, have you ever broken up with someone you were dating via text, over e-mail, or on Facebook? I will never forget the story from the new hire who found out his girlfriend broke up with him when he logged into Facebook and saw that she had changed her status to single. "I guess we're no longer together," he concluded. They never had to have a conversation! If you can just send your significant other a quick text that says "we r dun," then you haven't dealt effectively with a difficult person.

You Negotiate Every Day

As a manager, you undoubtedly will come across people with different perspectives, and you will have to negotiate and sell your ideas—on your own. You may be thinking, "Hey, I'm not a salesperson, and I'm not an executive. I'm a manager. I don't really need to negotiate." The truth is all good businesspeople negotiate at some point. Maybe you don't term it that, but you're selling ideas, persuading groups, and thinking through different perspectives every day. The fact is that you negotiate on some level each and every day.

Negotiate:

a : *to deal with*

b : *to arrange for or bring about through conference, discussion, and compromise*

You probably negotiate a lot more things than you think. If you've been in a relationship, you know what I'm talking about—from where you're going to eat (fancy French food or hole-in-the-wall burger joint) to what movie you're going to watch (*Swingers* or *You've Got Mail*) to how you will split the holidays amongst families (uh oh). You've probably negotiated over pizza toppings with friends, car purchases, and even buying a home, but you may have consulted your parents on a couple of those.

Now that you're in the workplace, you're negotiating and influencing all the time. Nell Madigan, Associate Dean, School of Labor and Employment Relations at the University of Illinois, says that an area of strength for millennials is that they "think differently and motivate by influence. That's what they respond to, and that's why they use this tactic." Since you don't rely on a strict hierarchy and "command and control," you are influencing and subtly negotiating all of the time.

Your generation doesn't like to bark out orders, so the art of negotiating is all the more important. You are negotiating up with your boss and senior leaders; you are negotiating down with your employees, and you likely are negotiating across with colleagues, customers, clients, and other departments.

As a part of the management team, you have a responsibility to support your company and executive decisions, but you also have a responsibility to the individuals you manage. You often may be the person to push for two team members to attend an important senior leader meeting. You negotiate their way to more exposure. Maybe you push for more training and development for your team. You have to negotiate the budget, and you advocate for more responsibility for your group. Likewise, you may sell a new corporate initiative to your team, trying to gain buy-in.

Furthermore, when working with your direct reports and your boss, there is always some give and take when discussing projects, timelines, and deliverables. Maybe you don't term it "negotiating" but you're absolutely conversing through ideas and going back and forth to arrive at an agreement. Informal and formal negotiations are happening all the time. Remember that the more you negotiate, the better you will get at it. Don't be afraid to jump right in. Since each and every negotiation is different, it's a skill that you will hone as you go along.

SHIFTING YOUR PERSPECTIVE
FROM FEAR TO FUN

I know that sounds like a bold shift, but I honestly love negotiating now. Lose your fear. It's not a tug-of-war where the one on the "losing" side ends up in the mud pit. There should be no "winners and losers." The goal of any good negotiation is for all parties to walk away satisfied with the decision. It's not a battle of the wits or a game of cat and mouse. By thinking about the person you are negotiating with as an ally and not an enemy to be conquered, you can enter the conversation with confidence. If you feel butterflies of nervousness setting in, then use the adrenaline to energize—not immobilize—you.

Sometimes, we can build things up in our head to be much bigger than they really are. Emil, a millennial at a large consulting firm, was getting burnt out on travel. He knew he wanted to talk with his boss about getting off the road and back in the home office more. He worried and stewed about how he would approach the topic for weeks and weeks. In his head, he was convinced his boss would be inflexible and tell him no way—without any consideration. He finally worked up enough courage and, before he could even finish building his case, his boss said, "Sure, I think that makes sense." All that worry and apprehension for weeks for no reason. There is a great quote by Mark Twain that I often remind myself of before and during negotiations, "I've had a lot of worries in my life, most of which never happened." The goal is for all parties to walk away satisfied. Remind yourself of this idea to help calm your fears and shift your perspective on negotiating.

It's Just a Conversation

Negotiation is a dialogue—a conversation. It's respectful and insightful. Everyone has a chance to talk, and everyone has an opportunity to listen. Contrary to popular belief, negotiation done right doesn't end with regrets, eye rolls, tears, yells, or right hooks. It's simply a conversation.

At work, the first few times someone has a different opinion than you or pushes against your course of action, you're not sure what to do or say. You're concerned with preserving relationships, so you tiptoe around ideas or feelings to avoid upsetting anyone. You're also a great collaborator, so your instinctive drive is to help someone or support that person's views. You have to be careful about being overly agreeable. No one wants or needs a "yes" person and definitely not a "yes" leader.

Courtney and I disagree on a lot of decisions, but it's been one of the most beneficial factors for our business. We both look at things differently and hearing each other's perspective helps us make better business decisions. I don't need someone who's going to agree with everything I say. I need employees who are going to bring their own ideas and opinions and think through different perspectives with me.

A millennial manager at a healthcare organization expressed how she sometimes felt like she "was being difficult" when she had a different viewpoint than her team. That is a notion that you must dispel. There doesn't always have to be consensus, and you don't want to fall into groupthink. Bringing up new and differing concepts truly is helpful to negotiations and working relationships. Maybe you will get everyone on board with this new position—and maybe you won't. Even if you decide on a different direction, there is value in the "devil's advocate." Your direction is stronger because it withstands the test of objections and skeptical queries.

LISTENING CRITICALLY: READING BETWEEN THE LINES

Millennials can get a bad rap when it comes to listening skills. Listening takes patience. With a go-go-go generation and drive, it can be difficult to be still—and just listen. Captain Mike Abrashoff advises leaders to "listen aggressively."[1] Try listening like you're having a test right after the conversation. I know you want to get an "A." You can pick up on subtle things like attitude, engagement levels, stress, and satisfaction by listening aggressively.

One thing that Leann Nicholson, a millennial manager at Cars.com, takes pride in is listening objectively and not taking sides or jumping to conclusions. Nicholson says, "I can see both sides of every situation, and I empathize and help people understand the big picture. There are few things that are absolutes. If I hear that something is important to an employee, we usually can find a way to adjust and agree."

Listening critically is the key to any successful negotiation and conversation. Marc Landsberg, CEO of socialdeviant, advises that you should "listen more carefully and with greater intensity to what's being said *to* you, versus *by* you. Understanding the needs of your audience will help you be more persuasive."

You're obviously listening to the words, but you also are listening between the lines and reading body language to get at the heart of the messages. Don't go into the conversation assuming you know what the person wants. Assumptions are one of the biggest barriers to listening. Don't assume, limit distractions, and open your mind and your perspective to get at the core of the communication. If you can understand what they're seeking or pushing for, you can customize your approach and present it as a win–win.

Let's look at you negotiating with your boss. As a millennial manager, you have two teams you're representing, so you may often find yourself negotiating up and down. In this case, you are negotiating for "work from home days" for your employees. You think they're responsible, hard working, and deserve a reward of flexibility. You also think it will boost productivity and engagement and, therefore, the bottom line. You know that this perk is not offered at your traditional firm currently, and you're not sure how receptive your boomer boss will be.

By listening attentively to your boss's point of view during your dialogue, you catch key words—*abuse the freedom; take advantage; everyone will want this; worried; productivity.* Although he hasn't said it directly, you can understand that your boomer boss fears that your employees won't be productive and that this perk will get out of hand. Now you can counter those fears. You can't cast them off as ridiculous, "Well, of course, they will be productive, silly!" You can validate and counter at the same time. "I can see how you might be worried about productivity when employees work from home. I was a little worried about that at first as well. But then I thought about the hours that they will gain back by not commuting or having coworker interruptions. You know how many interruptions we can have around here! This isn't something we have to roll out company-wide. We could even use my team as a three-month pilot to see how it goes." Just from listening attentively, you know how to dispel his worries and build your case. You even helped take out the risk by presenting your idea as a "pilot" and only a three-month trial. Listen critically and pick up on the subtle undertones and overtones.

Well known for his unconventional ways of doing business, Richard Branson, founder and chairman of Virgin Group, sums it up, "As a leader you have to be a really good listener. You need to know your own mind but there is no point in imposing your views on others without some debate. No one has a monopoly on good ideas or good advice. Get out there, listen to people, draw people out, and learn from them."

HAVING AN OPINION: YOUR VOICE

The idea of negotiating means that you have an opinion and you have a stance worth taking time for. Millennials function well under structure and with someone telling them what to do. As a result, I sometimes fear millennials move too quickly into implementation mode without thinking through the whole picture or creating a dialogue.

As a manager, you should always have an answer to, "What do you think?," and encourage your employees to embrace this practice as well. Now, you can't draw your line in the sand on everything. Obviously, not every one of your opinions is "right" or the best idea. Not every idea or perspective is worth fighting for, but some are. I know it can be hard to stand up for your opinions when it comes to your boss or your boss's boss. Keep in mind that you're "in the trenches" and your perspective is valuable. Have an opinion, find your voice, and stand up for it when appropriate. This doesn't mean be close minded to differing views. It means **don't fold the second someone voices an opposite concern.**

Let's look at a scenario from JB Training Solutions. Courtney supervises Nicole, who spent a lot of time enhancing all of our presentations. Nicole was working with a designer to improve the look and feel of our PowerPoint presentations, and she was spearheading the entire project. Soon after Nicole spent numerous hours on this project, one of our consultants recommended Prezi presentations and the unique and interesting elements that they bring to programs. Courtney was intrigued by Prezi, but she knew if she brought up the idea of changing our newly enhanced presentations, Nicole would be discouraged. Nothing like feeling like hours and hours of your time are flushed down the drain.

Courtney had to talk through the situation with me. Of course, my goal is to make our presentations the absolute best they can be. The first thing Courtney did was state that she too wants our presentations to be absolutely the best that they can be. I also didn't want them to discard a good idea right away without consideration. Courtney anticipated my thought, and she ensured that Nicole would explore Prezi and try it out with another presentation. Courtney said we could garner success from there and see if we should roll out this medium to our other Power-Points. That solution made sense to me. And that bought Courtney some time. She didn't have to address the idea of a new presentation right after Nicole finished a great job.

For this conversation to be a success, Courtney had to think through it. She needed to validate my concerns—that our content is the best that it can be and that we are showcasing our best work. She also had to give me a glimpse into the hard work and time that had been spent on the current enhancements. Quite honestly, sometimes, your bosses don't know all the inner workings on projects, and it's your job as manager to represent that well. It's not that I had a hard line, "We must have Prezi presentations," and, once I heard Courtney's perspective and the full story, then it made sense. If Courtney had come in very defensive or close minded, we could have ended in a very different place. Likewise, if she would have folded, we might have engaging Prezi presentations but a disengaged employee. We found common ground—we both want our product to be the absolute best it can be—and we left feeling that we would indeed achieve that.

Sometimes, It's Worth the Extra Time

Isn't it sometimes easier and faster just to follow orders? Doing your homework, building your case, and having a dialogue obviously take time. Sometimes, it's worth spending a little extra time and effort to push what you think is right or the best opportunity. This requires some confidence in yourself and your decision making, but as you grow as a manager, this is great proving ground to give, take, and see how things fall.

Let's say your boss comes to you and says the company is going through a big sales push, and he wants your team to begin cold calling. You remember going through this exercise a couple years ago, and you didn't find it effective. You discovered a process of finding warm leads through networks and LinkedIn that proved much more effective. You reached fewer people, but the quality of the leads was much better and yielded more sales. Your boss is a hard driver, and you know there will be a tough conversation to get his buy-in. Wouldn't it just be easier to go to your team and say, "We have to do cold calls; let's get started"? It's a lot easier, but it would be well worth the time to talk with your boss.

In my workings with millennials and millennial managers, I often find that you go into execute mode too quickly. Again, you're not a mindless worker bee paid to execute orders. You're a critical thinker and, if you have a better idea or alternative plan, then it's worth the extra effort to discuss it. Often, those are the conversations that lead to big wins. Let's say you convince your boss to let your team try making sales through networking and warm leads, and then you compare your results to other cold-calling teams. Your team and strategy wins by far and, now, you're respected as a confident leader with big ideas.

IT'S NOT ABOUT WINNING OR LOSING

Especially when negotiating with people at your company, you most likely have similar end goals. Chetan Borkhetaria, Global Learning Consultant at Lenovo, says, "If you have enough of a relationship and a sense of what is important to others, you can play with the puzzle and find a way to agree." When I was discussing Prezi with Courtney, it's not like I thought if I didn't convince her, then I was weak and I had lost the debate. It isn't about winning or losing.

Our team even negotiates our monthly goals. As you know, it's best if you decide on your team goals as a team, so that requires negotiating. Obviously, we want to push ourselves, but we want something that's attainable and inspiring. While we are negotiating goals, all of us have the same desire to make JB Training Solutions the best that it can be. We each share our perspective on our focus points and what's attainable yet still hairy enough to challenge us. When you're negotiating, don't think about winning and losing. You don't even have to think about "selling." Marc Landsberg states that all good ideas can stand on their own merits if you let them. He offers, "Make it easy for the audience to understand the value of the idea, versus the need for them to say yes."

Know What's in It for Them

When you can, do your homework before negotiations. Prepare, and know the value proposition for the other party. For example, you want

Will to take over billing for your team. It's a pretty big responsibility that will require a fair amount of time. You don't have the budget to offer Will a bonus or higher salary for taking on a larger role. What's in it for Will? Why would he agree to tackle this? Well, it would offer huge exposure to senior leaders and the CFO, and Will definitely aspires to be a manager. It also offers great skills and experience for moving up, which interests Will greatly. When you present this idea to Will, you lead with these points and frame the situation around what's in it for him. Since you're speaking in Will's terms, he sees you as on his side and is more agreeable. Now, will he ask for a raise or some extra perks for adding this responsibility? Maybe, but by knowing what he's really after, you can position your case. Although you can't offer him a raise now, this experience will position him well for a promotion down the road. You're not making false promises, but you're showcasing the value proposition.

Show That You "Get It"

Endorse them, and indicate that you understand their point of view. One reason negotiations go wrong is because one party doesn't feel validated. Say things like, "I see where you're coming from" or "I can understand how you would see it that way" or "That's my goal too." All of these phrases validate their point of view and perspective. When you can, show how your goals and perspectives align with theirs. If you don't give any concessions, the other party may feel cornered in a win–lose situation. Paraphrase their statements and agree where you can. "I understand that you need my team to help out with Project Thunder. From listening to you describe the project, I can tell that this initiative is really important to our department. I know you asked if we could have everything to you by Wednesday. I want to make sure we do an amazing job, and I feel like building in an extra day for my team will help us deliver great work. Do you think that would work?" Showing that you get them keeps you on the same team.

Don't Be Afraid of Silence

I have listened as many people talk and walk themselves right out of a negotiation. Silence is golden. Don't fear it. After presenting your case, and you get to "the ask," just wait after the question is raised. "Would it be okay if each of my team members has an opportunity to work from home once a week?" Pause. Wait. Don't say anything. Because the tendency is to just jump right in. "Or, if that's too much to start, then we could start with once every two weeks. . . . Actually, maybe even once a month would be fine to start." You've already backed yourself out of *the ask* before the person even had a chance to respond. Give the person time to process your request. That means although it seems a little awkward, just pause and wait. Let the other person jump to fill the silence.

Carve Out and Frame Your Win–Win

What does a "win" look like for the other person? Hopefully, you were listening. You want everyone to walk away satisfied, so wrap things up by framing the "wins."

"It sounds like we're both going to hit our goals here. You have the goal of running a fair and productive department, and I have the goal of offering flexibility to my productive team members. It sounds like we both agree that working from home once a week will be fair and may even increase everyone's productivity. We can regroup in three months to see how it's going." Frame your wins. This is what a strong relationship built on trust and communication yields—powerful outcomes and positive results.

WORKING THROUGH DIFFERENT PERSPECTIVES

Although brief, this gives you the fundamental tips for negotiating as a manager. As you're discovering, you negotiate each and every day— sometimes without even knowing it. The more and more you negotiate, the more confident you will feel and the more fun you will have with it. Keep reminding yourself that negotiating is not bad and that it's worth standing up for your opinions and ideas. As you go along, you and your team will feel more comfortable negotiating, exchanging different ideas, and arriving at the best conclusion. Negotiations build strong relationships of trust and respect. John F. Kennedy sends a powerful reminder, "Let us never negotiate out of fear. But let us never fear to negotiate." Create meaningful dialogue to create wins for your team and organization. Have an opinion, listen critically, and go for it.

Negotiate: Working Through Different Perspectives
◁ Telltale Tweets ▷

1. Negotiation isn't just about money. You negotiate every day—selling ideas, influencing decisions, and working through perspectives. #fun

2. Stand up for your perspective when needed. Listen first and know your value proposition. #momcannothelp

3. "If you have enough of a relationship & sense of what is important to others, you can play with the puzzle & find a way to agree." #wellsaid

11

---—⊙——---

ENGAGE: CONNECTING
TO THE BIG PICTURE

"The leader is the person who brings a little magic to the moment."
—Denise Morrison, President and CEO, Campbell Soup Company

Hawaiian shirt day, free food first Fridays, ping-pong tables, onsite laundry, or the amount of "flair" you wear on your uniform. Is that employee engagement?

Employee engagement. You've likely heard the term thrown around quite a bit. What exactly is it, and how do you get it? Although free food is always engaging for me, that is just a very small tactic in your larger strategy of building an engaged team. Employee engagement isn't defined by employee happiness or even employee satisfaction; the definition goes deeper. In the *New York Times* bestseller, *Building a Magnetic Culture*, Kevin Sheridan said that engaged employees:[1]

... possess an intellectual commitment and emotional bond to their employer.

... have an eagerness to exert both discretionary effort and creativity.

... become co-owners of their own engagement and commitment to improve.

Our interpretation of these characteristics is:

They have passion and enthusiasm for their company, and they're proud to say they work there!

They will go above and beyond and take initiative just because they want to. Now, that's a manager's dream.

They understand that it's not all "What can YOU do for me?" They know it's a give and take.

Now, can't you see why there is such a buzz about engaged employees? Engaged employees are an absolute joy for you and your organization! Your generation can excel in this area of building an engaged and empowered team. According to a 2010 survey by the Pew Research Center, "nearly six-in-ten younger workers (57 percent) say it is not very likely or not likely at all that they will stay with their current employers for the remainder of their working lives." Furthermore, only 23 percent of millennials think they will still be with their first employer after two years.[2]

The truth is you can help defy that statistic. The American Management Association states that "The cost of hiring and training a new employee can vary from 25 percent to 200 percent of annual compensation."[3] That's a lot of money. Turnover costs companies dearly, so you want to do your part in keeping your team engaged and away from their job-hopping tendencies.

Most millennials leave jobs because they're bored, disengaged, or ready for something new. After six months, millennials are asking for a promotion or a change in project. Millennials are accustomed to multitasking, getting information at the push of a button, and adapting to new technologies on a daily basis. Your generation likes to have this change in pace and energy in your work life as well. As a manager, be mindful of this predisposition because you want to make sure that your employees are always engaged and connected to work.

Courtney is a millennial, and she has worked at JB Training Solutions for eight years now. When she tells people about her "tenure," they say things like, "Oh, wow, you must really like it" or "You must be able to do the job in your sleep."

Courtney says, "Yes, I do really like my job, but no, I can't do my job in my sleep." That's a big reason she says she is still with the company after eight years. She has been engaged and pushed throughout. Every year, we take on a new business angle or challenge, so she is constantly using and honing new skills. She likes to see the results of her work, and I try to empower her as much as I can.

As a millennial manager, you can create that for your team. Marissa Mayer, the CEO of Yahoo!, speaks to some of the underlying drives of your team, "Employees, especially young people, want more than a paycheck."⁴ It used to be that employees went to work, worked, and didn't expect much more. It's not that clear cut anymore. Employees, and especially other millennials on your team, are looking for a fun, fast-paced, interesting, and challenging workplace—just like you are! Since you value these concepts, it's easy to build that in for your team. Engaged employees produce more, are stronger team players, and let's be honest, they're more fun. The Hay Group says companies with highly engaged workers grew revenues 2.5 times more than those with low engagement levels.⁵

"Engaging employees" is a large topic, and I will throw out a lot of ideas in this chapter. Some of them will work for you and your company culture, and some might not. Try them out. Be open to implementing a few risky ideas. Also, note that all of the aspects of CONNECT help engage and empower your team. For example, delivering feedback and communicating expectations are significant ways you can inspire your team, and navigating and adjusting your management style is a big contributor to engagement.

Now, how do you cultivate a culture of engagement? What do you need to do, and what should be your focus? Obviously, engagement looks different for different people. Something that engages one person might be terribly demotivating for someone else. Think back to our different communication and behavioral styles.

GETTING TO KNOW YOU, AND YOU, AND YOU

As a manager, you want to get in tune with your team. You need to sharpen your emotional intelligence to read between the lines and see the heart and core of your team. How's the morale? How is everyone functioning individually? How are they working together as a team? Who is excelling? Who needs an extra push or challenge? You may find that you learn a lot more from observing rather than talking. I urge you to step back, listen, and observe to get a real pulse on the engagement of your team.

Then get to know your employees individually. As a millennial manager, this is an area in which you excel. You're all about connecting to your people. Build a relationship by asking how your employees are doing. What's their life like outside of work? How was their weekend? Ask, but not in a creepy way.

Your team likes to know you care about them as a whole. What are their hobbies? What are the names of their family members? What are they passionate about? What motivates and inspires them? What demotivates them? You need to know what drives your employees, so you can reward, recognize, and encourage them on their terms. Getting to know them will go a long way in keeping them engaged and excited about work.

Show That You Care

It's so simple, but it makes a huge difference. Any time I read a book or article that applies to one of my employee's interests or hobbies, I pass it along. It sounds small, but if Nicole is running the marathon, it makes her feel special if I give her an article from Crain's magazine that shares tips from CEOs running the marathon.

If Allison loves all things British, I can take a picture of the "Keep Calm" store display and send it to her. Learn about birthdays, work anniversaries, weddings, new babies, new hobbies, or big events. You don't have to attend the baby shower or help throw the bachelor party, but a nice note or word of congratulations shows that you care. Even just share advice. "Okay, here is a list of all the restaurants you MUST visit in New Orleans." This shows your employees that you care for them as individuals.

Now, how do you determine what motivates someone? Of course, you can guess and go through a little trial and error. Or you could just ask. In one of our management courses, we recommend a fun exercise for managers to do with their employees. It's a quick team-building activity, but it gets at the root of some great ideas that will help you when it comes to engaging your team. It's a fun game of "Would you rather?" Feel free to share these questions with your team. Of course, they start out fun and lighthearted, but they then get at some good scoop. Maybe you're not going to send your employee on a mountain vacation, but you might buy them an iTunes gift card (instead of Starbucks) the next time you want to show appreciation.

Would You Rather...?
(You can only pick one!)

▷ Would you rather go on a mountain vacation or a beach vacation?
▷ Would you rather watch TV or listen to music?
▷ Would you rather be invisible or be able to read minds?

▷ Would you rather be stranded on an island alone or with someone you don't like?

▷ Would you rather receive a Starbucks gift card or an iTunes gift card?

▷ Would you rather be recognized with public praise or personal praise?

▷ Would you rather write the presentation or deliver the presentation?

▷ Would you rather be recognized with more flexibility or a spot bonus?

▷ Would you rather work independently or on a team?

▷ Would you rather eat lunch with a senior leader or get the afternoon off?

▷ Would you rather receive a gift certificate to your favorite restaurant or tickets to a sporting event? (equal value)

▷ Would you rather be given an open-ended project or a project with very explicit guidelines?

▷ Would you rather read a business book on leadership or watch a webinar on leadership?

▷ Would you rather be separated from your phone for a day or give up chocolate for a lifetime?

▷ Would you rather be separated from your phone for a week or go without Google for a lifetime?

This gives you great insight on the types of rewards and recognition your employees find motivating.

Now that you have some insight into your employees, let's take a look at the specific drivers of employee engagement. According to Sheridan's *Building a Magnetic Culture*, the top five drivers of engagement are:[6]

1. Recognition
2. Career development
3. Manager
4. Strategy and mission
5. Job content

If you think about it, those top three have to do with you—the manager. Besides the employee himself, who is mostly responsible for recognition and career development? The manager. This entire book is helping you become a more engaging manager, and you will learn more about "career development" in Chapter 13, "Teach: Being a Mentor—and Student." Let's break down the number one driver—recognition, so you can see where you can make a big difference.

RECOGNIZING AND REWARDING— CUSTOMIZED STRATEGIES

Recognition goes a lot further than the employee-of-the-month star on the bulletin board. Although trophies, ribbons, and certificates can be part of your strategy, I encourage you to think deeper and broader. There are several ways you think about this in connection with recognition, and I will cover a few overarching themes for showing recognition. You can recognize and reward your employees through praise, flexibility, visibility, responsibility, and autonomy.

Praise

Praise is often the form of recognition that comes to mind first. The great thing is that it can make a huge impact on engagement, and it doesn't cost a thing. That's actually an important element of many of the tips I will share. They don't cost a thing.

Now, there is public praise and private praise, and you want to make sure you are giving both. Employees, especially millennials, crave recognition through praise. Private praise is great to do in a meaningful way. When your employee is doing an especially good job, pull her in a one-on-one to tell her just that.

Ken Blanchard says, "Catch someone doing something right." Almost 100 percent of the time, when you catch someone doing something wrong, you say something. How often do you comment when you see someone doing something right? 10 percent? 5 percent? Try to catch someone doing something right today, and tell them right then and there.

For public praise, be creative. How do you feel when your boss congratulates you on an amazing job, and then he CCs your boss and others from your team? You feel pretty good, right? That doesn't cost anything —just two minutes of your time.

At your next team meeting, recognize employees in front of the entire team—and just watch them glow! As I have mentioned before, be specific. Anyone can say, "Malvin, you did a great job on the competitive analysis." This sounds a little better, "Malvin, I was really impressed by your resourcefulness and persistence with the competitive analysis. It gives us a really clear picture of where we are and where we need to be.

It is work like yours that helps make this team great." Just imagine how good Malvin will feel after you say that in front of your team. He feels valued, appreciated, and ready to tackle the next project with just as much, if not more, energy.

If you work with clients, customers, or external groups, sing your all-stars' praises to them. You can tell your client, "Lindsey, you're going to love working with Connor. He's very thorough and sharp, and he will be a great partner." That gives Connor the confidence and recognition he needs and deserves to begin a great partnership with the client.

"I praise loudly, and I blame softly," a great idea from Catherine the Great. Praise doesn't cost a thing, but it's incredibly powerful. Especially for your millennial employees who are accustomed to receiving positive accolades.

In fact, a Workforce Mood Tracker survey found that 69 percent of employees would work harder if they were better recognized![7] Despite this convincing statistic, I heard from one manager—let's call him Ebenezer—who was skeptical of this idea about praising employees. He was worried that if he praised employees too much, they would get complacent and not work as hard. Now, you're not giving praise for every little thing; you're giving praise for a job well done. It's not like "Congratulations, Abe, you showed up to work today. You're amazing! Hey, everybody, Abe is here! Let's give him a round of applause!" I encouraged the skeptical manager to try giving credit where credit is due and see if his team did indeed slack off. Ebenezer found just the opposite. The root of the idea is that people like to hear praise and they like to be recognized, so they want to do more things that will get them more praise. You're doing a really impressive job reading this book, by the way.

Flexibility

Flexibility comes in a few different forms: when, where, what. As I have discussed, flexibility might be one of the most motivating and engaging elements for your employees. I work with hundreds of companies and thousands of employees. Across the board, I am hearing that flexibility is what everyone is craving. It's an appealing reward for your high-achieving employees.

Flexibility in When

As more and more employees try to fit work into their lives, flex hours can be priceless. In fact, 82 percent of Fortune 100's Best Places to Work have virtual workforce policies.[8] Maybe a team member has obligations in the evenings, so starting work earlier but leaving work right at 5:00 PM is helpful. If there is an important project, the person tunes in early or late, but the work is getting done and it's on their own terms. When you give employees this type of flexibility and empowerment, they want to do a good job for you, and they want to prove that the system works.

At our company, when we achieved a goal, I would give a small but fun spot bonus of $50. I was finding that my millennial employees didn't seem overly impressed. The next time we hit our quarterly goals, I tried something different. I gave them an extra vacation day around the Fourth of July that was coming up, and you would have thought they won the lottery. They were ecstatic and motivated! I was finally speaking on their terms.

Flexibility in Where

With technology, employees can work when they want and where they want, and millennial managers are all for it! Now, nearly everyone has a "home office" and more and more companies are jumping on the work-from-home and telecommuting bandwagon. Case in point, 72 percent of employees say flexible work arrangements like telecommuting would cause them to choose one job over another.[9] Consider offering this perk to your employees. The hour they gain back in commuting often is put toward generating results for your team. Time and time again in our workshops and in our surveys, millennials say they would choose flexibility over an increase in salary. That's huge!

Furthermore, everyone seems to worry about this "productivity" idea when people aren't in the office. Employees tell me that they find working from home twice as productive because they don't have to worry about interruptions, drop-ins, or impromptu meetings. Who says that someone is being productive due to the mere fact that they are in the office building and sitting at a desk? Do you know Stanley from the sitcom *The Office*? Stanley is in the office, but he's secretly napping and often doing crossword puzzles.

If you have engaged employees, they will be productive wherever they are working, and empowering them with flexibility propels that engagement. As a millennial manager, you can begin pushing for this employee benefit. If it's not currently accepted or offered, present that as an amazing solution to recruit, retain, and engage your star employees.

Flexibility in What

Maybe you work in a business where you can't control the where and when. You work at a hospital or at a production facility, and employees have to be there on time at a certain time. Maybe your organization is still stressing the importance of "face-time." While you're pushing for flexibility for your team, begin offering flexibility in the work. One of our healthcare clients is doing just that. The client has flex schedules, but can't be as free with the "when" or the "where." So, the client is looking at the "what." This means things like job shadowing and job content.

This type of flexibility is especially helpful for your new hires. Just think about it. They have lived with a "semester mentality" throughout school. Everything could be measured in three-month increments. If they had a project or a hard class, it was bearable because it would change and something new would come along after three months. Now think about the workplace and companies that are slow to make decisions or have extended projects. Maybe a new employee takes part in a strategic plan where the end results won't be seen until five years down the road! They could have a hard time wrapping their heads around this extended timeline, and giving them more flexibility within and outside of the project could keep their engagement from slipping.

Also, think through new opportunities or "fun" projects that you can give your team. Is there a special project they can run? Can you give employees the flexibility to look at other positions, jobs, and responsibilities? Can you change some of the job content for your employees, so they can have flexibility and new challenges in what they do?

The bottom line is that flexibility is huge. It's huge. Your employees want it and crave it. Be creative about how you can use flexibility in the when, where, and what to engage and empower your team.

Visibility

Visibility is another great tool for showing recognition. Millennials especially love this idea of getting their name and face in front of senior management. If Taryn did an impressive job with her last project, can you take her to the next big meeting with senior leaders? Here, the benefits are two-fold. It's a learning experience for your emerging leader, and it also allows your rising star to get some exposure. What about asking if your boss would like to take Taryn to lunch to recognize her personally?

You can give them visibility with your key constituents, whether that is your clients, customers, board members, or different departments. This visibility recognizes your employees and keeps them engaged while also exposing them to critical parts of the business that allow them to expand their minds and take on larger roles. Many of these recognition ideas are win-wins. Meeting with senior-level clients is a perk for your employee, but it also helps them do a better job for you by gaining experience and new insights.

Finally, trumpet their successes. When someone on your team does a great job, talk about it. This is where "employee-of-the-month" awards, trophies, or plaques could come into play. Let's be honest, your millennials still love trophies. I will never forget the Facebook post from one of our clients. The employee had just won "Employee of the Month," and she had a picture of herself with the trophy on Facebook—she was so proud! To top it all off, the first comment was from her mom, "You didn't tell me about this! Congratulations!" Boomers also appreciate more formal recognition with a certificate or plaque that they can put in their office.

Another element of trumpeting success is giving credit. If you're presenting new ideas to your boss, but you know that Manisha came up with the majority of the ideas or did the hard work, absolutely give her credit. If Manisha wasn't there to hear your accolades, then let her know what you said. When your employees are doing some of the behind-the-scenes work, they really appreciate you being a champion for them. Employees work hard for those who work hard for them.

Responsibility

Giving more responsibility is a great way to engage and empower a star employee. It's important to note we're talking about star employees right now. If you have a poor performer who finally does something right, more responsibility might not be your first choice for recognition. That being said, your high performers are craving this stuff. They actively seek responsibility and consistently put themselves in a position to take on more, so they can learn, grow, and excel.

Give a Stretch Project

Lin, a millennial manager at a not-for-profit organization, notes, "Rudimentary assignments get rudimentary results. Challenge tends to motivate." A stretch project is a responsibility outside of a person's current skill set—it's going to make them stretch and push to be able to accomplish it. Maybe this is a responsibility that would help them take a step toward promotion. They might not get it perfectly the first time, but that's part of learning.

Many times, managers lament about what to give their employees to really push them. First, look at your project list. Is there something that you've been meaning to get to, but you just haven't been able to make it a priority? Hand it to your employee. Empower your employee with a couple items from your "B" list projects that are labeled important but not urgent. What about that business problem that you want to tackle? Have your employee lead a special project team to get it done.

At DICK's Sporting Goods, each year they hire a few high-potential Associates for their leadership development track. As part of the program, the Associates are given a stretch project where they must tackle a company challenge. The new Associates work on this project for months —the activities could include visiting stores, researching and analyzing data, speaking with company leaders, and getting in the trenches to discover new insights. It's incredibly eye-opening for them. They even have an opportunity to present their findings to some of DICK's most senior leaders. Now that's beautiful—responsibility paired with visibility. All of the high-potentials say these stretch projects are one of the most crucial elements in their development as an Associate. Consider how you can roll this out on a smaller scale with your team.

Another way to give responsibility is to position the individual as an expert. Do they have a certain skill that they could teach others? Can they lead training on the topic? Can they be the go-to expert when any department faces this issue? For instance, we work with OmnicomMediaGroup (OMG), who tapped some of their digital media employees to be experts and to train colleagues and managers. These digital media experts traveled to each of their U.S. offices and led training workshops. Normally, these employees would not have had this type of exposure or responsibility, but because they held the deep digital knowledge, they were positioned as subject-matter experts, and their skills and knowledge were heavily leveraged.

WWTBD—What Would The Boss Do?

As a manager who wants to foster growth of your employees, get out of the habit of sharing your opinion first. Wait. Any time your employee asks for your thoughts, turn it around and ask *them* before you answer. Don't jump in right away with your opinion. Rather, give your team members a few minutes to voice their ideas and share their perspective. It can be intimidating to follow the boss's perspective with your own—especially if it's different.

You may be surprised how many good ideas come out while you're just sitting back and waiting. Maybe Avery even has the exact same idea as you, but now that she voices the idea, she feels more buy-in and connected to it. It's much more fun to implement your own ideas rather than your boss's ideas!

This is what I did with Courtney, and this is what Courtney does for her team. It's easy for your team to come to you with a question and then implement your answer. Likewise, it's pretty easy and fast for you to just give them your answer, but you want to develop their critical thinking skills. Challenge yourself to always ask them "What do *you* think?" before sharing your thoughts. It gets them out of the habit of asking and executing and into reflecting and decision making. Often, they have the right answer when they step back and put themselves in the responsibility of being the provider of the answer. Who knew—they had the answer all along!

It also drives home that they need to come with a perspective. They can test their judgments in low-risk situations and conversations with their manager. Along these lines, try to solicit their point of view as much as you can. Again, this goes a long way toward building confidence in your people and gaining buy-in for projects. By getting them involved in more decisions and higher-level thinking, they are better able to perform in their job. They also feel more connected and invested in the project.

Finally, offer training before they need it. If one of your employees aspires to be a manager, can you get her to training courses that prepare her for this role before she even enters it? That way, she gains the skills so she can hit the ground running when she makes that transition.

Cars.com is on top of this idea of engaging employees with responsibility. The company has a large group of millennial employees who are interested in the management track, so management classes are offered through the company university for individuals *before* they become managers. As mentioned, sometimes companies don't offer any formal management training. If they do, it can be a few weeks or months into the new manager's role before they receive training. Cars.com is proactive, as the company wants its managers to feel comfortable and able to contribute from day one. Management also recognizes that it is incredibly engaging to give employees the responsibility of management training before they are even managers. You better believe these employees will want to stay with the company until they can take that exciting next step.

Autonomy

Autonomy is the freedom to bring your strengths and personality to your position and responsibilities. There are a few different things you can do to give autonomy to your employees. First, have them create their own, personal PUSH goals. Share your organization, department, and team goals, and they can align their goals with the bigger picture. Really encourage them to embrace something HAIRY.

Also, give them more autonomy in how they do their jobs. Issue the "do something you've never done before" challenge. Maybe that means thinking of a new process to track the logistics or implementing a new marketing message, but encourage them to embrace the position as their own. The challenge gives them the courage to think big and think differently.

Garry Tackett of CareerBuilder advises, "The world is much bigger and more complex than you know. Understand that whatever you are doing is a part of an ever-evolving process." Tackett goes on to say that it is important that you understand your current role and expected deliverables, "Trust that others are taking care of theirs, too. As long as you know what is expected of you and how it fits into the overall picture, you don't need the details of what everyone else is doing." Be comfortable taking a step back from the exact way your employee is completing a task, and focus on the end product or deliverable. Giving this autonomy empowers your people to step up.

BYOB Day

Sorry, it just means "Be your own boss," but quite a few companies we work with find beer cart Fridays engaging for employees. If you want to try an out-of-the-box idea, consider BYOB. This creative idea was brought to us by one of our clients. The company has a "be your own boss" day during which employees can do anything they would like—they are the boss. Employees don't come to work or check their e-mails. They can do whatever they wish, as long as it somehow helps the business. Employees might choose to run along the lake while brainstorming new ideas, visit the Museum of Science and Industry special exhibit to learn creative new insights, or work on a special project that combines a passion for music with business consulting. It's completely up to the employee, AKA boss. After the BYOB day, employees return and present their ideas to the company. Our client talks about how fired up everyone is after their BYOB day! They have implemented numerous creative ideas because employees had a chance to step back and think freely. Their company trusted them, rewarded them with autonomy, and the company was re-paid with an engaged workforce and some solid ideas.

Those are just a few ways that you can show your employees recognition—the number one driver of employee engagement. If you look through those ideas again, you will see that they are budget friendly and helpful for your to-do list. By giving autonomy and responsibility, you can get a few important projects off your plate while rewarding your team. Refer to this list often when you're stumped and want to offer creative ways to keep your team engaged.

SHOWING APPRECIATION: "THANK YOU"

Appreciation and recognition go hand-in-hand, but appreciation deserves its own category. Entire books have been written about showing employees appreciation. It's such a critical part of being a manager and fostering a positive environment, and it is so easy. Seriously, it is one of the simplest things you can do. "Thank you."

I conduct webinars to thousands of employees across the country, and I ask people what motivates them and how they would like their manager to show appreciation. You would not believe the number of people who say something along the lines of "a simple thank you." It's astounding. No one at their company sees their answers, so they're not being brown-nosers. They could say money, Starbucks gift cards, time off, or promotions. Granted, we do get answers along the lines of "$$$$$," MONEY!!, and the random "new pair of shoes." The truth is, about 75 percent say a simple thank you is all that they need.

For example, Samantha works at an architectural firm. During one especially hard week, she was cranking on proposals and putting in a lot of hours. She was tired and drained, but the principal of the firm told Samantha, "Thank you so much for everything you did this week. I know it was crazy, and you worked a lot of hours, but I'm so appreciative. We're lucky to have you." Samantha was wowed. Suddenly, she didn't seem quite as tired. Someone noticed—and in this case, that someone happened to be the founder and principal of the company. She noticed, recognized, and expressed appreciation. You see, Samantha previously worked at a design firm where she could work until 2:00 AM several days in a row, pitching in on projects without even a word of appreciation and recognition from her manager. Her new company and work environment was completely different. Samantha doesn't mind putting in extra hours because she knows her work is valued and appreciated—she receives a simple thank you.

When is the last time you told your employees thank you? I'm not talking about a passing thank you as they put something on your desk. As you may be catching on, I'm all about making communication direct, sincere, and specific. Any time someone on my team goes above and beyond, I try to thank them—specifically. Now, I may pair that expression of appreciation and verbal thank you with another perk or one of the responsibility ideas I discussed, but I absolutely include a sincere thank you. It could sound something like, "Thank you for dropping everything to put together this proposal. Judging from when I received this e-mail, you worked really late on this, and I can tell you put a lot of time and energy into it. Thanks for doing a great job."

When it comes to showing appreciation, there are countless things you can do. You could even write a personal, handwritten note—remember those? Oh the joy when I see a handwritten note amid the bills, junk mail, and magazines!

Then, as you know, personalize and customize your gestures of appreciation among your different employees. Aimee might appreciate you taking her to a "thank you" lunch at the new sushi place that just opened (her favorite!). For Garrett, you can show appreciation by telling him to take the morning off, so he can be there for his kids' first day of school (Taylor and Landon). For Heath, just buy him a box of Lucky Charms for breakfast at the office because he is always raving about that stuff. For Carrie, you can tell her that you will handle the expense report for this week! You know that this is her least favorite responsibility, so as thanks, you will take it off of her plate for a week. Again, all of these are particularly nice because they show appreciation, AND they show that you really know the individual. I could go on and on about fun ideas for showing appreciation.

Have fun thinking through creative ideas and add some personality. One of my favorite Zig Ziglar quotes is, "People often say that motivation doesn't last. Well, neither does bathing—that's why we recommend it daily." No need to be stingy with those thank-you notes. When I'm in the office, every single day when I leave, I tell my team thanks. The power of the thank you goes a long way.

BUILDING IN FUN: WORK HARD, PLAY HARD

When it comes to engaging your team, especially if you're managing millennials, building in fun is imperative. Millennials expect work to be fun. Building in fun can play out a few different ways. First, think about your team and its perspective. What does your team enjoy? How can you make the work day interesting and stimulating? How can you make sure the members are always learning and growing?

You want to foster an energized culture and spirit. It's something that you feel when you walk in the door. Lead your team with a positive attitude. If you have a positive attitude, fun usually follows. Negativity and cynical dispositions sour and dispel the energy. According to Helen Keller, "No pessimist ever discovered the secret of the stars, or sailed to an uncharted land, or opened a new doorway for the human spirit." It sounds like pessimists really miss out.

That's one of the biggest criticisms that we heard about bad bosses. Bad bosses are moody and negative. That keeps their team on edge—tense and anxious, hoping not to set off the big, bad negative boss. Try to lighten the mood and keep things in perspective. This is one area in which your generation excels. Help your team see the bright angle in situations, and you will build a lively and energetic culture—an environment that people want to be a part of and return to each day.

The ways for building in fun are countless. Don't be afraid to incorporate some new ideas. At JB Training Solutions, we always are trying something new. Some ideas include:

▷ Chili cook-offs and brown bag team lunches
▷ Lunch and learns—Lunch and educational presentations by team members
▷ Boggle breaks
▷ Morning yoga in the office
▷ Walking outdoor meeting
▷ Adventure lunches—Write down a bunch of directions on a piece of paper and see where you end up (Courtney ate at Taco & Burrito Place for her birthday/anniversary lunch!)
▷ Wise Up! Weekly educational sessions
▷ Wine Down Fridays—Everyone sips wine and "wines" down a busy week at 4:00 PM
▷ Decorate the office day (We've had Blackhawks, Royal Family, and Amelia Earhart themes)
▷ Ring the Bell—If you seal a deal or accomplish something big, ring the bell!
▷ Stress relief day—Massage therapist on site
▷ Contests! (Best hair, most creative cubicle, best team logo)
▷ Marshmallow dodge ball (Now, we're talking!)

This list goes on and on and on. They're usually more fun to implement if you or your team think of them yourselves, so I'll stop the brainstorming list there. As I referenced in Chapter 8, "Own It: Taking—and Giving—Responsibility," there is a significant value in taking a pause and inserting fun.

EMPOWERING YOUR PEOPLE: YOU CAN DO IT

Although it sounds like a tall order, you can boost engagement by empowering individuals in their jobs. This goes hand-in-hand with giving them ownership. How many companies do you know that are stifled with bureaucracy? No one can really get anything done because no one has the power to make a decision. Someone has an idea or a business solution, but it has to be floated to management, and then it has to be sent to legal. Then, everyone has to meet, but nothing is really decided. Then, five months later, when you get a tentative "go ahead," you have lost all of your energy and excitement. At that point, the problem or challenge probably needs a new solution because so much time has lapsed. So, you go through the whole process again. Now that's stifling and discouraging.

I referenced Zappos in the amazing way that management gives its employees autonomy. I especially love an example from Tony Hsieh's book *Delivering Happiness: A Path to Profits, Passion, and Purpose.* Hsieh is the CEO of Zappos, and he wanted to test—and even prove—what amazing customer service his company has. He called his company—which sells shoes and clothes—posing as a customer wanting to buy something very different. He was on a business trip with some clients, and they arrived at their hotel late one night well after the kitchen was closed. The group was starving for food, but no one knew of any pizza places in town. On a hunch, Hsieh bet his clients that Zappos' 24/7 customer service was so amazing that they could call the 1-800 number, pretend to be a customer, and the agent who picked up the call would find them a place to buy pizza in Santa Monica at 2:00 AM. This was not a routine question or a product offering, and the employee who answered that call definitely did not have a script for this one. The employee didn't have to check with the higher-ups. She was empowered from day one to do what she needed to do to provide great customer service. Therefore, she did what any great customer service agent would do—she found the pizza! She quickly researched and discovered several pizza places that were still open and that delivered. That had nothing to do with selling shoes, but she did help the customer. The CEO got his pizza and proved the strength of a culture of empowerment.[10]

Furthermore, one of our clients—Centro—has secured the number one spot on Crain's Chicago Best Places to Work list for two consecutive years. Centro has a laundry list of exciting employee initiatives, and the majority of their managers are millennials. One idea that really drives Centro and its employees is the "Employee Manifesto" written by CEO Shawn Riegsecker. It talks about the values that the company upholds and, importantly, that they emphasize a key aspect of responsibility and empowerment. "*Every employee is responsible for his or her own improvement, the improvement of the corporation, and the improvement of those around them. Lasting success can only be achieved through dedication to the growth and wellbeing of the individual, not the corporation.*"

To me, this is a powerful testament of empowerment and speaks to how a manager and an employee need to meet halfway. You're offering it to employees, and they're expected to step up to the plate and take that on for the betterment of themselves and the organization. From the moment you enter Centro's office, you can tell that all employees take this message to heart. Centro empowers its people and expects employees to rise to the occasion. On multiple occasions, I have been standing in the waiting room, and employees who passed smiled and asked if I had been helped. They weren't the receptionist, but they felt the responsibility to ensure a visitor had a positive experience. No one told them they should do that; they just had that sense of responsibility and ownership.

It's all about building a team culture that is rewarding, inspiring, and inviting. You want people to *want* to do an amazing job. Tanja Nitschke, millennial mentor and HR Business Partner at Groupon, echoes this sentiment, "I like the idea of being a career manager versus a job manager. Here are the goals, *now, how can we get there? How can we leverage your strengths?*"

CONNECTING TO THE BIG PICTURE

Engage and empower. "Empowerment is a term of management. The key is to pull back and stow away one's ego as the joy comes in watching your people soar and aspire to do great things at a level that derives from your confidence, your trust and leadership in them," explains Nava Yeshoalul, Staffing Business Partner, Global Business Organization at Google. "Engagement is a term of leadership. The leader has the responsibility to remove barriers. If you really want your employees to develop judgment and wisdom, then they have to be allowed to make (and own) their decisions—creating a work culture that fosters the collective community to act in empowered ways."

This is where you can make an impact on the bottom line and the future of your organization by involving your people and activating their passions. You can customize your appreciation, recognition, and rewards for your team, and they will keep generating and customizing great results and positive outcomes for you. Experiment with different ideas and discover what works. Offer praise, flexibility, or visibility, and follow up with a little responsibility or autonomy to help connect employees to the big picture. Pepper in the "thank yous" and sprinkle in the fun. This is a mandate made for millennials. You want to be a part of a rewarding and engaging environment. If you build it, they will come—and play—and stay.

Engage and Empower: Connecting to the Big Picture
◁ Telltale Tweets ▷

1. An engaged and empowered team will go above and beyond for you and your organization. Help them see how they make a difference. #inspire

2. There are so many options for recognizing your team! Praise, flexibility, visibility, responsibility, autonomy, and more! #byob #thankyou

3. It's not all work and no play. Build in some fun to keep up the positive energy and high team morale. #marshmallowdodgeball

4. Recognize, appreciate, empower, challenge, and engage to feed positive results and passionate people. #hungry #momentum

12

---○---

COLLABORATE:
MAKING IT HAPPEN

"If I have seen further it is by standing on the shoulders of giants."
—Isaac Newton

Stop, Collaborate, and Listen. Think about some of the great visuals of teamwork that adorn walls and offices. There's the TEAMWORK poster with the reverent rowing team—"Together we achieve more." Or the poster of the diverse team members all putting their hands together before they "break" and lift their hands in the air exuberantly. Then there is the flying V poster representing how the geese in the front create "uplift" for those behind them, and the geese at the back honk to encourage the ones in the front to keep up the pace. Finally, you can't forget about the colony of bees touting that each and every bee has a very specific role and job to do.

Put aside some of these typical metaphors for a moment and really think about teamwork and what it means. A strong team is powerful. Moving. Resilient. Seemingly unstoppable. A great team has that energy, that spark—you can feel it when you're there—almost like static. The individuals on the team know each other's strengths, feed off of each other's ideas, and they challenge, push, and support each other. They're never satisfied with the first answer or the easiest answer. They love hurdles, obstacles, and curveballs because that is when they really get to perform, reach, stretch, stretch, stretch—and prevail. An achievement or team accomplishment is savored, but not for long, because the fun is in the sprint, the journey to the top.

You can build that. But it takes work and discipline.

Even today's prominent business leaders admit the most difficult part of their job is building and leading a team. Take the late Steve Jobs, for instance. Jobs obviously made extraordinary contributions at Apple, but he spoke openly about his struggles in "the people part" of his role as CEO. Jobs learned from mistakes, and his analogy for what builds strong teams was spot on: "My model for business is the Beatles. They were four guys who kept each other's negative tendencies in check. They balanced each other, and the total was greater than the sum of the parts. And that's how I see business. You know great things in business are never done by one person. They're done by a team of people."[1]

This is what your generation is all about. It's all about teamwork and working together. From all of our interviews with millennial managers, the idea of collaboration and teamwork stood out brightly. It's about connecting. Millennials side with Helen Keller on this one, "Alone we can do so little; together we can do so much." Instead of issuing orders, you love to ask for everyone's opinion and consider all ideas. Sheryl Sandberg of Facebook says, "I go around the room and ask people, 'What do you think?'"[2] This is the millennial manager. You want to hear every voice and every perspective because everyone deserves to have a say.

Now many tips for building a great team and fostering an environment of collaboration can be found throughout this book. Everything CONNECTs. Part of collaborating is communicating expectations, delivering feedback, getting to know your people, and adjusting your style. If you're putting these lessons into practice from the other chapters, you're likely fostering a collaborative spirit.

We won't bore you with too many of the how's since collaboration is ingrained in your work style, but I will cover some of the intricacies of maintaining a collaborative but action-oriented team from having the right people in the right roles to running a productive meeting.

MATCHING THE PERSON WITH THE RESPONSIBILITY

Do you have the right people in the right roles? Jim Collins spoke to this idea in *Good to Great* when he said the Level 5 leader gets the "right people on the bus."[3] Do your people have the skills to do the job, or can they learn the skills?

At Leo Burnett, when I was in charge of recruiting and hiring, this was a big focus for me. I looked for matches between the job and the person, and I didn't try to put a square peg in a round hole. I know what you're thinking, "Brad, believe me, I would love to have more control over the hiring and firing. However, that is not the case." Nonetheless, you can still build a strong team by putting people in the right roles.

Play to people's strengths. A great book by Marcus Buckingham, *First Break All the Rules,* talks about focusing on strengths instead of always trying to improve weaknesses.[4] Focus on what you're good at! Just think about how programmed we are to improve our weaknesses. If you look at personal business goals, they often revolve around weaknesses. A good writer has a goal "to become a better presenter" and a great team player sets a goal "to be more of a leader on the team." Has the writer ever thought to set a goal to become an even better, an even more amazing writer? That's her strength and passion. Why shouldn't she hone it instead of focusing on improving a weakness that she's not very excited about? Why can't the team player simply focus on being a better team player? Help your team members foster their strengths.

Ashley Nuese of Avatar HR Solutions said, "I like to find out what my employees are good at and then give them more of that." Now, I know that you can't do this all the time. Sometimes, Digby the creative, big thinker is going to have to do the research or data entry. You also want well-rounded team members who can pitch in when needed, but where you can, match your people's strengths with the job responsibility and encourage them to bring their strengths and style to all of their tasks. Trying to force-fit people to positions or responsibilities is a blow to team dynamic. Everyone feels it. Just consider this example.

From time to time, we answer questions submitted to an HR advice column, basically a *Dear Abby* for the workplace. A reader submitted a question along the lines of:

> *One of our managers is an introvert by nature, and I'm supposed to find training that will change him into an outgoing and jovial extrovert. Do you think we will see results from this training?*
>
> —*It's Doomed, HR generalist, Baton Rouge, LA*

"It's Doomed" is right. It is doomed to fail if they really want to transform an introvert into a gregarious extrovert. My questions are,

"Why do you think this person should be an extrovert? What goals do you think are achieved through extroversion? For example, do you want the person to be more engaging? Do you want him to show more confidence?" Let's look at the underlying goals and see how they can be reached without trying to change the fundamental nature of the person.

If you really need an extroverted person in the role, then you probably need to put an extrovert in that role—but challenge yourself. What are your goals, and can they be achieved by an introverted person? Do you want the manager to build strong relationships, connect with people, and engage with team members? Both extroverts and introverts can do that—they just have different ways of going about it. To build a strong foundation for a collaborative team, match a person's strengths with the job responsibilities while being open to the different ways they achieve the end goal.

COLLABORATING TO TAKE ACTION: JUST DO IT

One thing we heard from older generations is that millennials spend too much time in the "collaboration zone." You want to hear from everyone, and you want to solve problems together, but you must know when to move from information gathering to the decision-making stage. I think there are a couple things coming into play here that make it difficult for millennial managers.

First, there is a little trepidation in making the wrong decision, and second, you don't want to offend or upset someone by the decision you make. Do you know that feeling when you're sitting around the table, everyone has shared their ideas, you've gone around and around, and there almost is this collective sigh of "Soooo…"? *SO*, what's the decision? What are we going to do? As a millennial manager, you might be tempted to say, "Well, it sounds like we all need to think a little more on this one. Let' marinate on it and decide next time." Now, I'm not saying that you shouldn't take time to think through decisions, but pushing off decisions can become an epidemic. Dan Jessup, Head of People Strategy, Groupon, has a sound recipe for making collaboration a success, "Start with diplomacy, add humility, finish with decisiveness and context. Bake for 30 minutes."

There are collaborative decisions, but sometimes, you need to call the shot—"finish with decisiveness." You are the manager. Have a perspective. Make a choice. If you feel that your team is getting hung up on the idea-generation stage, set a timer for 15 minutes. Give your team (and yourself!) 15 minutes to discuss the issue. Then, at the end of the time, make a decision. If it's a bigger discussion and everyone needs time to mull, set a timeline. "Let's all think about this tonight, and then tomorrow, we will set the timer for twenty to thirty minutes and come to a decision after that." At that point, maybe you have consensus, and maybe you call the shot.

Just Say It. Just Do It

Just commit. Just go for it. I have already talked about making mistakes and expecting some failures. Not everything is going to go just as planned, and maybe you won't make the best decision. Sometimes, you just have to jump and take the plunge. Make a decision and own it. Commit. This is what *your* managers want more of from millennial managers. They love the collaboration, but they want to ensure the decision making and decision implementing is close at hand. Remember that there are few decisions that you will make that will cause your company to crumble.

To Collaborate, You Don't Have to Accommodate

You don't have to say "yes," agree, or go along with everything in the name of "going with the flow" or being a "flexible" and collaborative leader. If you have a lot to get done by the end of the day, you can let Jack know that you could use some help when he asks if he can leave early for a softball game. If Mia asks if she needs to customize the proposal or if she can just send the standard version, you can tell her that she needs to customize it even though that will take up a lot of her time. No one likes to be *that* person, but when you need to draw the line, you should.

Bradley Aldrich, millennial manager and Of Counsel, Wolfe Law Group, says that he is constantly evolving as a manager: "At first, my management style was hesitant to weak and nonexistent. I had never had to tell anyone what to do, and I was nervous about stepping on toes. As I have moved along, I've become a little more firm—but still pretty casual on the spectrum. I make a conscious effort to have good relationships, but now, I'm more comfortable giving clear directions and setting expectations."

There's a profound difference between being unreasonable and being a leader who wants to get the best from the team. After talking with millennial managers, I concluded that part of this hesitation about decision making is affected by a desire to be liked. There is a real fear of being seen as the authority figure or the bad guy. You collaborate and try to reach consensus because you want everyone on your team to be pleased by the decision. Gregory Tall of Robert Morris University asserts, "Some of your best decisions will be unpopular ones. Have the courage to communicate candidly and the confidence to follow your instinct." Sometimes, millennial managers back down to uphold their value of flexibility, to please others, or to prevent conflict. You don't have to accommodate to collaborate. Make a decision and stand by it—even if the going gets tough.

The truth is conflict isn't all bad. Conflict can be beneficial and build stronger teams. In general though, millennials tend to back down if they feel tension or if they think someone doesn't like their decision. You have to realize that it's not that they're against *you*; they just may be against your opinion. That's okay. It's not personal. My wife and I disagree from time to time, but we know that we're both on the same team and that we both have the same end goals. Work together and collaborate, but don't feel like you always have to accommodate and dodge conflict. Remember, you're the manager.

MANAGER OR BFF? DRAWING THE LINE

There is a fine line between being a manager and being a friend. For millennial managers who want to foster relationships, help individuals grow, and collaborate, this can be a hard line to draw, especially if they're managing others around their age. People are realizing that they often spend more time with the people they work with than their own families! Now wouldn't that make the days more enjoyable and work more do-able, if you enjoyed the people that you were with eight or more hours a day? These people do not have to be your best friends or the individuals you would choose to hang out with on a Saturday night. You can respect, value, and enjoy the people on your team without being "Best Friends Forever."

In our interviews, we found that this is one of the biggest challenges for millennial managers. You want your people to know that you care for them, but you also want to be able to hold them accountable and give them constructive criticism. When was the last time you told your friend three ways that they could be a better friend? When was the last time you worked through a development plan to get your friends to where they need to be? Friendship training, maybe?

The fact is friends are equals, and you probably accept each other just the way you are. The end goal is to just be friends. At work, the standard is different. Work has to be accomplished, there are quite a few end goals, and you're challenging each other to be the best you can be. Millennial manager Conor Gee admits that it's more difficult when you're around the same age as the people you manage. When speaking of his millennial employee, Conor said, "It was great. We got along really well at work, so it was like 'Does this extend outside of work?' and if so, what does that look like? The more you become their friend, the harder it is to be their manager. It doesn't mean you can't do both, but in certain situations it needs to be clearly defined."

Do your employees really need another friend? Who knows. Could they benefit more from having a mentor and manager that challenges them? Definitely. Don't forget Mrs. Stanley!

Vince Lombardi captured this fine line when he said, "The leader can never close the gap between himself and the group. If he does, he is no longer what he must be. He must walk a tightrope between the consent he must win and the control he must exert." You have to keep that level of authority or influence with your direct reports. If you're partying with them on most weekends, it's hard to command respect at the Monday meeting. If you're always making comments on a direct report's Facebook page and posting pictures of the two of you, it's harder to say you're not playing favorites when you give her the next cool project. If you eat lunch with one of your employees every single day, you may have a tough time telling her the comments she made at the meeting were inappropriate.

This is an area that can be tricky for many millennials. I don't want you to walk away from this section thinking you have to be a cold, distant autocratic taskmaster with your team just because you're the boss. I simply am saying there needs to be a line. The best way to think about it is that there's a difference between "being friendly" and "being friends" with your team. Here's a pocket guide:

Friendly: Attending some group happy hours with your team

Friends: Staying out 'til 2:00 AM after the happy hour grinding it out at the club

Friendly: Having a drink or two and chatting with your team at the holiday party

Friends: Getting so drunk you end up crashing on your direct report's couch

Friendly: Engaging in an occasional game of Words With Friends with a direct report

Friends: Spending two hours a day in your direct report's office playing Scrabble

Friendly: Hanging out with your direct report at the water cooler

Friends: Making out with your direct report at the water cooler

Watch the gray areas, and draw a line. Having strong relationships with your team is critical to group success. Where the "friends" thing becomes an issue is when the relationship gets taken advantage of. If your direct report and friend shows up late and hungover one day and says, "C'mon boss, cut me some slack, you saw how much we had to drink last night," then it's an issue. If you have trouble giving a team member constructive feedback because she's your friend and you're worried about how that will affect your friendship, then it's an issue.

If you don't maintain influence, then you will struggle to do everything you have learned in this book. Would you tell your friend that she is not ready for a promotion? Would you lay out expectations, set goals, and deliver feedback with your direct report who is your friend? We're not saying it can't or doesn't happen, but being a friend and manager can be tough territory.

MANAGING THE COLLABORATION ZONE: TEAM MEETINGS

Meetings, meetings, meetings. The official collaboration zone, and now you're in charge of them. You may hate running team meetings and you may love it, but the truth is that a lot rests in your hands as the leader of these massive time-takers. Meetings can move you forward, or they can be a colossal waste of time. Let's talk about how to avoid the latter.

First, you want to meet with your team on a routine basis. Depending on the size of your team, maybe that's once a week or once a month. If you have a smaller team, maybe you meet a couple times a week. Meetings can be highly collaborative and productive—if you run them efficiently. As a millennial, I am betting that you enjoy your team meetings. It's a perfect time to build relationships, get to know your people, and have some fun. You can also see how this could be a recipe for disaster if not managed well.

The first tip I have for running good meetings doesn't sound too engaging, but you can still incorporate fun in the realms of "maintaining order and control." If your meetings get too far off track, then your team sees your meetings as a joke, and participants will have a reason to skip out on the next one, show up late, or play "Words With Friends" the entire time. Chetan Borkhetaria, Global Learning Consultant at Lenovo, enjoys a lot of team meetings and offers, "Collaboration goes well with a clear sense of purpose and ownership. What's really important is identifying roles and responsibilities, and you must constantly clarify these. For example, sometimes we don't have a note taker, but you must identify this person. CO—**LABOR**—ATION. *Work together.*"

To keep everyone on track and focused, have an agenda that includes a start time and an END time. This prevents that killer thirty-minute turned two-hour meeting that snuffs out creativity and productivity. It sounds so simple, but most meetings don't have agendas. How do you know if you're accomplishing what you need to accomplish? How do you know if you're being effective? How do you keep all of those two-minute updates from turning into thirty-minute updates? Have an agenda and stick to it. One of our clients, TPN, takes this point seriously. The company is guided by Six Sigma principles around meeting efficiency —specifically, enforce on-time start and stop and allot three-minute and two-minute reports to keep things moving along. Most people would round up and make it a nice, five-minute report, but TPN knows that the team appreciates this efficiency.

Share Responsibilities

Who says you need to be talking the entire time?—even if that's *your* favorite part. Assign different responsibilities to team members, so they feel like it's *their* meeting and it creates buy-in for your team. If you have a part or you know you might be called upon, you're much more likely to pay attention. Furthermore, this is a great way to recognize and develop your people through responsibility and visibility. Your team members can hone their organizational, strategic, and presentation skills by having a tangible part in the meeting.

Keep on Keeping on

Please, keep things moving. There's Tangent Tamara, Derailer Devra, Questioning Quentin, and Jokester Jeremy. Maybe you get off topic, but it's your job to not let this spiral out of control. You can use your agenda as a way out, and you can fall back on our next tip.

Table Discussions

Your team may launch into some really interesting and important agenda items, but they're not exactly timely or relevant. You can discuss the topic with an individual off line or you can put it on the agenda for the next meeting. I know this may be hard to do in the spirit of lively discussion and team building. As you build more trust and get to know your team, you will gain more intuition on when it's more productive to table discussions or let them go.

Allot Time for Feedback and Questions

How many times have you walked out of a meeting and you're not sure what was decided? Far too often, I'm afraid. Unfortunately, what happens in meetings, usually stays in meetings. The thing is people talk and talk and talk and, all of a sudden, you are out of time and everyone leaves. *So what happened? Did we decide anything? Where did we leave it? Soooo what's going on?*

Always leave about five minutes for questions, wrap up, and next actions. "So now what?" should always be at the end of every meeting. Now what do we do? Did you discuss next actions? Have they been assigned? Divvy up next actions right then so no one is confused stepping out of the meeting. Let your team voice any questions or concerns, so everyone is onboard.

Add Some Fun—Seriously

True to the values of millennials, you need to incorporate some fun at meetings. Meetings don't need to be all work and no play. You can still have very effective, fun meetings. Bring your own ideas and personality, but I have included a few suggestions for making meetings more engaging and interesting:

High/low—Have everyone state their high and low from the previous day or week.

Reflection question—You pose one question at the beginning of the meeting and everyone has to answer it. Questions can include:

▷ What's a blocker for you at work right now?
▷ What is taking the majority of your time at work and outside of work?
▷ What project are you most excited about?
▷ What did you accomplish yesterday?
▷ What do you plan to accomplish today?
▷ What one thing do you wish you did more of?

Delegate the creation of fun. Assign team members a meeting, and they are responsible for an ice-breaker or short activity to get the group going. This takes something off of your plate, and it empowers your group to take ownership of the success of your meetings.

Think outside the conference room. Hold a meeting outside or in a different room. Have a stand-up meeting, or have everyone sit in different seats than they normally do.

Have a quotable quotes jar. There are some funny things, hilarious people, and interesting situations at your workplace, no doubt. These are the entertaining situations and quotes that need to be captured. Have team members write down their quotable quotes or situations seen or heard around the office. Every meeting, read one or two quotes to get everyone laughing.

Keep a positive spirit. Sure, you're busy, stressed, tense, or deadline driven. There is a lot going on—always. Your attitude and outlook at meetings sends a powerful message. You should be a transparent leader, but no one enjoys negative, despondent transparency. For fun, try playing the unfortunately/fortunately game. If anyone says "unfortunately" during the meeting, then someone must counter with a fortunately statement. For example: "Unfortunately, we just heard that we didn't win the new business pitch." Someone can respond, "Fortunately, we don't have to sleep at the office anymore or eat potato chips for dinner." It's a lighthearted way to keep a positive atmosphere.

These are just a few, simple ideas for building team relationships while still running an efficient meeting. If done right, meetings are a great venue for collaborating, communicating, and decision making.

CONTRIBUTING TO A COLLABORATIVE COMPANY AND COMMUNITY

I have talked a lot about collaborating on your team and focusing on your role, but you operate within a larger organization. It's crucial to keep your team connected to the company culture and aligned with the overarching goals. When everyone feels like they are part of a community, employees feel connected to something bigger than themselves.

That sense of togetherness and community at your company is so important. Many of the techniques for building a strong team culture apply to the company at large. CONNECT. Live and breathe your company values and mission. For example, our client Hu-Friedy has six core values that its employees uphold—TRIERS: Teamwork, Respect, Integrity, Excellence, Reliability, and Social Responsibility. These values bring each and every employee together. Your millennial employees especially love this connection to the bigger picture.

You want to contribute to a "we're in this together" company culture. One of my favorite examples of positive company culture comes from Umpqua, a Pacific Northwest bank. Umpqua has a 15-minute "motivational moment" every morning.[5] At each of its locations, every morning, the entire group takes a moment to have some fun. Each day an employee leads the event. It can be anything they want. They can have a dance party, sing a song, do a little yoga, and my personal favorite, play marshmallow dodge ball. This happens for ALL employees across ALL levels and locations. The entire company can take a few minutes to relax and play together to get the motivation they need to work hard together. It's a great, short way to build community and have some fun. A team and organization is only as good as its weakest link. It's important to keep everyone engaged, energized, and pulling for each other. This is when you realize:

"Oh, Alex isn't that bad; he's actually pretty cool now that he's not in front of that spreadsheet."

"Veronica actually isn't as uptight as I thought now that we're not racing to get our RFP out."

Finally, the comment that we hear most often: "It was good to see _____ in a different light."

Everyone in the company doesn't have to be friends. You can have a strong working relationship and company culture built on trust and respect—without having an office full of BFFs.

Collaborate With Your Community

Connecting, collaborating, and volunteering in the community can go a long way in bringing your organization together. Is there a pro bono project that ties into your business? Can you help out with a local charity? While volunteering, you're not talking about deadlines and projects, and you get to hang out with your team while helping others. It is about connecting and doing meaningful work.

At JB Training Solutions, we volunteer with Chicago Scholars. We're all about career success, so it makes perfect sense that we would work with a not-for-profit dedicated to helping underprivileged teens get into a great college, succeed there, and then land a solid job. One evening, we read applications and interviewed students together and, after the interviews, we all sent around nice texts because we felt such a strong connection with the students and the cause. We loved meeting Julian, Lexus, and Yesenia, and we enjoyed hearing from the aspiring engineers, lawyers, doctors, and teachers. It made our team stronger and connected us to the bigger picture—a true millennial aspiration.

MAKING IT HAPPEN

Collaborate and work together. Foster a team environment, so you can knock through challenges and capitalize on opportunities. Set your team on a path toward success by collaborating—not accommodating—

and making big decisions. Choose being friendly over being friends to maintain your influence, and enjoy the ride as your energy, intensity, and collaborative spirit propels your team forward. Anne Price offers, "In the coming years, people management will become more and more critical, and the companies who thrive will be those with strong managers with the emotional intelligence to know how to motivate, encourage, show compassion, nurture talent, and perform selflessly." You can be that manager.

Collaborate: Making It Happen
◁ Telltale Tweets ▷

1. A strong team is powerful. Moving. Resilient. Seemingly unstoppable. You can build it, but it takes hard work & discipline. #collaborate

2. Watch the fine line between friend and manager. You can be friendly without being a friend. Maintain your level of influence. #noBFFs

3. Collaborate and work together—but take action. Lead productive meetings. Just do it. Just say it. Just decide. #productivity #chalant

4. Make a difference in your company culture and your community. Be the change you want to see. #gandhi #challenge

13

---⊙---

TEACH: BEING A MENTOR—AND STUDENT

"The task of leadership is not to put greatness into people, but to elicit it, for the greatness is there already."
—John Buchan

Who's your Mrs. Stanley? Who is your role model? Who is the person who gave you the push, the leg up, the insight, the new perspective—just because. There have probably been quite a few people in and out of your life who influenced you. For me, one of those people was my first boss at Leo Burnett. Looking back, I realize just how little I knew back then, but with Leo Burnett's culture to grow and promote from within, my boss was my mentor and champion. If you think about it, you have had teachers, mentors, coaches, tutors, professors, bosses, and colleagues all along the way who have helped and pushed you. You have spent a large part of your life learning and soaking it all in. Now you have the chance to pay it forward to your team. Not too fast, you're still a student. Even as a manager and teacher, you still have a lot to learn. That's one of the first lessons you can teach your people—everyone—including yourself—should always be learning and growing. Patti Grace, U.S. Director of Learning and Development for OmnicomMediaGroup, encourages millennials to "be well read and knowledgeable about not only being a manager of *process* but also being a leader of *people*. Develop an acute awareness of your need to always *learn* and develop your leadership skills."

At JB Training Solutions, everyone is a teacher and a student. We can all learn from each other and teach each other. We are always moving forward, growing, and learning.

Katie Drinan, the Vice President, Employee Relations at MB Financial, says that the majority of its top young performers report into their high-potential senior leaders. You can have the chicken or the egg debate over that one, but there is no doubt that there are both teaching and learning moments in these high-performing partnerships.

"No matter how you define your path to success—whether it involves balancing your personal and professional responsibilities, having a job where you can make a difference, enjoying open and honest communication, or using the latest technology, it will be critical to take advantage of the training and development opportunities available to you," says Jill Smart, Chief Human Resources Officer, Accenture. "It may be surprising, but one of those opportunities will involve learning from the different generations in your workplace. Just as your expertise with social media may help more seasoned managers, they will have a great deal to teach you." Be a lifelong student and teacher.

The millennial managers we talked to showed great passion for this topic. You may not think you have that "teaching" aurora or inspirational persona, but it doesn't have to be anything fancy or prophetic. Don't feel like everything you say has to be a quotable quote that battles Ken Blanchard or Zig Ziglar for that next teamwork poster. It doesn't need all the fanfare; just make every opportunity a "teaching" or a learning moment. Teaching is more of a mindset. Everything that you do can be a teaching and learning moment.

PROVIDING THE SKILLS AND INSIGHT: TRAINING AND STORYTELLING

Teach the Hard Skills

There are so many ways to be creative and teach your employees the hard skills of the job. There are job shadows, rotational programs, stretch assignments, special projects, delegation, business book clubs, and formal training. If you're working on a new task, have your direct report watch you, shadow you, or pitch in. If she can listen in on one of your calls or attend a meeting with you, let her join you, observe, and be a sponge. This hands-on experience is priceless. If there are computer skills, product insights, or competencies that need to be enhanced, connect your employees with more formal training. Try to instill a love for learning.

Teach the Soft Skills

Soft business skills are all those competencies that surround the job that are incredibly indicative of whether an employee is successful or not. Topics include time management, initiative, diversity and inclusion, business etiquette, communication styles, teamwork, writing skills, working across the generations, and so much more. Especially help your millennials and new employees in this area. Of course, there is formal training for these hot topics, but you also can be creative with imparting this knowledge. Try holding "lunch & learns" where you discuss an important issue, or have different employees host a quick "Wise Up!" educational session each week. Finally, one of the most powerful ways to teach the soft skills is to lead by example and share your experiences and stories.

Tell a Story to Teach

Story telling is an amazing and engaging way to teach your employees. Many great leaders and mentors are great storytellers. It's difficult to remember the hard data or the stats that proved your point, but it's easy to recall the story that dramatized the learning point. It becomes etched in your memory. Do you remember that last book that you just couldn't put down? Courtney says she is the world's worst for making and breaking the "just one more chapter" promise to herself. She just can't pull herself away from the story! That's the type of attention and energy that you can bring from your team with a good story. Stories are great for making information stick and for bringing lessons to life.

This reminds me of a story. One of our clients—Sofia—worked at a consulting company. She was talking about this idea of "quality over quantity" with her direct report, and she wanted to reinforce how important the quality of her work is. After really emphasizing this point, a few errors in formatting and content were made, so Sofia thought of a story of when she was in her direct report's exact position. She said something like:

> *I know we've been talking a lot about the quality of our work lately. I know that everyone has a lot going on, that we're juggling responsibilities and moving at a fast pace. Even though we have the urge to "just get things done," we have to make sure we're taking that step back to look at our work and make sure it's as professional and buttoned up as it can be. I'm sure from your perspective, you may be getting frustrated. You put a lot of time into a project, and then you feel like I nitpick a few typos and formatting issues.*
>
> *I remember when I was putting together a big proposal for a client, and I had spent hours on it. One of my boss's comments was that after one of the bullets, I needed to put an extra space. That instance is etched into my brain because a part of me was like "What?!" I put this whole thing together and I get a comment about a missing space. Then the other part of me really understood the push for excellence and flawless execution in all that we do. From that point on, I looked at all of my documents, presentations, and e-mails with an eye for the critical because it's those little things that can make a difference. Now, I don't want you to think that I don't have appreciation for the larger work that you do, but I'm really thankful that my boss was tough on me at first. When I was starting out, he didn't let anything slide, and that made me a better and more buttoned-up professional.*

In that instance, Sofia was able to give feedback by drawing a relation to herself by telling a story and explaining the bigger picture. It's always nice when people know you went through the same trials that they are experiencing.

Tell Stories to Relate and Show Understanding

As a leader, stories are a great way to share experiences, learning points, and show that you understand. Just imagine a grandfather and grandkid sitting on the front porch, "You know son, when I was a young boy...." Those are the stories and lessons that stick with us for a lifetime. Bring that to life for your team.

I still recall the power of a story from my early career days. I was an account executive at Leo Burnett working on the McDonald's account. It was an incredibly busy, frenetic, and high-profile account to work on. We ran at 100 miles an hour 12 to 14 hours a day. One day I made a mistake at work relating to a commercial we were running. A big mistake. A mistake that ended up costing the company more than I made in a year. It was devastating, and I felt horrible. I spent the day sitting in meetings with lawyers, producers, and senior management trying to figure out what happened and how to move forward. I went home that night feeling worse than I ever had in my whole life.

At about 9:00 PM the phone rang. It was Jerry Conner, Executive Vice President in charge of the McDonald's account and my boss's, boss's, boss's, boss. The head cheese. As I reluctantly picked up the phone, two thoughts raced through my head. Best-case scenario he chews me out; worst-case scenario he fires me. He began the conversation with a story. He told me about an Account Executive many years ago at Burnett who had made a mistake. Like mine, this was a colossal blunder that cost the company tens of thousands of dollars. The person who made the mistake felt miserable, but learned from the error and went on to have a very successful career. Of course that person was Jerry himself.

Instead of calling to reprimand me, he called to boost my spirits. I'll never forget the power of that story and how it made me think very differently about that company and more importantly about Jerry.

Tell Stories to Share a Vision and Paint a Picture

The speech by a great leader that instantly jumps to mind is Martin Luther King Jr.'s, "I Have a Dream" speech. King told a story and painted a picture of a world that was so vivid and touching that it sends chills down your arms. He uses descriptive words drenched in emotion to paint a picture of his vision. He talks about the sweltering heat of injustice, and the crowd can almost feel the oppression boiling from Mississippi and Georgia. Then, King inspires hope that the hot, sweltering, and unwelcoming states will become an oasis, and the crowd envisions people of all colors and backgrounds sitting down to share a meal together. King continues and makes it real. He hopes that one day his four children will "live in a nation where they will not be judged by the color of their skin but by the content of their character."

I have a dream today!

King had a dream. He had a dream and a story that everyone could grab a hold of.

Another great story teller is Karen, the President of a Chicago not-for-profit organization. Every time you're with Karen, you hear an amazing story, and her little anecdotes share her vision for the organization and for a better Chicago. The last time Courtney met with Karen to discuss ways our organizations could work together, she was jotting down notes and her bracelet made a little jingle. She took the moment to explain how that bracelet was given to her by the very first class of students. They have now been thriving in their careers for several years, and every day, it serves as a reminder to Karen. Futures are bright. All of a sudden, their meeting was more personal and more vivid. Courtney was connected to the students, not just the idea.

What's your story? What stories do you have that can help you lead your team? Everyone has stories, it just takes some time to sift through them and conjure up those details. It's like preparing for an interview with all of those behavioral questions: *Tell me about a time that you overcame an obstacle*, or, *Tell us about a time you had to deal with a difficult customer and how did it go.* Just like an interview, you want to prepare and think through your experiences and background so when the opportunity arises, you have a few stories top-of-mind. Think through some of the below questions. Don't merely think of one-word answers. What are the details of the situation? How would it relate to your team to deliver a teaching moment?

▷ When did you overcome an obstacle, and how did you deal with it?
▷ When did you have to deal with a difficult person, and how did you overcome it?
▷ When did you have to work on a long-term project, and how did you get through it?
▷ When have you failed? How did you learn from that experience?
▷ When did you think outside of the box to come up with a creative solution?

▷ When have you gone above and beyond the call of duty, and how were you rewarded?

▷ When was a time that you were juggling a lot of responsibilities and projects? How did you get through it?

▷ Describe a time when preparation and practice really paid off for you.

▷ When was a time that you set an aggressive goal and met it? What about a time when you fell short of your goals?

▷ Describe a time when you were scared to take a risk or try something new. How did it turn out?

▷ Is there a time where you took the high road instead taking shady measures just to win? How did that go?

Take some time to shape your thoughts and answers to these questions, and then never miss an opportunity to have a teaching and learning moment. You want to keep your team in a constant stage of growth, learning, and advancement, and as a millennial manager, you're all about that.

EVALUATING PERFORMANCE: NEVER MISS A LEARNING MOMENT

If your employee performs well or not so well, it's a teaching moment. Go over all the things that were effective, so that it's molded in her memory, and your employee is sure to repeat that success.

When our company won a big proposal with a Fortune 50 company, we were thrilled. We likely beat out larger companies with more resources. We felt like we did a lot of things right with the proposal. We built relationships with team members, customized our content to fit the company's needs, and immersed ourselves in its business and needs. We went above and beyond to wow the company by showcasing our work via webinar and making more formal presentations to its senior team. Inevitably, there were some things we could have done a little better.

We wanted to make sure we could emulate this success, so our team sat down afterward and put together our AAR—After Action Review—as inspired by Captain Mike Abrashoff of the USS Benfold.[1] We listed all of the things we did well, and we brainstormed things we could have done a little better or should change the next time around. It was enlightening.

First, it was fun to talk about all the things we did well, and we congratulated those individuals on the strengths they showed and ideas they came up with to make the project a success. In that regard, it was a good team-building activity. Then it was inspiring to look at the things we could do better too. It reinforced the fact that we can never get too comfortable or confident. It's like when the number one ranked team loses to the worst team in the league. We always have to be sharpening our game and improving, even in the face of big wins. The list that we put together was a "cheers" to our high points and a push for our low points. It was our challenge to expect greater and greater things from ourselves and our team.

Think about having an After Action Review with your team. Challenging yourself and your team means being "unfailingly self-critical." AAR doesn't let good get in the way of great. It's pretty simple to conduct with your team. In your informal AAR, consider the questions:

What did we have planned?

What did we actually do?

What did we do well and why?

What can we improve and how?

You could put together something as simple as shown below.

After Action Review

This was the plan.	This is what happened.
To wrap up the program in Q3	Program wrapped up in Q4
To partner with client's subject-matter expert to understand content	Learned more on our own due to hectic schedules of senior leaders
Things we rocked.	Things we could improve.
Set up in-person meeting to fully understand needs and interests	Get right people on team earlier, so they feel connected from the start
Asked a lot of good questions; listened more than we talked	Gain buy-in from higher-ups or the main decision maker right away
Presented our proposal instead of just e-mailing it	Tell more stories and anecdotes to explain our perspective (even more!)

How often does your team actually get a chance to debrief after a project? Usually, you're just racing to the next thing. AAR gives you time to celebrate your successes and challenge yourself for the next big thing. To be sure, AAR is not a checklist with a "good" and "bad" column. Daryl Sneed, Chief Talent Officer, Sg2, says you should always view teaching and learning as much more than a checklist. "True mastery cannot be assessed simply by 'how much' someone knows," asserts Sneed. "It is in the observation of how knowledge is personalized and creatively used across varying situations that give indication to true competence and achievement." Evaluating performance through an AAR is a good time to take a breather, reflect, teach, and nurture creativity and true competence in problem solving.

NURTURING CREATIVITY: FOSTERING PROBLEM SOLVERS

Outside of teaching new responsibilities, you also want to teach employees how to have an open and creative mindset. Even if you work in a creative field, there are naysayers, rules, regulations, and budgets that inhibit some great ideas. Think about ways you can generate more creativity on your team. Wouldn't it be great if your team could always think outside the box when it comes to solving problems? As manager, you can help instill a culture of creativity.

Being creative is a challenge, however. It seems like our laughs and our imagination shrink and shrink as we get older. A child laughs more than forty times in one day, and an adult laughs less than eleven. After years of conditioning to color in the lines and do as you were told in school, all of sudden, you're at work and you have to think of innovative solutions to solve real-world problems. Anne Pramaggiore, the CEO of ComEd, advises, "Don't be afraid to color outside the lines. If you are too keenly focused on the road ahead, you may miss the amazing detour that offers you more."

Remember that you can't say "Be innovative" or "Be creative" to make it happen. Often, the best ideas come when you step away from work instead of putting your nose to the grindstone—"must be creative, must be creative." As a manager, you can't necessarily teach creativity but you can nurture it and give your people the tools to foster it.

One thing we've done at JB Training Solutions is to first pick a problem we're trying to solve. Then, we open the dictionary and randomly point at a word. We brainstorm all the ideas that relate to that word and answer our problem. This is a light-hearted example, but we actually were planning our ten-year anniversary celebration, and we wanted to try out some of these creativity exercises. Our random word was fashion, so we thought of all the ideas for our party that were inspired by the word fashion. Ideas ranged from a business attire fashion show to having our company logo man on the catwalk. The exercise opened our minds, got us thinking outside of the box, and encouraged the free flow of ideas. Don't worry, there was no catwalk at the celebration.

Being a creative problem solver isn't easy. Thomas Edison reflected, "Many of life's failures are people who did not realize how close they were to success when they gave up." It's easy to throw in the towel and to not rise to the occasion. It's easier to say it can't be done or think you don't have time to figure it out. As a manager, you can help your employees get over this hump and this doubt. Push them and teach them to give it another shot and to not fear failure. Another persistent man, Winston Churchill, said, "Success is not final, failure is not fatal: it is the courage to continue that counts." Challenges bring out the courage, persistence, and determination in your team.

DELEGATING: TEACHING THEM TO FISH

Another challenging way to teach your employees new skills and knowledge is through delegation. "Managing is getting paid for the homeruns someone else hits," says Casey Stengel, Hall of Fame baseball manager. Delegating can be hard work. Remember you were promoted because you did your last job really well—now you have to let go of that control and empower someone else to own that responsibility. Tyler Micenheimer, a millennial and HR manager at PepsiCo, said that one of his favorite parts of managing was that he didn't have to worry about some of the smaller details that weren't his strong suit. When it comes to delegating and teaching new tasks, you want to give:

Direction: The what and when of doing the job
Autonomy: The "how" of the responsibility
Authority: The power to decide
Responsibility: The ownership of success and failure
Accountability: The reliability to finish a job well

Space: Room to succeed or fail
Credit: Acknowledgment for a job well done

Delegating is about letting go. "Things do not grow in the shadow of great trees." This is a quote from Constantin Brancusi. Have you ever heard of Constantin? Probably not. What about Rodin? Most of you likely have heard of Auguste Rodin, the great sculptor and creator of *The Thinker*. Well, Constantin studied under Rodin. In the shadow of Rodin, Constantin was never able to break out and build a name for himself. For your employees to grow and reach the next level, you have to give them the space, freedom, and responsibility to branch out on their own.

There are a few things you want to avoid when it comes to delegating. There are quite a few bosses out there who do some of these things in the name of being a good boss, "empowering" their people, or "delegating."

A Few Things NOT to Do

Dumping Without Help or Input

"Vic, I know you've been asking for more responsibility. Here's your chance! We need to turn our department into a profit center. This has never been done before. It's quite the challenge, and you can present your recommendations to our department head in two weeks. Go gettum, buddy!"

That's not delegating, that's dumping. It's a big project that has never been done before, and you provided little to no direction. If you're giving your employees a fairly large project that they've never done before, you want to offer them a little perspective.

If you don't have any guidelines and you're not sure what you want, let them know that. Say, *"Vic, this is a very open-ended project. Honestly, I'm looking forward to hearing your perspective on this idea. I don't expect you to have all the answers, but spend some time thinking through the project, look at what our competitors are doing, and be sure to chat with Willie in Marketing. He will offer great perspective, and he's familiar with this type of initiative. Let's touch base at the end of the week once you've had a chance to do those things."*

Checking in TOO Much

On the flipside of the macromanager who dumps work is the micro-manager who hovers over work and checks in TOO much. *"Daphne, how's it going? Are you finished with that part yet? So where are you with it then? I thought you said it was going well?"*

You have to give your employee space to succeed or fail. Micromanaging projects stifles creativity and counteracts the reasons for delegating anyway. If you check in too much, your employees will always use you as a crutch, and they may never gain the confidence to complete the project on their own. Establish check-in points at the onset of the project, and stick to those. If your employees come to you before the check point, you can support them, but really encourage them to think through it on their own. Failing is a big part of learning. If you start to feel that little twitch of wanting to take control and complete it the "right" way, think about how important it is to trust your employees. Believe and trust that they will produce great work.

Don't Let Them Get Too Far Off Track

There is nothing worse than cranking on a project for two weeks and then realizing you weren't even close. You were in left field, and your boss wasn't even at the game. For employees, it's really discouraging when they feel as though they've wasted time, spun their wheels, or accomplished little. Employees want to contribute to meaningful work, and it is disheartening if they keep finding that they're off base and constantly redoing their work. Check points or check-ins help prevent this from happening. Even if it's as simple as a one-minute debrief in the morning, you can sometimes catch if the direction is getting too far out there. To maximize productivity yet provide learning moments, look for the balance in providing autonomy and direction.

Refrain from Assigning Only Menial Tasks

BORING. Sure, one great thing about being a manager is that you can delegate all the things you dislike doing. Filing—delegated! Data entry —delegated! Administrative duties—delegated! "I'm the best boss ever."

Some of those responsibilities are important for your team to learn, and you do want to free up your time to work on more important tasks, but you want to ensure you're delegating a balance of fun, meaningful projects and menial tasks.

**Don't Clear Room for Fantasy Football Research
or Pinterest Prowling**

Dumping your Friday to-do list on your team so you can hit the beach that afternoon is not very engaging. As a manager, you have to walk the walk and talk the talk. If you're constantly dumping work so you can have more fun outside of work, resentment will begin to build on your team. You're basically saying that your life and time are more important than theirs. They may start to feel unappreciated, disrespected, or bitter as they envision you with friends and a martini while they are fiddling with an Excel sheet.

Don't Blame Your Team for Reasonable Misses

Our Director of Training, Jeff Hiller, says, "If you delegate a task and it doesn't go exactly as planned, think twice before blowing up at your employee or giving them tough criticism." If they gave their best effort and came close, then it sounds like a "win" in the delegating game. They won't be able to do it as good as you the first time. When there is a reasonable miss, this is the perfect time for spot coaching and giving them specific feedback on how they can take it to the next level. You have to be okay with it not being exactly as you would have done it. If you did your due diligence with your check-ins, then you should have already curtailed any "major" misses.

Delegating is hard work, but it's a key part of being a "teacher." It can be difficult to let go of some of your old duties—you were just so good at them and you knew the exact way to do it! You've got to let go of that mindset. Delegation is the only way your direct reports can learn and grow. Importantly, delegation frees you up to work on projects more appropriate for your level.

Here's the deal. It's easy to do your old job. You did it well (which got you promoted). It's fun to do your old job because you had it down to a science. It's hard to do your new job. It's different, and it presents new challenges and forces you to pick up new skills. Many newer managers especially tend to gravitate back to their old job, but I can guarantee you this. Senior management will not come to you two years from now and say, "Eric, you're *still* doing your old job really well. We're going to promote you again!" If you're stuck in the details, you're not looking up to see the big picture of what your team or organization needs.

MENTORING AND COACHING: A LEG UP

"The mediocre mentor tells. The good mentor explains. The superior mentor demonstrates. The great mentor inspires, encourages, and takes you into the trenches," said author and businessman Navtaj Chandhoke. Serving as a mentor and coach is priceless in the development of your team. You give knowledge, confidence, and an outsider's perspective. You can often see in someone what they can't see in themselves.

Now, mentoring is less about telling; it's more about asking, sharing, and showing. Think about a few of the great mentor-mentee relationships on the big screen and in real life. There was Socrates and Plato, Yoda and Luke Skywalker, Zina Garrison and Serena Williams, and even Usher and Justin Bieber. The big thing about coaching is not giving the answers. Josef Albers says, "Good teaching is more a giving of right questions than a giving of right answers."[2] When your employee asks you a question, you can say,

What do you think?

What's your idea?

What do you think happened there?

What do you think you could have done differently?

You're not giving the answers. Importantly, you're not creating a "mini me." You're molding and shaping a new leader. There is one common thread in two strong female leaders—Madeline Albright, the first female U.S. Secretary of State, and Condoleezza Rice, the first female African-American U.S. Secretary of State. They both had a mentor in Josef Korbel.[3] Josef Korbel was Madeline Albright's father, and she credits him for influencing and pushing her education and career pursuits. Korbel also served as Condoleezza's mentor at Stanford, and he pushed her to specialize in the Soviet Union and even to serve as Provost of Stanford. Korbel challenged both women to be the best. He was still able to challenge them without molding them—they each have very diverse political points of view.

As a mentor and coach, you walk the talk. If you talk a big game but don't back it up with action and followthrough, your employees see right through it. If you stress the importance of training and development to your team, but you skip out on the next training session or work on your computer throughout the session, then you're not setting a good example. If you teach your employees to build amazing client relationships, then you can't bad-talk the client in front of them. Not to scare you, but you're the manager, and they are watching you!

Expect Greatness

Give them the benefit of the doubt that they will achieve and be downright awesome. When your people know that you believe in them, they start to believe in themselves. At JB Training Solutions, Nicole is an amazing member of our team. She's a hard worker, and she keeps everyone on track heading up our operations and logistics. For some reason, Nicole doesn't think she's very creative. Every time she would say she wasn't creative, we challenged her. It came down to us telling her that she couldn't say that anymore because her comments become a self-fulfilling prophecy. She stopped talking negatively. We expected greatness, and now Nicole often is the one to add an interesting idea or opinion to our business discussions. Expect positive results, and they often follow. It's just like the student who is told that he is a troublemaker throughout grade school. In fact, the student lives up to his name and is a troublemaker. Likewise, Nicole lived up to the idea that she can be creative.

Push, challenge, ask insightful questions, and teach. Be that manager that expects greatness. Share your knowledge and experiences through storytelling and nurturing creativity. To teach hard skills, delegate responsibilities without dumping or micromanaging. Give your employees an opportunity to rise to the occasion and meet your expectations of excellence. Paul Spiegelman, CEO of The Beryl Companies, explains, "Leadership is about constant curiosity and learning. Gain from others with more experience from you, and in return, give to those with less." Pay it forward to teach your employees and give them a leg up—just as that someone did for you.

Teach: Being a Teacher and Student
◁ Telltale Tweets ▷

1. Be like Mrs. Stanley. Take the time to teach. Give your people a push, a leg up, an insight, a new perspective—just because. #noble

2. Delegate responsibility to empower your team. It's about letting go. "Things do not grow in the shadow of great trees." #whoisconstantin?

3. Help your employees see what they can't see in themselves. Mentor, coach, and expect greatness. #usherandbieber

14

LEADING WHEN THINGS GET STICKY

"May your trails be crooked, winding, lonesome, dangerous, leading to the most amazing view. May your mountains rise into and above the clouds."

—Edward Abbey

There will be ups and downs, curveballs and fastballs, hurdles and pits, storms and sunny days. As a manager, you will have every analogy hurled at you. A theme that you have heard echoed throughout this book is that it won't be easy to lead and inspire a team. Sometimes, decisions and routes will be crystal clear, but more often, the situations that you encounter and the circumstances that you face will float around in the murky gray of uncertainty. Every now and then, things just get downright sticky.

Unfortunately, management doesn't come equipped with a magic wand that makes all of those sticky situations that you don't like disappear with a slight wave of the hand. "If you don't like something, change it; if you can't change it, change the way you think about it," says children's book illustrator Mary Engelbreit. In this chapter, I will help you reframe your thinking about those typical management trials and tribulations.

When talking with millennial managers, there were three scenarios that we heard time and time again as being prevalent and extra sticky. How do you manage your peers? How do you manage people older than you? How do you manage a virtual team? All of the tips that I have offered throughout the book apply to these situations, but I have some specific tips to help you navigate each sticky situation successfully.

MANAGING YOUR PEERS: FROM BUDDY TO BOSS

One day, they are your colleagues and buddies—the people you go to happy hour with, take coffee breaks with, and the people you may even complain about your boss with. Then, the next day, you're their boss. Sticky. All of a sudden, you find yourself wondering what you should and shouldn't say to your former colleagues—poking fun at your boss, complaining about the finance department, and chatting about clients over drinks no longer seems appropriate.

One of the biggest obstacles that millennials say they face is managing their peers. How do you go from friend to manager? How do you draw boundaries or command respect? This can be a touchy situation. Your coworkers and pals might be happy for you, but there also may be some questions there. *Why did he get the promotion and not me?* To make the transition from peer to manager, there are a few things to keep in mind.

1. Go all in. You are the manager. Just because you were given the promotion or the title change, doesn't mean you automatically are seen as the leader. The first period of your transition is critical as your friends question your role and maybe even wonder how much they will be able to get away with. Assume your role with a humble confidence—an openness to ideas with a strong self-assurance in your leadership abilities.

2. Determine your boundaries. Right from the start, you must set clear expectations and boundaries when managing your peers. Millennial managers have a tendency to treat their team like equals and friends, and millennial direct reports are very open to this idea. It's your job to make clear what is acceptable and what is not.

One millennial manager at a real estate firm recalled this story of a poor-performing millennial intern—Ivan—who did not have a clue about boundaries. One fateful morning, Ivan the intern texted his manager telling her that he would not be able to come into work . . . because he was still hungover. The millennial manager was infuriated. First, Ivan hid behind technology and texted her instead of calling—at a time when he already should have been at work no less. Second, Ivan had the audacity to tell his manager that he was hungover. The millennial manager alerted human resources about the reason Ivan the intern was not showing up for work and said that his pay should be docked—copying Ivan. Although his manager was about his age, Ivan did not see the boundaries—he crossed the line. Needless to say, Ivan did *not* receive an offer for a full-time position.

Drawing the boundaries and setting expectations need to fall in the manager's court. For example, maybe as peers, everyone would go out for happy hours together, but now as manager, you don't go or you only stay for a drink or two. It's not that you can't have fun as a manager, but what happens when your direct reports start talking negatively about the vice president on the second drink? Do you say something or do you let it go? Either way, you're not in a spot to do much good for yourself. If you don't say anything, your inaction is condoning their behavior. If you do say something, you're the snooty manager who can't relax. You lose either way, and it's best not to put yourself in that situation.

3. Find the balance between power-hungry authoritarian and friendship-preserving pushover. Admittedly, millennials who are now managing their former peers are in a tough spot, and there are opposite ends of the spectrum that managers tend to jump toward. Your goal is to land somewhere in between. On one hand, some newly promoted millennials are excited to be in charge! To show their peers that they are now the leader, they take a more aggressive and commanding management style. They assert their power and give out orders to make it clear that they are no longer a peer—they are the BOSS. This usually breeds contempt and frustration amongst team members. *Who does this guy think he is? He was doing the same thing I was doing yesterday, and now, all of a sudden he has all the answers?*

On the other hand, some managers jump to the other end of the spectrum to not come off too bossy or arrogant. They are so concerned with hurting feelings or preserving friendships that they never really take on a management role at all. They get lost in the collaboration and friendship zone, and don't take on leadership responsibilities. Phillip Schreiber of the Holland & Knight law firm notes that millennial managers need to be wary of favoritism. This is not to scare you, but something you should be aware of. Schreiber says, "If the perception is that you are showing favoritism, you are at risk for discrimination claims, and you also can run into employee relations problems. It's really about the perception a manager creates when working with his or her team."

Your goal is to find a comfortable spot in the middle of power-hungry and pushover. This is where you will be most effective. Rocci Primavera, Director of Finance Development Programs, Abbott Laboratories, speaks to this idea of walking the fine line, "Teach with an informal, highly collaborative, and give-and-take style. Don't unconsciously act superior in any way—perhaps trying to prove that you deserve your manager role." Remember, **you can be assertive AND nice.** You can be friendly without being a friend.

4. Chat it out. If there are some people who are really struggling with your situation, you need to have a conversation. Maybe they are bitter or resentful or maybe they just miss your friendship. Talk about it. Set aside time for a one-on-one to hear what's going on. This is when you want to do less talking and more listening. Ask a lot of probing questions, and it's best to address the proverbial elephant in the room. Here are some ideas on how to start.

I can imagine it may seem a little different since I've become manager. I've noticed you seem a little distant, so I wanted to see what was going on.

Ever since I took on this new role, I feel as though you've been really short with me and wanted to see what was up.

Obviously, things have changed a little bit since I've become manager, and I wanted to hear your thoughts and see how we could best work together.

Try to empathize. Even if your colleague knows you are the better person for the job, they still may be bummed or discouraged that they didn't get a promotion. Show that you're on their side and that you want them to be successful so that they too can move up and take on more responsibilities.

5. Find a mentor. Is there a manager inside or outside of your organization whom you respect and admire? Use them as an adviser or mentor. You undoubtedly will have sticky situations that arise. In the past, you likely chatted through workplace sticky situations with your former peers that you now manage. Having a mentor gives you a great third-party, objective view of the situation, and you can play off their years of experience. They likely have faced very similar challenges and opportunities, and it's nice to have a sounding board.

MANAGING SOMEONE OLDER THAN YOU: BUILDING CREDIBILITY

You have likely seen a few movies or read books where the young people think they know more than they do. They cast off advice from their elders and end up in quite a mess. To be honest, if you're a millennial manager supervising older employees, they likely are skeptical of your performance. Thirty-four percent of U.S. workers say they are older than their bosses. Fifteen percent say they work for someone who is at least 10 years younger, according to a 2012 CareerBuilder survey, and the majority agrees that it can be difficult to work for someone younger than they are.[1]

Think again about a few business icons of your generation—the individuals who started Facebook, Google, and Groupon. They are young. Especially with the technology surge, it's not uncommon that more and more CEOs and leaders are closer to college than retirement. It's more likely, but on the flipside, for your boomer employees, you might be the same age as their son or daughter.

In the first chapters, you looked at the different generations and came to understand how millennials are viewed by older generations. Xers and boomers don't always see eye-to-eye with millennials—so what happens when you're their boss?

Employees who are older than you want to see that you're knowledgeable, action oriented, and have your stuff together. Tyler Micenheimer, a millennial and HR manager at PepsiCo, said he has learned a few things through managing employees who are older than him. "Credibility must be gained through interactions. You can say whatever you want, but you have to act and prove yourself or there is a credibility gap," says Micenheimer.

Get to know the style of those who you are managing that are older than you. Note that they may not be as excited about collaboration and doing everything as a team. For example, according to CareerBuilder, sixty-six percent of workers ages 55-plus prefer to skip the process and dive right into executing workplace projects.[2]

With this perspective in mind, we have some ideas for you.

1. Know your stuff. They're skeptical. They think you're young and don't know much. Prove them wrong. Study up. Knowing your stuff gets down to preparing, researching, learning, and being a sponge, so you're ready to lead your team forward. If you don't seem knowledgeable or on your toes from the start, your employees' suspicions will be confirmed—you're too young and inexperienced for the job.

Now, that doesn't mean you're a know-it-all or that you have an ego bigger than your boots. Micenheimer says, "There is a fine line between being assertive and being cocky." Older generations would have a hard time deciding which is worse—a clueless millennial or a know-it-all millennial. Know your stuff; don't flaunt your stuff. You can ask questions and request insights from your team. Knowing your stuff is also different from knowing everything. You want to maintain that humility—leaders who can't admit that they made a mistake or won't change courses don't make it very far.

2. Respect their experience, but don't be intimidated by it. Admit it; they have more experience than you. Your older employees have some amazing insights and breadth of knowledge brought to them by their years at work and in life. See it as a value and not a threat. Lauren Dufour, millennial manager at Discover Financial Services, manages some employees about twice her age. Dufour advises, "What helped me was showing that I was on their side. Getting their buy-in went a long way. I also asked those experienced professionals to teach me; it built rapport and helped me to get up to speed a lot quicker. Anytime you have a new manager, it's nice to have someone who remains modest and willing to learn."

One of the biggest beefs that we hear from older employees is that millennials have no regard for their experience. That's when they start thinking that "you're a little know-it-all" and an "entitled kid." Show that you respect the perspective that they bring to the table. Future conversations will go more smoothly, and your relationship will be stronger.

Although you want to give them respect, you also don't want to be ruled by "the way things have always been done" or "that has never worked before." As the leader, you have to push back when experience is keeping the team's perspective narrow and close minded. You bring a new perspective to the table and, as a leader, you don't want new and fresh ideas to be squashed before they are even thought through. If you find that an older employee is often jumping in to voice a negative opinion or push down new ideas, here are a few phrases you can try out:

> *"Ella, we value your experience and knowledge when it comes to this topic, but at this point, we really want to open our minds to new ideas and things we haven't tried before. I ask that everyone refrain from critiquing ideas in our brainstorming stage."*

> *"Letty, at this time, we want to focus on solutions instead of the challenges of our strategy. I know that you have great experience in this area, so I know you can add solid perspective when it comes to getting through this."*

> *"Vince, I'm so glad you have already had an opportunity to go through this situation. Since this is new to some of us, I know you will help us get through this with flying colors. I know you're skeptical right now, so why don't we set up some time to talk in depth."*

3. Have confidence. Remember, you're in your position for a reason. If older employees are skeptical of your position and authority, they're looking at your words and actions to either confirm or deny these preconceptions. Use powerful talk and confident body language when leading meetings and communicating one-on-one. Don't make age an issue. Often, millennial managers are the ones who are more worried about the situation than their older direct reports, so they tiptoe around issues and don't assert their authority. Being wishy-washy or indecisive is a sure sign of immaturity to an older worker. It's not a bad idea just to be the boss. Xers and boomers are accustomed to having a leader. Trust your decisions and communicate them confidently.

4. Share information and experiences. You share your skills, and have older employees share theirs. Think of it like a reverse mentor relationship. Prevent the brain drain by helping your older workers unload all the information and skills they have learned over the years. Nancy Harris works at a global energy company, and she shares, "As a manager, it's important to learn from everyone on your team, regardless of years of experience, everyone has something to offer." Harris goes on to say that it's crucial to listen and learn from all. Maybe your boomer employee wants to learn the latest on marketing via social media, and you want to learn about the pros and cons of the last billing systems change. Now you're both gaining skills you need to be most effective.

5. Try to see the whole picture. Significant others, children, college tuition, aging parents, retirement, and more—oh my! Flexibility, rewards, and recognition may take a different form for your older workers. Maybe to celebrate a job well done, you usually call a team happy hour—but your Xer employee can't attend because he has to pick up his kids or your boomer just wants to beat traffic and get home to enjoy dinner with her husband. Sometimes, millennials are more likely to check into e-mail in the evening, but maybe your boomer employee draws the line. Take these different styles and situations into account when making decisions. You want to be inclusive and not everyone is drawn to your millennial management style.

Having a diverse team representing different skill and experience levels puts you at an advantage. Make the most out of your team and individuals by adjusting your style, respecting experience, and stepping up to be a confident leader who is willing to learn and willing to lead.

MANAGING VIRTUAL TEAMS: WORKING TOGETHER WHEN APART

It's time to work together—even though you're apart. The workplace is becoming increasingly mobile, so managing remote employees is starting to be the norm. Currently, twenty to thirty million people work from home at least one day a week.[3] As millennial managers, you support this trend and you will push for it to be even more prevalent.

Although most of the CONNECT tips still apply when managing a remote team, there are a few specific things to consider.

1. Set crystal clear expectations. Work with your employee to determine work hours, communication schedules, boundaries, conference call and feedback protocols, and more. To set the partnership up for success, be as direct and clear as possible. Don't assume anything. Develop an operating agreement for your team to serve as a guideline for how everyone can work together successfully even though you're not all in the same location.

2. Resist the urge to micromanage. This is especially true for any Type A personalities, who find it unsettling to not actually see the progress or work getting done. Distance may tempt you to check in more often, but your employees will actually value and grow from their independence. Telecommuter Jayme Muenz said: "I communicate with my manager mostly via e-mail and have biweekly one-on-one meetings over the phone. My hands-off manager allows me to be autonomous and confident in what I do."

3. Be creative with recognition and appreciation. You already know how important recognition and appreciation are to building an engaged team. To show appreciation for a job well done, pick up the phone to call for no other reason but to say thank you and chit-chat for a few minutes about how your employee is doing. When working remotely, receiving something tangible can go a long way. Send a handwritten thank you note or put together a small package of some of their favorite things (York peppermint patties, Starbucks card, and Purdue football bobble head) as a token of your appreciation.

As a fun way to help a remote employee feel connected and recognized, send video messages to say thanks or to celebrate fun occasions. Send a "Happy Birthday" video from the team. If you have several remote employees, make a "traveling award" that is mailed each week to an employee who has gone above and beyond. These seemingly silly gestures will help the team feel connected, and it will promote a culture of engagement.

4. Give and receive regular feedback. Making time for feedback can be especially difficult when you are managing remotely. Feedback still can be a daily occurrence, but it doesn't have to be formal. If a coworker did a great job on a sales call, let her know right after the call and point out specific instances that were impressive. If there was a mistake in the weekly report, let her know immediately. Call or video conference her; you never want to give constructive feedback over e-mail. Ideally, you can deliver the individual's formal reviews in person.

5. Make some face time. At least once a month, organize a conference call with the entire team. If possible, use video conferencing. If fiscally possible, get the whole team together at least once a year. Use this time to focus on team building and getting to know one another in addition to discussing business matters. This will go a long way in working together successfully even though you're apart.

LEADING WHEN THINGS GET STICKY

"Adversity is a fact of life. It can't be controlled. What we can control is how we react to it." There will be difficult situations and tough decisions that you will face every day. The going will get tough. This is where you find out what you're really made of. This is when you define yourself and your leadership legacy. "If you aren't in over your head, how do you know how tall you are?" If you uphold the lessons you learned throughout this book, and you CONNECT, you likely will navigate your way toward an effective resolution and positive opportunity. Step up when things get sticky.

Leading When Things Get Sticky
◁ Telltale Tweets ▷

1. When managing your peers, find the balance between power-hungry authoritarian and friendship-preserving pushover. #balance #influence

2. While managing someone older than you, respect and learn from their experience, but don't be intimidated by it. #proveyourself

3. Work together even when you're apart. Be creative with engaging employees you don't always see face-to-face. #trust #fromadistance

CONCLUSION:
GO FORTH

"Around here, however, we don't look backwards
for very long. We keep moving forward, opening up new doors
and doing new things, because we're curious ... and
curiosity keeps leading us down new paths."

—Walt Disney Company

I will never forget the day the "ideal work environment" changed. I was interviewing candidates for a position at JB Training Solutions in 2008. We were looking for a bright, hard-working recent college graduate to join our team. We are not a Leo Burnett when it comes to size or glamour, so I would ask "What is your ideal work environment?" to understand what the candidate was seeking. If a candidate answered along the lines of "fast-paced, large company," then I knew the position would not be a good fit.

The new answers to this question jolted me, just like the interview of the candidate from Princeton who worked on a leaderless team. I interviewed six candidates from six different schools, and interestingly I received a slightly different version of the same answer from everyone. Now, I also travel to college campuses across the country to advise students on getting a great job and excelling in the workplace. Being tapped into these universities and their career centers, I knew that this answer wasn't simply the answer "du jour."

Every single person of whom I asked this question gave an answer along the lines of, "I want to work in an environment where I can contribute to meaningful work, grow and develop, and make an impact at the company." Wow. Answers that I was accustomed to receiving typically revolved around how large or small the company was. "Fast-paced" was an adjective I often heard. In fact, if I had been asked that question when I was a college student, I would have answered, "My ideal work environment is a company that pays me money." Now, your generation was rocking my world yet again. Instead of describing a workplace, millennials talked about their place in the work—how they connected.

Your generation peels back the facade of the glamorous office building downtown, looks past the "pace" of the office, and considers the fundamental roots and meaning of the work. Your generation wants to grow and develop—while you are contributing. You want to make a difference, and you are attracted to organizations that get it.

Now you can help build it.

As the new business leaders, this is the type of environment that you will build, foster, and develop. You want work to be more than just work. You want it to provide meaning and development for yourself and your employees. Maybe you're not saving lives every day, but your duties and responsibilities are making an impact and a difference. Winston Churchill states, "The price of greatness is responsibility."

This is it. This is your time. This is your time to bridge the gap between the hierarchal leadership style of senior leaders and the collaborative, casual approach of your peers. You already are rewriting the rules for the workplace; don't stop once you enter management—and leadership—and mentorship. Don't lose that energy. Stick by your ideals for leaving a legacy as a leader. Cheryl Ryan, millennial manager at Centro, shared, "It would mean a lot if I could help shape and develop someone's career to help them move forward—whether inside or outside of work. To know that I helped people find their passion in their career and gain a sense of accomplishment—that's the legacy I would like to leave."

We heard more echoes of Ryan's sentiments toward people management rather than process management. You want to be known for . . .

> . . . *Empowering individuals*
> . . . *Helping people find their passions and have a sense of*
>   *accomplishment*
> . . . *Shaping and developing their careers to help them move forward*

. . . Being someone who gets things done and listens to problems
. . . Making the right decisions that were the most effective
. . . Hard work and fairness
*. . . **Getting people to see what they couldn't see in themselves***

You have learned a lot, and you have the tools. Leonardo da Vinci reminds, "I have been impressed with the urgency of doing. Knowing is not enough; we must apply. Being willing is not enough, we must do." At the end of my workshops, participants take the time to write down just three things that they will put into practice right away. Before you even finish these last sentences, write down three management PUSH goals.

You took a glimpse at each of the generations and learned about making the transition from individual contributor to manager. You heard the cries of millennials and senior leaders in their manifestos, and you have countless nuggets of management advice from your peers, artists, captains, entrepreneurs, and historical figures. You know how to CONNECT as a leader. Communicate, Own it, Naviate, Negotiate, Engage, Collaborate, and Teach.

Go forth. This is your guide. You can connect to your people, to results, and to the big picture. You can go forth, rewrite the rules of management, and forge a path toward open and collaborative leadership. Just CONNECT.

MILLENNIAL MANAGER MANIFESTO

I am a millennial manager. Manager 3.0.

Just listen to us roar.

It's you, me, him, her, millennial, Xer, boomer. It's us—all together.

We are bridging, minding, respecting, and connecting the gap.

We are making a difference, rewriting the rules, and charging ahead little by little.

And with all of us, little by little is actually pretty big.

I am adjusting, adapting, and stretching—because I get you—and you and you.

We're bringing different strengths and perspectives. And we're working hard.

There's people and passions, progress and profits. And it's all connected.

We're all connected.

I am ready to talk, ready to listen. Ready to go.

We're figuring it out, we're working together.

I am a millennial manager.

ENDNOTES

INTRODUCTION: NOT BETTER, NOT WORSE—JUST DIFFERENT

[1]David M. Gross and Sophfronia Scott, "Living: Proceeding with Caution," *Time,* July 16, 1990, pp. 1-9.
[2]Gross and Scott, "Living."
[3]Gross and Scott, "Living."
[4]Gross and Scott, "Living."

CHAPTER 1: TALKIN' 'BOUT YOUR GENERATION

[1]Society for Human Resource Management, *Intergenerational Conflict in the Workplace.* Poll (Alexandria, VA: Society for Human Resource Management, April 29, 2011). http:// www.shrm.org/Research/SurveyFindings/Articles/Pages/IntergenerationalConflict intheWorkplace.aspx
[2]Condoleezza Rice. Keynote address at the Society for Human Resource Management 2012 Annual Conference and Exposition, Atlanta, June 24, 2012.
[3] Rice, Keynote address.
[4]Society for Human Resource Management, *Intergenerational Conflict in the Workplace.*
[5]Joyce A. Martin, Brady E. Hamilton, and Stephanie J. Ventura."Births: Final Data for 2010." *National Vital Statistics Report,* August 2012, *61* (1), 3.

CHAPTER 2: MILLENNIALS DEFINED

[1]Neil Howe and William Strauss. *Millennials Rising: The Next Great Generation* (New York: Random House, 2000).
[2]Howe and Strauss, *Millennials Rising.*
[3]Howe and Strauss, *Millennials Rising.*
[4]Howe and Strauss, *Millennials Rising.*
[5]Howe and Strauss, *Millennials Rising.*
[6]Howe and Strauss, *Millennials Rising.*
[7]David Brooks, "It's Not About You," *New York Times*, May 30, 2011. http://www.nytimes .com/2011/05/31/opinion/31brooks.html

[8]Howe and Strauss, *Millennials Rising.*

[9]Theodor Johann Tonsing, *Generation Y at Work* (South Africa: Bala Publishing, 2009).

CHAPTER 3: FROM INDIVIDUAL CONTRIBUTOR TO MANAGER

[1]Hope Yen, "More Than Seven in 10 U.S. Teens Jobless in Summer," *USA Today*, June 12, 2012. http://usatoday30.usatoday.com/money/economy/story/2012-06-12/teen-jobs-disappearing/55555506/1

[2]Neil Howe and William Strauss, *Millennials Go To College: Strategies for a New Generation on Campus* (New York: Paramount Market Publishing, 2007).

CHAPTER 4: DEFINING MANAGEMENT CHARACTERISTICS: SHAKING IT UP

[1]Liz Wiseman and Greg Mckeown, *Multipliers: How the Best Leaders Make Everyone Smarter* (New York: HarperCollins, 2010).

[2]Jeffrey Henning. "Employee Engagement Survey: The Gallup Q12." *Survey Research & Enterprise Feedback Management, Voice of Vovici Blog.* Jeffrey Henning, June 16, 2009. http://blog.vovici.com/blog/bid/18535/Employee-Engagement-Survey-The-Gallup-Q12.

[3]Judith Aquino, "Gen Y: The Next Generation of Spenders," *CRM* magazine, February 2012. http://www.destinationcrm.com/Articles/Editorial/Magazine-Features/Gen-Y-The-Next-Generation-of-Spenders-79884.aspx

[4]Stephanie Castellano, "Tuning in to Trust," *T&D Magazine*, September 1, 2012, 66 (9), 18.

[5]Shia Kapos, "Who Wears the Pants? Crain's 40 Under 40 Feted at Union League Club," *Crain's Chicago Business*, January 13, 2012. http://www.chicagobusiness.com/article/20120113/NEWS07/120119888/who-wears-the-pants-crains-40-under-40-feted-at-union-league-club

[6]Ani, "Corporate Experts Call for 'Hoodie' Zuckerberg to Step down as Facebook CEO," *Yahoo! News*, August 20, 2012. http://in.news.yahoo.com/corporate-experts-call-hoodie-zuckerberg-step-down-facebook-062219758—finance.html

[7]Andrew Mason, "The World's 50 Most Innovative Companies," *Fast Company*, 2011. http://www.fastcompany.com/most-innovative-companies/2011/

[8]Twitter Benefits & Perks. https://twitter.com/jobs/benefits

[9]EventBrite Careers. http://www.eventbrite.com/jobs/

CHAPTER 5: REWRITING THE RULES OF MANAGEMENT

[1]Malcolm Gladwell, Keynote address at the Society for Human Resources Management 2012 Annual Conference and Exposition, Atlanta, Georgia, June 25, 2012.

[2]Cathy Benko and Anne Weisberg, "Mass Career Customization: Building the CorporateLattice,"Deloitte.http://www.deloitte.com/view/en_US/us/Insights/Browse-by-Content-Type/deloitte-review/35912ee3fad33210VgnVCM100000ba42f00aRCRD.htm

[3]"By the Numbers—50 Facts about Millennials" Edelman Digital, June 1, 2011. http://www.edelmandigital.com/2011/06/01/by-the-numbers-50-facts-about-millennials/

[4]Jose A. Berrios, Speech at the Society for Human Resources Management 2012 Annual Conference and Exposition, Atlanta, June 25, 2012.

[5]"By the Numbers—50 Facts about Millennials."

[6]Pew Research Center. "Sleep with Phone." In *Millennials: A Portrait of Generation Next*. Washington, DC: Pew Research Center, 2010.

[7]Nick Shore, "Turning on the "No-Collar" Workforce," *MTV,* March 15, 2012, http://www.mediapost.com/publications/article/170109/turning-on-the-no-collar-workforce.html

[8]Shore, "Turning on the "No-Collar" Workforce."

CHAPTER 6: LEADING YOUR TEAM: CONNECT

[1]Mike D. Abrashoff. *It's Your Ship: Management Techniques from the Best Damn Ship in the Navy* (New York: Warner Books, 2002).

CHAPTER 7: COMMUNICATE: JUST SAY IT

[1]Seth Godin, "Willfully Ignorant vs. Aggressively Skeptical," *Seth Godin's Blog*, August 15, 2009. http://sethgodin.typepad.com/seths_blog/2009/08/willfully-ignorant-vs-aggressively-skeptical.html

[2]Robert Half International and Yahoo! HotJobs, "Generation Y: What Millennial Workers Want: How to Attract and Retain Gen Y Employees." 2008, Menlo Park, California. http://www.rhi.com/GenY

[3]Rachel Emma Silverman, "Top New Year's Resolutions," *The Juggle Wall Street Journal Blog*, December 29, 2011. http://blogs.wsj.com/juggle/2011/12/29/top-new-years-resolutions/

[4]Rachel Zupek, "8 Embarrassing Situations at Work," CareerBuilder.com, last modified January 11, 2009. http://www.careerbuilder.com/Article/CB-1379-The-Workplace-8-Embarrassing-Situations-at-Work/

[5]Jim Collins, *Good to Great: Why Some Companies Make the Leap . . . and Others Don't* (New York: HarperCollins, 2001).

[6]Kerry Patterson, Joseph Grenny, Ron McMillan, and Al Switzler. *Crucial Confrontations* (New York: McGraw-Hill, 2005).

[7]BrainyQuote.com. Xplore Inc. Accessed November 12, 2012. http://www.brainyquote.com/quotes/quotes/c/colinpowell38124.html

CHAPTER 8: OWN IT: TAKING—AND GIVING—RESPONSIBILITY

[1]Mike D. Abrashoff, *It's Your Ship: Management Techniques from the Best Damn Ship in the Navy* (New York: Warner Books, 2002).

[2]Mr. Youth and Intrepid. (May 2010): Millennial, Inc: What Your Company Will Look Like When Millennials Call the Shots. New York: Mr. Youth and Intrepid.

[3]Rotter, J.B. Generalized expectancies for internal versus external locus of control of reinforcement. *Psychological Monographs,* 1966, *80,* 1-28.

[4]Jean Twenge, Stacy Campbell, Brian Hoffman, and Charles Lance, "Generational Differences in Work Values: Leisure and Extrinsic Values Increasing, Social and Intrinsic Values Decreasing," *Journal of Management,* 2010, *36* (5), 1117-1142.

[5]Jim Collins,*Good to Great: Why Some Companies Make the Leap . . . and Others Don't* (New York: HarperCollins, 2001).

[6]Collins, *Good to Great.*

[7]Abrashoff, *It's Your Ship.*

[8]Jim Collins, "The 10 Greatest CEOs of All Time: What These Extraordinary Leaders Can Teach Today's Troubled Executives." *Fortune Magazine,* July 21, 2003. http://money .cnn.com/magazines/fortune/fortune_archive/2003/07/21/346095/index.htm

[9]Nathan Furr, "How Failure Taught Edison to Repeatedly Innovate," *Forbes,* June 9, 2011. http://www.forbes.com/sites/nathanfurr/2011/06/09/how-failure-taught-edison-to-repeatedly-innovate/

[10]Myles Brown, "The 25 Biggest Fails in NBA Playoff History," *Complex,* April 15, 2011. http://www.complex.com/sports/2011/04/the-25-biggest-fails-in-nba-playoff-history/michael-jordan

[11]Bruce Mills, "Stay Focused on your Business," *Mills Way* Blog, October 1, 2012. http://www.millsway.com/tag/inspiration/

[12]Erica Swallow, "TaskRabbit's Leah Busque on Staying Competitive," Entrepreneur .com, April 12, 2012. http://www.entrepreneur.com/article/223323#

[13]Abrashoff, *It's Your Ship.*

[14]Aman Motwane, "Modern Management Is Obsolete—Are You Ready for the Next Level?" Presented at the Society for Human Resources Management 2012 Annual Conference and Exposition, Atlanta, June 25, 2012.

[15]Barry Boyce, "Wisdom 2.0: The Digital World Connects," *Shambhala Sun,* July 2011. http://www.shambhalasun.com/index.php?option=content&task=view&id=3720&Item id=0&limit=1&limitstart=0

CHAPTER 9: NAVIGATE: MANAGING THROUGH THE UNKNOWN

[1]Rob Marsh, "6 Things Sara Blakely Said About Starting a Small Business," Logo-Maker, March 12, 2012. http://www.logomaker.com/blog/2012/03/12/small-business-quote-of-the-week%E2%80%94sara-blakely/

[2]Kevin Freiberg and Jackie Freiberg, *Nuts! Southwest Airlines' Crazy Recipe for Business and Personal Success* (New York: Broadway Books, 1996).

[3]Abraham Maslow, "The Theory of Human Motivation," *Psychological Review,* 1943, 50 (4), 370-396. http://psychclassics.yorku.ca/Maslow/motivation.htm

[4]Mark Thomas, *Mastering People Management: Build a Successful Team—Motivate, Empower and Lead People* (London: Thorogood, 2007).

[5]Nelson Mandela, "Mandela in His Own Words," CNN.com, last modified June 26, 2008. http://edition.cnn.com/2008/WORLD/africa/06/24/mandela.quotes/index.html

CHAPTER 10: NEGOTIATE: WORKING THROUGH
DIFFERENT PERSPECTIVES

[1]Mike D. Abrashoff, *It's Your Ship: Management Techniques from the Best Damn Ship in the Navy* (New York: Warner Books, 2002).

CHAPTER 11: ENGAGE: CONNECTING
TO THE BIG PICTURE

[1]Kevin Sheridan, *Building a Magnetic Culture* (New York: McGraw-Hill, 2012).

[2]Pew Research Center, *Millennials: A Portrait of Generation Next* (Washington, DC: Pew Research Center, 2010).

[3]Gillean Smith, "Love Thy Employees or Make the Cut? You Decide." Examiner.com, February 28, 2011. http://www.examiner.com/article/love-thy-employees-or-make-the-cut-you-decide

[4]Carmine Gallo, "Google's Marissa Mayer: 3 Leadership Traits She'll Bring to Yahoo." Forbes.com, July 17, 2012. http://www.forbes.com/sites/carminegallo/2012/07/17/googles-marissa-mayer-3-leadership-traits-shell-bring-to-yahoo/

[5]Hay Group, *Are You Missing Something? Engaging and Enabling Employees for Success* (Philadelphia: HayGroup Insights, 2010).

[6]Sheridan, *Building a Magnetic Culture*.

[7]Workforce Mood Tracker, *The September 2011 Report: The Impact of Recognition on Employee Retention* (Southborough, MA: Globoforce, 2011).

[8]Kevin Sheridan, *The Virtual Manager: Cutting-Edge Solutions for Hiring, Managing, Motivating, and Engaging Mobile Employees* (Pompton Plains, NJ: Career Press, 2012).

[9]Telework Research Network, *The Bottom Line on Telework: California Government Workforce,* 2011. http://www.teleworkresearchnetwork.com/wp-content/uploads/down loads/2012/03/CA_State_of_Telework_9-18-11.pdf

[10]Tony Hsieh, *Delivering Happiness: A Path to Profits, Passion, and Purpose* (New York: Hachette Book Group, 2010).

CHAPTER 12: COLLABORATE: MAKING IT HAPPEN

[1]BMN News Team, "The Business Wisdom of Steve Jobs," BRANDMAKER News, October 5, 2011. http://brandmakernews.com/features/brands-we-love/2908/the-business-wisdom-of-steve-jobs.html

[2]BrainyQuote.com, Xplore Inc, 2012. Accessed November 13, 2012. http://www.brainy quote.com/quotes/authors/s/sheryl_sandberg.html

[3]Jim Collins, *Good to Great: Why Some Companies Make the Leap . . . and Others Don't* (New York: HarperCollins, 2001).

[4]Marcus Buckingham, *First, Break All the Rules: What the World's Greatest Managers Do Differently* (New York: Simon & Schuster, 1999).

[5]Pamela Meyer, *From Workplace to Playspace: Innovating, Learning and Changing Through Dynamic Engagement* (San Francisco: Jossey-Bass, 2010).

CHAPTER 13: TEACH: BEING A MENTOR—AND STUDENT

[1]Mike D. Abrashoff, *It's Your Ship: Management Techniques from the Best Damn Ship in the Navy* (New York: Warner Books, 2002).

[2]Josef Albers, *Interaction of Color* (New Haven: Yale University Press, 2006).

³Meg McCollister and Ann Mesle, "What Do Madeleine Albright and Condoleezza Rice Have in Common? Czech Mentors!" *Shifting the Balance* Blog, April 13, 2012. http://shiftingthebalance.com/tag/condoleessa-rice/

CHAPTER 14: LEADING WHEN THINGS GET STICKY

¹"CareerBuilder Survey Identifies Generational Differences in Work Styles, Communication and Changing Job," Career Builder.com, September 13, 2012. http://www.careerbuilder.com/share/aboutus/pressreleasesdetail.aspx?sd=9/13/2012&id=pr715&ed=9/13/2099

²"CareerBuilder Survey Identifies Generational Differences in Work Styles, Communication and Changing Job."

³Telework Research Network. The Bottom Line on Telework: California Government Workforce, 2011. http://www.teleworkresearchnetwork.com/wp-content/uploads/downloads/2012/03/CA_State_of_Telework_9-18-11.pdf

BIBLIOGRAPHY

In addition to the sources cited in the endnotes, the authors read the following resources and found them helpful.

David Allen, *Getting Things Done: The Art of Stress-Free Productivity* (New York: Penguin Group, 2011).

Arleen Arnsparger, "4GenR8tns: Succeeding with Colleagues, Cohorts & Customers," 2008. http://www.generationsatwork.com/articles_succeeding.php

Kristin Birmham, "Inside Facebook's Hackathons: 5 Tips for Hosting Your Own," *CIO*, August 12, 2012. http://www.cio.com/article/714320/Inside_Facebook_s_Hackathons_5_Tips_For_Hosting_Your_Own?page=1&taxonomyId=3004

"Birth Data," Centers for Disease Control and Prevention, October 3, 2012. http://www.cdc.gov/NCHS/births.htm

Jody Davenport, *Corroborating the Expectations and Predilection of Millennials with the Andragological Principle of Self-Directed Learning* (Ann Arbor, MI: ProQuest LLC, 2010).

Edelman and StrategyOne, *The 8095 Exchange: Millennials, Their Actions Surrounding Brands, and the Dynamics of Reverberation* (New York: Edelman and Strategy One, 2011).

Ellen Frankenburg, "The Next Generation Really is Different," The Frankenberg Group. http://www.frankenberggroup.com/published-articles/articles-written-for-family-business-magazine/158-the-next-generation-really-is-different.html

Haya El Nasser, "The Office Is Shrinking as Tech Creates Workplace Everywhere," *USA Today*, June 5, 2012. http://usatoday30.usatoday.com/money/workplace/story/2012-06-05/tech-creates-workplace-everywhere/55405518/1

Kevin Freiberg and Jackie Freiberg, *Nuts! Southwest Airlines' Crazy Recipe for Business and Personal Success* (New York: Broadway Books, 1996).

Geoffrey James, *Success Secrets from Silicon Valley: How to Make Your Teams More Effective* (New York: Random House, 1996).

Peter Jennings, "Top Ten Suggested Names," ABC World News Tonight, 1219/97 abc.com poll.

Heather Kerrigan, "Results-Only Work Environment Goes Public Sector," *GOVERNING*, April 2012. http://www.governing.com/topics/public-workforce/gov-results-only-work-environment-goes-public-sector.html

Richard Koch, *The 80/20 Principle: The Secret to Achieving More with Less* (New York: Doubleday, 2008).

Leslie Kwoh, "More Firms Bow to Generation Y's Demands," *The Wall Street Journal*, August 22, 2012. http://online.wsj.com/article/SB10000872396390443713704577603302382190374.html

Jack Marshall, "How Agencies Court Millennials," *Digiday*, March 27, 2012. http://www.digiday.com/agencies/how-agencies-court-millennials/

Pew Research Center, *Millennials: A Portrait of Generation Next* (Washington, DC: Pew Research Center, 2010)

Claire Raines, "Generations at Work: Managing Millennials," 2002. http://www.hreonline.com/pdfs/ManagingMillennials.pdf

Tom Rath, *StrengthsFinder2.0* (New York: Gallup Press, 2007).

Joe Reynolds, "The Case for Building Your Employees a Tree House," *Inc.*, December 1, 2011.http://www.inc.com/joe-reynolds/the-case-for-building-your-employees-a-tree-house.html

Stuart Rojstaczer and Christopher Healy, "Where A is Ordinary: The Evolution of American College and University Grading: 1940-2009," *Teachers College Record* 2012, *114* (7) 1-23. http://www.tcrecord.org/content.asp?contentid=16473

Dan Schawbel, "Millennials vs. Baby Boomers: Who Would You Rather Hire?" *Time Magazine*, March 29, 2012. http://business.time.com/2012/03/29/millennials-vs-baby-boomers-who-would-you-rather-hire/

Angel Soria, "Get the Skinny on Perks at Top Social Network Companies," *Salty Waffle* blog, August 15, 2012. http://www.saltywaffle.com/get-the-skinny-on-perks-at-top-social-network-companies/

Glenn Stanton and Andrew Hess, "Generational Values and Desires," *Focus on the Family*, June 2012. http://www.focusonthefamily.com/about_us/focus-findings/family-formation-trends/generational-values-desires.aspx

Frank Stephenson, "For the Love of Me." *Research in Review* (Florida State University), Summer 2004, 16-31.

"Top Small Company Workplaces," *Inc.*, 2010. http://www.inc.com/top-workplaces/2010/11-cool-workplace-perks.html

Jean Twenge, *Generation Me: Why Today's Young Americans Are More Confident, Assertive, Entitled—And More Miserable Than Ever Before* (New York: Free Press, 2006).

Chuck Underwood, *The Generational Imperative: Understanding Generational Differences in the Workplace, Marketplace, and Living Room* (North Charleston, SC: The Generational Imperative, Inc, 2007).

WorldOne Research, "LexisNexis Technology Gap Survey," 2008. http://www.lexisnexis .com/media/pdfs/LexisNexis-Technology-Gap-Survey-4-09.pdf

Ron Zemke, Claire Raines, and Bob Filipczak, *Generations at Work: Managing the Clash of Veterans, Boomers, Xers and Nexters in Your Workplace* (New York: AMACOM, 2010).

INDEX

ABOUT THE AUTHORS

BRAD KARSH (Chicago, IL) is President and Founder of JB Training Solutions, a company focused on helping professionals achieve more in their careers. A workplace and generational expert, he appears regularly on CNN and has been quoted in *The New York Times, The Wall Street Journal,* and dozens of other publications.

COURTNEY TEMPLIN (Chicago, IL), herself a millennial manager, is Chief Operating Officer at JB Training Solutions and sits on the board of the Chicago Society for Human Resource Management, where she leads the Emerging Leaders Initiative.

Other Titles Available for Managers in eBook Format:

2600 Phrases for Effective Performance Reviews   978-08144-28702

2600 Phrases for Setting Effective Performance Goals   978-08144-17768

101 Tough Conversations to Have with Employees   978-08144-13494

AMA Business Boot Camp   978-08144-31658

Quick Team-Building Activities for Busy Managers   978-08144-27699

People Styles at Work . . . and Beyond   978-08144-13432

For more information, please visit: www.amacombooks.org

About AMACOM

Who We Are: AMACOM is the book publishing division of the American Management Association. AMACOM's broad range of offerings spans not only the critical business topics and leadership challenges of today and tomorrow but also the issues that affect our lives, our work, and our world.

What We Publish: AMACOM publishes nonfiction books on business, management, leadership, HR, training, communications, career growth, personal development, marketing, sales, customer service, project management, and finance.

About Our Authors: AMACOM authors are experts in their fields, unrivaled in their knowledge, experience, and reputation. They are world-class educators, successful executives, business owners, trainers, consultants, and journalists—all eager to share their insights and techniques with a broad audience.